JUST DESERTS:
Sentencing Based on Equality and Desert

JUST DESERTS:
Sentencing Based on Equality and Desert

Richard G. Singer
Professor, Rutgers University Law School
Visiting Professor, Cardozo School of Law

Ballinger Publishing Company • **Cambridge, Massachusetts**
A Subsidiary of Harper & Row, Publishers, Inc.

International Standard Book Number: 0-88410-799-X

Library of Congress Catalog Card Number: 79-915

Printed in the United States of America

Library of Congress Cataloging in Publication Data

Singer, Richard G.
  Just deserts.

  Bibliography: p.
  1. Sentences (Criminal procedure)—United States. 2. Prison sentences—United States. I. Title.
KF9685.S56   345'.73'077   79-915
ISBN 0-88410-799-X

※

Acknowledgments

No book is solely the work of one person, and this volume is no exception. Notions, thoughts, concepts are worked out over a long period of time, with too many people to be able to mention them all. Specifically, however, there are persons who have made a gift to me of their time, and their criticisms, and they should be acknowledged, with the usual caveat that they cannot in any way be held accountable for the mistakes of fact or thinking that are presented here: Alex Brooks, a colleague at Rutgers Law School who blue penciled the first chapter with a fine and sensitive eye; James Harris, whose acquaintance began with deserts sentencing and will continue; Simon Rosenzweig, whose antipathy toward deserts sentencing caused me to rethink its validity; and Andrew von Hirsch, who graciously reviewed the drafts despite the differences between us that the book details. Also, my thanks to my wife, Anne, who read an early draft and gave cogent comments.

Two students at Rutgers Law School have worked hard and long on some of the materials, and they should be acknowledged: Alexander Greer and Martha Jacoff. Finally, to those who graciously accepted draft after changed draft and were still smiling at the end of all that typing, proofreading, and editing: at Rutgers Law School, Mary Gardner, Marie Todd, Stella Lovelace, Helene Wright, Josephine Walker-Lewis, and especially Genevieve De Perty; and at Cardozo Law School, Dorothy Walsh.

To Laurel

Contents

✳

List of Tables

Introduction

I'd like to get away from earth awhile
And then come back to it and begin over.
May no Fate wilfully misunderstand me
And half grant what I wish and snatch me away
Not to return

Robert Frost, Birches

Three years ago, Andrew von Hirsch, a professor at the
Rutgers School of Criminal Justice and reporter for the
Committee for the Study of Incarceration, issued the Committee's report, *Doing Justice*.[1] The report called for major sentencing
reform, with a philosophical outlook on the purposes of punishment
that, while debated in the philosophical journals,[2] had rarely been
articulated in a more general arena for nearly a century: commensurate deserts. The proposition, more fully explored in Chapter 2, was
that punishment, *qua* punishment, was a legitimate goal of the sentencing process—indeed, that it was the *only* legitimate goal of the
sentencing process.

---

[1] A. VON HIRSCH, DOING JUSTICE (1976).

[2] The literature on punishment is rich. Extensive bibliographies can be found in J.
KLEINIG, PUNISHMENT AND DESERT (1973), J. CEDERBLOM and W. BLIZEK, JUSTICE AND
PUNISHMENT (1977); and G. EZORSKY, PHILOSOPHICAL PERSPECTIVES ON PUNISHMENT
(1972). A far less comprehensive list can be found in the bibliography at the end of this
book.

At the same time, there was a growing dissatisfaction with present sentencing systems from both a theoretical and a pragmatic point of view. This dissatisfaction adopted "commensurate deserts" as its rallying cry. But, as Chapter 10 seeks to show, there has been enormous misunderstanding of that term, and it has become increasingly abused. Whether this misunderstanding is wilfull or not, it threatens to seriously jeopardize the acceptance of the deserts model. Legislatures throughout the country, sometimes in the name of desert, are enacting legislation that in all likelihood neither von Hirsch nor anyone on the study committee would endorse. All that appears to have been heard, or at least comprehended, is that the deserts notion gives legitimacy to punishment: the limitations that the duration or intensity be moderate and that nonincarceration be preferred in most instances seem to have been ignored. Moreover, the commensurate deserts position that rehabilitation should not be considered in determining the length or type of punishment has been distorted to the position that rehabilitation, as a goal of the criminal justice system, should be abandoned.

In part, this may be due to the fact that *Doing Justice* was concerned with articulating the principles of a philosophy of sentencing, rather than dealing with the technical problems of implementing its program. The debate between retributivists and utilitarians, after all, had been largely a philosphical one. Since utilitarians had clearly won the day in legislative enactments, desert philosphers had rarely attempted—or been asked to attempt—to show how their program would work in real legislation; their primary goal had been to show the foibles of utilitarian punishment. This is not to say that there were no hints in *Doing Justice* of how the commensurate deserts model could be legislated; but the book held only the barest outlines of a plan. This was not true, however, of another book published almost simultaneously by the Twentieth Century Fund.[3] This book attempted to detail a method of promulgating a commensurate deserts sentencing system. Perhaps because its suggestions were considered unreasonable, but more likely because it was overshadowed by the earlier-published *Doing Justice, Fair and Certain Punishment*'s more detailed approach to desert sentencing has not had the influence it merits.

Still, legislatures and parole boards have moved ahead with incredible alacrity. Since 1974 at least a dozen have accepted sentencing reform, much of it in the name of just deserts. At least a dozen other legislatures have the issue still pending, and several legislatures that have rejected the notion are likely to reconsider the approach in the next few years. In many of these, the legislation is called commensu-

---

[3] TWENTIETH CENTURY FUND, FAIR AND CERTAIN PUNISHMENT (1976).

rate deserts, but scarcely resembles the philosophical notion. It may turn out that, thirty years from now, just deserts theorists, confronted with what has been done in their name, will have to say of just deserts sentencing, as Shaw is reputed to have said of Christianity, and rehabilitationists are now lamenting: "It was a nice idea; it's too bad it was never seriously tried."[4]

The present work is intended (1) to restate and reexamine the commensurate deserts approach to sentencing and to demonstrate that many of the so-called legislative reforms in sentencing are in fact inconsistent with the philosophies underlying both *Doing Justice* and *Fair and Certain Punishment*; and (2) to offer some tentative thoughts on some of the philosophical and implementation problems those books only tenuously discussed, but which need discussion as implementation is being considered around the country. As the work itself demonstrates, there is no consensus among commensurate deserts theorists themselves on the implementation of the philosophy. Moreover, I could surely make no claim to holding the "truth" of commensurate deserts. Instead, the book seeks to explore in a tentative fashion some of the issues raised by the philosophy and its implementation. If it makes any contribution at all toward that end, it will have achieved its objective.

One final point—many of the changes suggested in this book could be supported on nondesert grounds. That I have not explored those grounds in depth does not mean that I would reject the result; the focus here, however, is on what the desert theory, in practice, would appear to require.

[4] Since the appearance of DOING JUSTICE and of Dean Norval Morris' earlier book, THE FUTURE OF IMPRISONMENT (1974), the critics have inveighed against those authors because of their "political naivete," arguing that desert gives the legislature a justification for enhancing punishment. Now, as legislatures proceed to do just that, the critics exclaim: "I told you so." See, e.g., Clear, *Correctional Policy, Neo-Retributionism and the Determinate Sentence,* 4 JUST. SYS. J. 26 (1978). Clear, and others, endow even von Hirsch and Morris with too sweeping powers, assuming that harsher penalties would never had occurred had it not been for their (misguided) attempt to make the justice system more just.

JUST DESERTS:
Sentencing Based on Equality and Desert

Chapter 1

The Death of the
Indeterminate Sentence

THE DECLINE OF THE MEDICAL MODEL

For well over half a century, this country has relied primarily upon the indeterminate sentence to deal with criminals.[1]

There is scarce need to expound at length upon the system—its basic premise was that the criminal was morally "sick" and could be "rehabilitated" (through Christian love and strict discipline) like any other sick person. As with all "illnesses," however, the degree of the individual's disease and his recuperative possibilities would differ.[2] Therefore, "cure" would take an indefinite period of time,

---

[1] In 1900, four states had indeterminate sentence laws, while forty-one had good time laws. By 1915, twenty-six states had adopted full indeterminate sentencing. Miller, *At Hard Labor: Rediscovering the 19th Century Prison*, 9 Issues in Crim. 91, 99 (1974).

[2] See, for example, the first principle of the first meeting of correctional professionals in 1870: "Crime is thus a sort of moral disease, of which punishment is the remedy. The efficacy of the remedy is a question of social therapeutics, a question of the fitness and measure of the dose." Principle Nine declared: "[W]e believe it will be little, if at all, more difficult to judge correctly as to the moral cure of a criminal, than it is of the mental cure of a lunatic." Transactions of the National Congress on Penitentiary and Reformatory Discipline, Principles of Penitentiary and Reformatory Discipline Suggested for Consideration by the National Congress (and adopted by that body), 548, 551 (1871). Compare the remark that "The diagnosis and treatment of the criminal is a highly technical medical and sociological problem for which the lawyer is rarely any better fitted than a real estate agent or a plumber." H. Barnes, The Story of Punishment 265–66 (1930). I am not suggesting, of course, that criminologists universally agreed that criminality could be medically controlled or cured; the "medical model" merely holds that crime can be dealt with *as though* it were a disease and subjected to "scientific" (i.e., expert) cure. Nevertheless, the fact is that many criminologists did see

and release should be based upon the prognosis by the parole board—the experts, the analogs to medical doctors. Inside the prison, as inside the hospital, therapy would continue apace, but those who did not participate in therapy could not expect early release; release would depend on "cure."

We never fully believed this thesis, however. Had we, our legislatures would have simply passed sentences of zero-to-life for all crimes and left the rest for the parole board. Whether because of a latent distrust of the medical analog, a remembrance of the lex talionis (which required an eye—but *no more than* an eye—for an eye, and therefore enunciated proportionality as a concept of punishment), or for some other reason, we retained maximum sentences well below life imprisonment for most crimes. Nevertheless, maximum sentences, as set by the legislature, did increase through the first several decades of the twentieth century, reflecting a combination of zeal for the individualized, "medical" approach to crime and, in the face of apparent increases in crime, an increasing realization that, if the "medicine" didn't "work," perhaps the incapacitation allowed by indeterminate confinement would.

The growth of the indeterminate, individualization model was accelerated by other quasi-scientific approaches to the problem of crime. Lombroso, for example, argued that criminals could be detected by their physiology.[3] The massive eugenics movement which swept this country in the early decades of the twentieth century promised to abolish crime by removing hereditary criminality through sterilization of the "carriers."[4] Throughout the early twentieth century, reformers

---

in science, including medicine—particularly psychology and psychiatry—the hope for a crime panacea.

[3] C. LOMBROSO, CRIMINAL MAN (1876). Lombroso's thesis was refined in the twentieth century by E. KRETSCHMER, PHYSIQUE AND CHARACTER (1925) and W. SHELDON, S. STEVENS, and W.B. TUCKER, THE VARIETIES OF HUMAN PHYSIQUE (1940). See also E. FERRI, THE POSITIVE SCHOOL OF CRIMINOLOGY (1901). Compare, as well, the statement, in 1924, that perhaps one-third of all convicts had "gland or toxic disturbance" which caused the criminal behavior. Schlapp, *Behavior and Gland Disease,* 15 J. HEREDITY 11 (1924), quoted in H. BLOCH and F. FLYNN, DELINQUENCY 123 (1956). Bloch and Flynn devote a full chapter to body factors related to delinquency, covering body types, endocrinology, and other medical disciplines. There is, of course, a modern analogy: the XYZ Klinefelter syndrome.

For a survey of the history, and current attempts to link crime and physical disorders, see Shah and Roth, *Biological and Psychophysiological Factors in Criminality,* in HANDBOOK OF CRIMINOLOGY 101–73 (D. Glaser, ed., 1976) (attaching an extensive bibliography).

[4] The notion that criminality was hereditary was spurred by the study of the Jukes. R. DUGDALE, THE JUKES—A STUDY OF CRIME, PAUPERISM, DISEASE AND HEREDITY (1877). This was continued in H. GOODARD, THE KALIKAK FAMILY (1912).

In the early 1900s several states provided for sterilization of some criminals. The first

of the criminal justice system, and particularly of corrections, embraced the promises that the social sciences offered—classification of offenders by scientific means and then cure, again by scientific means, of their specific difficulties.[5]

In short, through the 1940s, the search for a "scientific" method of dealing with criminals, and hence crime, was widespread. Many criminologists believed (or hoped) that somewhere there was a solution—a scientific solution—to the problem. Not surprisingly, this scientific approach to criminality was accelerated by the growth of psychiatry, which seemed to reaffirm that most behavior disorders (of which criminality was surely one) were both diagnosable and curable. Psychiatry tnus came to be seen by criminologists as the type of medicine that could give us most insights into crime and its cure. One example of this movement was the passage of sexual psychopath laws during the 1930s and 1940s;[6] another was the initial attempts (now somewhat successful) to abolish the *M'Naughton* rules of insanity in the substantive criminal law and to replace them with more flexible

---

case involving such a statute upheld it as against a challenge on "cruel and unusual punishment" grounds. State v. Feilen, 70 Wash. 65, 126 p. 75 (1912). Thereafter however, the statutes were invalidated, at least as applied to prisoners, as punishment for crimes. See Davis v. Berry, 216 F. 416 (S.D. Iowa 1914) (due process grounds, but a lengthy discussion of eighth amendment grounds as well); Mickle v. Henrichs, 262 F. 687 (D. Nev. 1918) (Cruel and unusual punishment). States continued, however, to enact such laws, one of which was declared unconstitutional, but only on the equal protection grounds that not all equally culpable criminals were subject to sterilization, in Skinner v. Oklahoma, 316 U.S. 535 (1942). For general discussions, see Felkenes, *Sterilization and the Law*, in NEW DIMENSIONS IN CRIMINAL JUSTICE 111 (H. Becker, G. Felkenes, and P. Whisenand, eds., 1966); Kindgren, *Sixty Years of Compulsory Eugenic Sterilization: Three Generations of Imbeciles and the Constitution of the United States*, 43 CHI.-KENT L. REV. 123 (1966); O'Hara and Sanks, *Eugenic Sterilization*, 45 GEO. L.J. 29 (1956).

[5] See, e.g., H. BARNES, THE EVOLUTION OF PENOLOGY IN PENNSYLVANIA, esp. pp. 6–7, 406–407 (1927). Consider, also, that the notion of prediction tables and scientific approaches to consort groups, delinquency factors, and so forth are widely acclaimed at the time. The work of the Gluecks is probably the most exemplary of this type. See S. and E. GLUECK, ONE THOUSAND JUVENILE DELINQUENTS: THEIR TREATMENT BY COURT AND CLINIC (1924); JUVENILE DELINQUENTS GROWN UP (1940); UNRAVELING JUVENILE DELINQUENCY (1950).

[6] From the mid-1930s, when Michigan passed the first "sexual psychopath" law, through the early 1950s, states seemed in a race to pass such statutes. The story is well recounted in S. RUBIN, THE LAW OF CRIMINAL CORRECTION, ch. 11, secs. 14–17 (2d ed. 1973). The Supreme Court held such a statute constitutional in Minnesota ex rel. Pearson v. Probate Court of Ramsey County, 309 U.S. 270 (1940). Twenty-six states had passed some statutes by 1962, and most of these are still extant, although a few have been invalidated on grounds of vagueness or lack of full due process. See, e.g., Specht v. Patterson, 386 U.S. 605 (1966). The writing on the subject is almost interminable. Some samples are Hacker and Frym, *The Sexual Psychopath Act in Practice: Critical Discussion*. 43 CALIF. L. REV. 766 (1955), Sutherland, *Diffusion of Sexual Psychopath Laws*, 56 AM. J. OF SOC. 242 (1950); Swanson, *Sexual Psychopath Statutes: Summary and Analysis*, 51 J. CRIM. L., C. & P.S. 215 (1960).

rules that would allow psychiatrists more freedom to testify in criminal trials.[7]

By the mid-1950s, then, the medical-scientific-psychiatric approach to crime and criminality had reached a position of substantial prestige. Presentence reports were to have both social science data for the prediction of the individual's likelihood of recidivism and the potential for rehabilitation and, where ordered, a psychiatric evaluation of the offender. Prisons became "correctional institutions" and prisoners became "residents," "clients," or even "patients." The notion of a treatment approach to criminality became widespread.

Almost simultaneously, however, attacks on psychiatry, and consequently its ability to deal with criminality, began to surface. Some, like Thomas Szasz, argued that "mental illness" was simply another way of labeling deviancy from prescribed norms of conduct.[8] Rather than an objective, impartial, scientific process, argued Szasz, psychi-

---

[7] The so-called *M'Naughton* rules, developed by the House of Lords in what was effectively an advisory opinion, essentially stated that the defendant was legally insane—and hence not responsible for his acts—only if he did not know (1) the nature and quality of his act or (2) the difference between right and wrong. 10 Cl. & F. 200, 8 Eng. Rep. 718 (H.L. 1843). The rule was criticized as being restricted to "knowledge" or "cognitive processes," contrary to developing psychiatric opinion during the twentieth century.

The *M'Naughton* critics argued that psychiatrists were unable to fully explain the defendant's mental illness, but were restricted to questions of "cognition." This belief has now been proved unfounded. A. GOLDSTEIN, THE INSANITY DEFENSE (1967). Professor Goldstein has shown that most state courts received all psychiatric evidence proffered, without strict regard to the wording of *M'Naughton*. Furthermore, Jerome Hall has vigorously argued that *M'Naughton* always envisioned the broadest reliance on psychiatric testimony. J. HALL, PRINCIPLES OF CRIMINAL LAW (1960). Whatever the merits of this position, it was surely not the perception shared by most jurists in the early 1950s.

In 1953, The British Royal Commission on Capital Punishment proposed replacing *M'Naughton* with a more liberal test of insanity. Almost simultaneously in this country, Judge David Bazelon, speaking for a major federal court in an historic opinion, Durham v. United States, 214 F.2d 862 (D.C. Cir. 1954), basically adopted the position of the Royal Commission. One year later the initial draft of the Model Penal Code provisions on insanity was published which, while not adopting in toto the *Durham*–Royal Commission test, greatly broadened the defense of insanity. American Law Institute, Model Penal Code §4.01 et seq. (Tent. Draft #4, 1955).

Durham's eminence, however, was short-lived. The rule was swiftly modified by a series of opinions that recognized the inability of psychiatry to specify mental illness. Perhaps the pivotal point in this process was the reversal, almost literally overnight, of the position of doctors at Saint Elizabeth's Hospital in the District of Columbia, where *Durham* was applicable, as to whether sociopathy was a mental illness. *In re* Rosenfeld, 157 F. Supp. 18 (D.D.C. 1957). Doubts began to burgeon about this "science" that could change definitions of "mental illness" by a majority vote. Twenty years after *Durham*, the D.C. Circuit itself overruled it, adopting instead the Model Penal Code test. United States v. Brawner, 471 F.2d 969 (D.C. Cir. 1972). But *Durham* had opened the way for a reevaluation of *M'Naughton*, in any event.

[8] T. SZASZ, THE MYTH OF MENTAL ILLNESS (1961).

atry was simply a subjective, arbitrary method that allowed indefinite confinement of "undesirables" in mental hospitals under the fiction that they could be treated.

A second attack on the very notion of psychiatry as a method of dealing with deviancy came from the behaviorists, led by B. F. Skinner.[9] This school argued that "mental illness" was too vague a concept for scientific study. Moreover, since the ultimate goal of treatment was to normalize the conduct of the patient (here they implicitly agreed with Szasz and others that deviancy was the predicate of intervention), behaviorist techniques allegedly achieved this change of conduct more easily and without the cluttering fiction of "mental illness." Therefore, psychiatry was irrelevant to the ultimate goal of behavior change.[10]

A third attack on psychiatry focused on the actual conditions in mental hospitals. Here, the motivations and approaches were mixed. Some critics, like Dr. Morton Birnbaum, argued that hospital conditions were so inadequate that mental patients were not receiving the treatment to which they were entitled and that a legal right to treatment should be recognized so that the treatment that psychiatry offered could be obtained.[11] Birnbaum did not question, however, that the treatment could be efficacious.

Other critics of conditions in mental hospitals were less clear. Erving Goffman argued that mental hospitals were "total institutions" in which patients were, in fact, deprived of their autonomy,[12] but Goffman did not explicitly declare whether he believed that treatment could work, if afforded. Ken Kesey's novel, *One Flew Over the Cuckoo's Nest*,[13] was less ambivalent—the conditions he painted were a living hell, and there was little doubt from his sketch that he believed that all

---

[9] B.F. SKINNER, THE BEHAVIOR OF ORGANISMS (1938); SCIENCE AND HUMAN BEHAVIOR (1953); WALDEN TWO (1948); BEYOND FREEDOM AND DIGNITY (1971); ABOUT BEHAVIORISM (1974).

[10] Behaviorism, at least in a mild form of the token economy, was instituted in some mental hospitals as early as the early 1960s and has spread from there. There have been some attempts, virtually all now abandoned, to institute behavior modification programs, ranging from the token economy to more virulent forms of aversive conditioning, in prisons. See Singer, *Consent of the Unfree: Medical Experimentation and Behavior Modification in the Closed Institution*, 1 J. LAW AND HUM. BEH. 1, 32–43 (1977). Latent fears of determinism and soul-wrenching primordial questions about human autonomy are raised by such programs. These were highlighted by Anthony Burgess' novel, A CLOCKWORK ORANGE (1963), which popularized the fear that behavior modifiers would remove whatever free will was left in the human race. Strident attacks on the involuntary application of behaviorist techniques to mental patients and prisoners increased; the therapeutic state" became the enemy of liberty, and the "right to be different" was advanced by many. See, e.g., N. KITTRIE, THE RIGHT TO BE DIFFERENT (1970); R. SINGER and W. STATSKY, RIGHTS OF THE IMPRISONED (1974).

[11] Birnbaum, *The Right to Treatment*, 46 A.B.A.J. 499 (1960).

[12] E. GOFFMAN, ASYLUMS (1960).

[13] K. KESEY, ONE FLEW OVER THE CUCKOO'S NEST (1962).

total institutions would remain so: their only function appeared to be (echoes of Szasz) to hold deviants and to make them (as McMurphy is made in the end of the book) nondangerous to the staff as well as to society at large.

Some of these attacks, of course, were accurate. Moreover, the secrecy in which these activities were carried out—behind the grey walls of mental hospitals and, to some extent of prisons—added to the concern of the critics. Kesey's book, which overstated the conditions of mental health treatment in most states, was accepted as gospel, since it appeared not unreasonable on its face and since no one else—except the protesting doctors—knew better. The only, or major, defenders of the system were doctors themselves, and their obvious self-interest deprived their protestations of any influence at all. Moreover the defenders of the system typically felt compelled, erroneously, to deny that any abuses were occurring. When some abuses were proved, the entire defense, both of the good and of the bad, became more suspect.

The same movement occurred in penology. During the 1960s, civil rights demonstrators—many young, reasonably affluent, often white—were incarcerated, if only for a short time, in local jails and sometimes in large prisons. With the protests against the Viet Nam war, this phenomenon was repeated. When these persons were released, as had occurred in the 1920s when draft resisters were released, they revealed the conditions of prisons and the abuses they had experienced. And, because they were young, white, affluent, and clearly not "criminals," they were believed (and rightly).

The onset of "poverty" litigation, spurred by what then seemed to be a relatively innocuous opinion of the United States Supreme Court,[14] but which in retrospect is clearly a watershed in the entire civil liberties movement, similarly increased the scrutiny to which prisons were subjected. Federal judges visiting prisons, perhaps for the first time in their lives,[15] saw the intolerable conditions of solitary confinement, overcrowding, and idleness that had been invisible behind the three-foot-thick walls of penal institutions throughout the country. The

[14] In Monroe v. Pape, 365 U.S. 167 (1961), the Supreme Court held that state citizens could sue in federal court state officers who violated their constitutional rights. The decision really only reaffirmed a long-standing interpretation of a century-old statute, but coming as it did at the outset of the civil rights movement, it gave proponents of civil rights activities a method of avoiding supposedly prejudiced state courts. The remedies, moreover, were virtually unlimited—damages, injunctions, writs of prohibition—and over the past dozen years have proliferated even more astoundingly. In recent years, federal courts have appointed prison monitors, human rights commissions, ombudsmen; in other litigation, receiverships have sometimes been established under the aegis of the court to run local governmental units, such as school boards. The impact of *Monroe* cannot be underestimated in the entire spectrum of civil rights litigation.

[15] J. BENNETT, I CHOSE PRISON (1970).

slaughter at Attica, combined with the revelations (after the riot was quashed) of the conditions of that prison, reinforced much of the criticism: prisoners were not, in fact, being "treated," "rehabilitated," or "reformed" in those institutions. Instead—a cry heard 200 years earlier in criticism of the first prison and echoed by every critic since then—prisons were "schools of crime," warehouses in which men spent agonizing years decaying, shunted out of the mainstream of society, and when they were released, precluded from entering that society fully by a battery of discriminatory, irrational, mean-minded "civil disabilities." The caption "correctional facility," which had been proudly worn by new prisons in the 1950s and 1960s, became a mark of scorn and derision in the 1970s. The final straw of this particular camel's load was Robert Martinson's study—which essentially concluded that coerced programs of rehabilitation in prison rarely, if ever, affected the recidivism rate of prisoners who participated in them, probably because the prisoner did not wish to be rehabilitated, but participated only to obtain early release.[16] Martinson's conclusion was seized by anti-indeterminacy forces and his findings somewhat distorted by both liberals (who opposed "conformity" programs) and conservatives (who sneered at rehabilitating the prisoner).

If prisoners were not being rehabilitated in the prisons, and if social science and psychiatry could not aid in that endeavor, what then was the parole board doing when it determined whether a prisoner had been "rehabilitated" and was "ready to rejoin society"? The revelation by the President's Crime Commission Report in 1967 that in twenty-five states parole board members were employed only part time raised even more serious questions about whether these boards were, in fact, composed of professionals able to espy the advent of rehabilitation. Further investigation indicated that, in terms of ability to predict "relapse" of the "disease"—recidivism—the board members were no better than the "lay" public.

Finally, and perhaps most melancholy of all, we lost hope in the juvenile justice system—the paradigmatic rehabilitative treatment system. Even if one does not accept, at least wholly, Platt's thesis that the entire movement toward juvenile justice was constructed as a method of restricting immigrant and black children,[17] by the mid-1960s it often appeared to be just that. Moreover, in 1966, the United States Supreme Court sounded its final disappointment: "There is evidence . . . that there may be grounds for concern that the child

[16] D. LIPTON, R. MARTINSON, and J. WILKS, THE EFFECTIVENESS OF CORRECTIONAL TREATMENT (1975).

[17] See A. PLATT, THE CHILD SAVERS (1969). See also D. ROTHMAN, THE DISCOVERY OF THE ASYLUM (1971).

receives the worst of both worlds: that he gets neither the protections accorded to adults nor the solicitous care and regenerative treatment postulated for children."[18] A year later, the Court underscored this by making the juvenile system increasingly more like the adult system.[19]

By the early 1970s, then, the hope of criminologists that science, in the form of medicine, psychiatry, social work, and so forth, would find a solution to the crime problem—a solution that was both compatible with our belief in liberty and our visions of the perfectibility of mankind—stood in tatters, dealt blow after merciless blow from all sides for an entire decade and more.[20] The criticism was for the most part deserved and needed telling. But the rehabilitationist theory, which had for so long promised salvation, now appeared not only as an empty promise, but as an intentional deceit, repeated only to perpetuate jobs and power. The reaction, as any reaction to crushed hopes, was jolting—the movement to commensurate deserts drew some of its greatest energies from disillusioned rehabilitationists.

THE UNMAKING OF JUDICIAL DISCRETION

At the same time that the medical model, which upheld one leg of the individualization theory of sentencing, was being undercut, another historical tide eroded a second leg. In many aspects of our lives, a growing concern with discretion was noticeable. Schools, military commands, hospitals (in regard to doctor staff positions), and many other so-called "insular communities," into which the courts had earlier absolutely refused to intrude, now became the subject of both judicial inquiry and public debate. The culmination of this distrust with discretion, of course, was the decision of the United States Supreme Court in *United States v. Nixon.*[21] The cry to abolish (not merely limit) discretion, grew loud.[22]

Judicial discretion in sentencing remained strangely aloof from these attacks for a substantial period of time. Disparity of sentences, of course, had been long recognized: in the early 1960s, both the Director of the United States Bureau of Prisons[23] and the Attorney General of

[18] Kent v. United States, 383 U.S. 541, 546 (1966).

[19] *In re* Gault, 387 U.S. 1 (1967).

[20] Professor Zalman has a supplementary, if not contradictory, analysis—that the disenchantment with discretion derives from the evidence of some failures of the welfare state. Zalman, *The Rise and Fall of the Indeterminate Sentence*, 24 WAYNE L. REV. 45, 857 (1977–78).

[21] 418 U.S. 683 (1974).

[22] See AMERICAN FRIENDS SERVICE COMMITTEE, STRUGGLE FOR JUSTICE (1971).

[23] Bennett, Countdown for Judicial Sentencing, 25 Fed. Prob. 22 (Sept. 1961).

the United States[24] had bemoaned it. In 1957, Congress had passed legislation funding "sentencing institutes" where federal judges could learn how to sentence more evenly.[25] And experimentation in sentencing councils, or other types of group sentencing, arose here and there. But in general, until the mid-1970s, judicial sentencing, with all its discretion, was not seriously challenged. Even reform standards, such as those of the American Bar Association, sought to regularize the sentencing hearing and the process of sentencing or to establish appellate review, but did little to restrict the actual choice of sentence.

There may be many reasons why the concern with disparity in judicial sentences initially focused on establishing appellate review of sentencing, rather than on reexamining the purposes of sentencing. Discretion was a necessary part of the medical model of sentencing. It should not surprise, after all, that different judges sentenced offenders to different terms for the same crime, because the crime was relatively unimportant, merely the catalyst that initiated the system. If that was true, then only in rare cases would the discretion be so badly mishandled that one could speak of abuse of discretion; and in such instances, an appellate court could act.

Moreover, appellate review of sentences itself was generally ill-received. In 1974, in incredibly strong dictum,[26] the U.S. Supreme Court spoke out sharply against appellate review of sentences. The argument that the trial judge had "seen" the defendant throughout the trial, had been able to assess credibility, and the like[27]—while hardly true because of the excessive rates of plea bargaining[28]—still had allure.

What, then, has happened in four years to concentrate our focus not on establishing an appellate tribunal, but on the sentencing judge? In part, I believe, time simply caught up with the judiciary. In part, it was the appearance of a highly intelligent, thoughtful book on sentencing by Marvin Frankel—a federal judge[29] who had actually *seen* "individualized" sentencing at work; his blast at his own colleagues for lawless sentencing surely contributed to the concern for controlling discretion, rather than simply reviewing it.

Finally, there was a simultaneous growing crescendo not against judges who released white collar criminals, but against those who

[24] Kennedy, Address, 30 F.R.D. 422 (1961).

[25] 28 U.S.C. §334 (1964).

[26] Dorszynski v. United States, 418 U.S. 424 (1974).

[27] Brewster, Appellate Review of Sentences, 40 F.R.D. 79 (1965).

[28] See State v. Leggeadrini, 75 N.J. 150, 380 A.2d 1112 (1977), acknowledging that where the defendant pleads guilty, appellate review of sentences is more likely to be meaningful.

[29] M. FRANKEL, CRIMINAL SENTENCES—LAW WITHOUT ORDER (1973).

allegedly released too soon the real criminals; the movement against judicial lenience in sentencing also played its part.

LAW AND ORDER AND THE SENTENCING PROCESS

In contrast to those who argued that the medical model was too harsh and led to excessively long sentences and to those who argued that judicial discretion often operated crudely against the young, black, violent offender and in favor of the middle-aged, white, "business" offender, stood the proponents of simply harsher sentences—the law-and-order contingent.

This book is not the place to debate whether there has, in fact, been an increase in the crime rate, or simply in the reported crime rate, or a mixture of both, as well as other factors. (Indeed, there is some indication that the rate—real or reported—is inching downward at this very time.) But it seems clear that in the late 1960s and early 1970s there was a growing perception that the criminal justice system was becoming incredibly overworked. Plea bargaining, condemned for nearly one hundred years by judicial decisions and criminological critics, suddenly received sanction from the United States Supreme Court[30] as an efficacious method of dealing with the ballooning number of offenders, both violent and nonviolent. City streets appeared to become more dangerous to walk, possibly due to the increase of criminals, possibly because of the increased vulnerability of victims. There appeared to be an epidemic drug addiction problem, which itself allegedly generated more crime. Recidivism rates were published as higher than ever, although that figure is enormously suspect, even in the best of times. Rehabilitation seemed not to work; deterrence, and if not deterrence, incapacitation, seemed like the answer.

These cries are the perennials in the garden of reaction to a perceived breakdown in the criminal justice system; they have occurred in every generation. And, perhaps, without the other factors already mentioned, these cries, like those of the 1920s, 1930s, and 1940s, would have had little effect in fact upon the correctional or sentencing systems. In combination with the other elements outlined in this short history, however, they provided the final, vital link in the movement for the demise of the indeterminate sentence.

[30] Santobello v. New York, 404 U.S. 257 (1971).

Chapter 2

Sentencing Reform, Equality, and Proportionality

Every just scheme of punishment must be fair. And part of fairness is equality. Prima facie, equality would demand that two offenders who have committed the same offense receive the same sentence. Yet the medical model of punishment as well as the other utilitarian schools of punishment—deterrence and incapacitation—impose different sentences upon offenders who have committed the same crime and confine them for different lengths of time. How, then, can they claim that they are fair? Is it not clear that they lead by definition to inherently unequal, and hence unfair, treatment?

The issue is important, for it demonstrates the need, which will be reconsidered later, to reassert the definition of equality. Equality, as we know, is not treating all people alike; it is treating similar people similarly and dissimilar people dissimilarly. And to determine the "similarity" of persons, the goals or criteria of the system must be considered.

Thus, the utilitarian would argue that to impose the same sentence upon all persons who committed the "same" crime is in fact not equal, because it does not consider the utilitarian goals of the system. The offender must be held for as long as necessary to achieve those goals; any other mechanism would be unfair and hence unequal. Thus, if a school system, whose purpose was to teach persons to read at a certain grade level, released one student at the age of twenty-three, while releasing another at the age of fourteen, it would not indicate that it had treated them unequally or unfairly: it simply took longer to achieve the goal with one student than with the other. To have released the first student at age fourteen would have been unfair and unequal, since neither he nor society (the indirect beneficiary of high reading levels) would have achieved the benefit sought.

To justify facially unequal sentences, then, the utilitarian must show two things: (1) equal access to the tools of rehabilitation, deterrence or (anti-)incapacitation; (2) release at the time—the precise time—that benefit is achieved. Retention after the time the status had been achieved would be unfair and hence unequal. One method to test the fairness of a system of utilitarian punishment, then, is whether it can and does achieve this type of equality.

UTILITARIANISM AND EQUALITY

Inaccurate Prediction
The goal of crime control through rehabilitation and incapacitation requires some prediction of future behavior—how the offender will behave when released from the institution. In order to assure equality—even within the terms of the system—there must be accuracy of prediction. Yet the data are far from encouraging: most students agree that prediction methods are crude and very often wrong.[1] This inability to predict accurately undermines the medical-incapacitative arms of the utilitarian school.

Deterrence and Crime Control
A second utilitarian goal is crime control through deterrence: the sentence imposed on the offender should be sufficient to deter both him (specific deterrence) and others (general deterrence) from further criminal acts. Here again, however, the evidence that any sentence deters is weak.[2] Furthermore, the argument that continued incarceration lowers the crime rate[3] is also suspect.[4]

---

[1] See, e.g., von Hirsch, *Prediction of Criminal Conduct and Preventive Confinement of Convicted Persons,* 21 Buff. L. Rev. 717 (1972); Ennis and Litwack, *Psychiatry and the Presumption of Expertise: Flipping Coins in the Courtroom,* 62 Calif. L. Rev. 693 (1974). Even those who argue that we can predict agree that, at best, the rate is, for nonviolent offenders with past histories of criminality, between 62–70 percent. Even this would give a very high rate of "false positives"; whether it is "too" high, of course, is a subjective judgment to be balanced with the deprivation of liberty that occurs on the basis of the predictions. See U.S. Parole Commission, Selected Reprints Related to Parole Decision Making (1977).

[2] See generally, F. Zimring and G. Hawkins, Deterrence (1973). N. Walker, Sentencing in a Rational Society 59 (1971).

[3] See J. Wilson, Thinking About Crime (1975).

[4] Current figures indicate that police "clear" only 20 percent of all property offenses and approximately 35 percent of all "person" offenses. Of persons arrested for property offenses, only 15 percent are actually convicted and only 5–10 percent actually incarcerated, the rest receiving probation. The conviction rate is higher for person-person

At the very best, the evidence is uncertain as to whether any of the utilitarian aims are, or can be, achieved by our current sentencing process. If they cannot be—or if the precise time at which they are achieved cannot be accurately determined—they are unfair, even under their own terms, to offenders. While recognizing each of these goals as desirable in the abstract,[5] therefore, the commensurate desert

---

offenders, but not by much. Thus, of all property crimes reported only 2–3 percent of the offenders are incarcerated. Of all personal crimes reported, the rate is somewhere in the vicinity of 10 percent. Additionally, the general consensus is that at least 50 percent of all property crimes (some estimates are as high as 80 percent) are unreported; of all person-person crimes, probably 50 percent go unreported. Thus, releasing all property offenders would—assuming that every one committed another crime—increase the property crime rate by no more than 1.5 percent, and probably by less than 1 percent. Personal offenses might increase—again assuming 100 percent recidivism—by 2.5 percent. This would thus, at best, increase the total crime rate by less than 4 percent, since most offenses are property crimes. Moreover, given what we actually know about recidivism rates (between 30–60 percent appears to be the best estimate), we would be talking about a total increase in actual crime of less than 2 percent. One response to this argument, however, is that a 100 percent recidivism rate (one new crime per every released prisoner) is misleading—that a small number of offenders actually commit most crimes and if we could determine who they are, and incapacitate them sufficiently, crime rates would go down. Corollary to this position is the assumption that, e.g., even this handful would account for a wider spread of crime than would the easier assumption that each released prisoner would commit one more crime—i.e., that of one hundred offenders, even if ninety did not recidivate, the remaining ten would commit in excess of one hundred crimes. See C. SILBERMAN, CRIMINAL VIOLENCE, CRIMINAL JUSTICE, ch. 3 (1978); Shinnar and Shinnar, *The Effects of the Criminal Justice System in the Control of Crime: A Quantitative Approach*, 9 LAW & SOC. REVIEW (Summer 1975). In partial response to this assertion, VanDine, Dimitz, and Conrad recently conducted a much more sophisticated analysis that concluded that incarceration of every violent offender for a period of five years would reduce the violent crime rate no more than 4 percent and probably closer to 1–2 percent. Van Dine, Dimitz, and Conrad, *The Incapacitation of the Dangerous Offender: A Statistical Experiment*, JOURNAL OF RESEARCH IN CRIME AND DELINQUENCY 22 (January 1977). Whatever the precise figures, or even best guesses, the argument that punishment in fact reduces the crime rate is dubious at best. Moreover, it is not clear that incarceration actually reduces the crime rate at all, since in many crimes, the "replacement" coefficient of crime may operate so that some person, otherwise marginally law abiding, fills the vacuum left by the incarcerated offender. This seems true, for example, in gambling and narcotics offenses and is arguably true in other areas as well. In any event, prophecies such as those made by Professor Wilson that long-term incarceration of armed robbers and burglars would reduce the incidence of those crimes by 20 percent seem serendipitous at best. See Wilson, *supra* note 3. Hospers, *Punishment, Protection, and Retaliation*, in J. CEDERBLOM and W. BLIZEK, JUSTICE AND PUNISHMENT 21, 26 (1977), cites Maya Pines as quoting wardens to the effect that if the entire prison population were released tomorrow, the nation would be no less safe than it is now, but these are merely subjective judgments as well.

[5] A misleading statement is that of Bedau that "retributivists in principle are fundamentally indifferent between the state of the world in which there is no crime, and the state of the world in which there is a wide variety of horrible crimes each of which is punished fully and exactly as retribution requires." Bedau, *Concessions to Retribution in Punishment*, in J. CEDERBLOM and W. BLIZEK, JUSTICE AND PUNISHMENT 51, 69 (1977). This is equivalent to saying that retributivists care about neither flowers, poetry, nor poverty, simply because they do not believe that punishment should be used to affect those aspects of life. The retributivist may well care about crime rates; the sole claim of

school of sentencing contends that because of their highly tenuous nature and the slim likelihood of achieving them, we should be much more modest[6] in our aims or, at best, in our premises for determining suitable punishment. Given the failure of the police to secure arrests, particularly of property offenders, and the exceptionally low rate of both successful prosecution and ultimate confinement, it is not possible to prove that sentences handed out to that miniscule proportion of offenders whom we catch will have any significant deterrent effect.

Access to Programs

It is unnecessary to develop at length here the argument that prisoners in fact do not have equal access to programs by which they may become rehabilitated or to demonstrate that it is no longer necessary to incapacitate them. The facts of prison life are sufficiently well known that again, at best, the utilitarian is put in a difficult, perhaps impossible, position of justifying differential sentencing. At the very least, the system is prima facie violative of equality, even under its own terms.

In short, even within their own goals, the proponents of utilitarianism cannot demonstrate that offenders are equally treated; the individualization model of sentencing that utilitarianism requires fails to reach even tolerable levels of equality.

COMMENSURATE DESERTS, RETRIBUTION, AND EQUALITY

But the weaknesses in the utilitarian position are not limited to pragmatic ones of whether, in fact, the goals are achievable either presently or at some future date. Critics argue that the essence of utilitarianism—using one person to achieve another's happiness—is morally repugnant, because it uses one person as a pawn for the good of

---

the retributivist is that it is not the role of punishment, and of the agencies that punish, to try to affect the crime rate.

[6] Professor Zalman, in a stimulating article, has suggested that the desert call for modesty in goals for which we use the sentencing system is symptomatic of a larger societal disenchantment with the welfare state. Zalman, *The Rise and Fall of the Indeterminate Sentence*, 24 WAYNE L. REV. 45, 857 (1977–1978). This thesis is somewhat grandiose, since at least some supporters of a desert model reject neither the possibility nor the desirability of meaningful programs, but only the proposition that the sentencing process should be used to achieve that end. Thus, some desert supporters might well call for increased education, vocational rehabilitation programs, even increased community aid after incarceration, all of which reflect the welfare state, and still not seek to achieve rehabilitative ends through sentencing or corrections. Indeed, as noted in Chapter 7, most desert theorists argue that rehabilitation programs in prisons should be expanded, not terminated. Nevertheless, Zalman's hypothesis is an intriguing one and warrants further examination.

others; it is concerned with the "greatest good of the greatest number," even if some have to suffer, unequally, to achieve that good.

Another way of making this point is to say that utilitarians are interested in justice in the aggregate, rather than with distributive justice. Jon Kleinig has put it well[7]:

> Apart from the internal difficulties posed by the classical accounts, it does seem highly implausible to analyse justice in terms of utility. There is no place in these accounts for questioning the justness of a law which maximised advantages at the expense of equality of treatment, for justice would simply be the maximisation of advantages. Yet criticize on this basis is what we quite frequently want to do. Consider two courses of action B and C, whose consequences can affect four people, P, Q, R and S. Let us suppose that the performance of B will give P six units of advantage, Q one unit, R one unit, and S one unit, totalling nine units of advantage. It seems quite proper here to consider the choice between B and C as one between utility and justice respectively (without, for the moment, making the further claim that the performance of C is better). The trouble with utilitarian attempts to analyse justice is that they confuse two quite different sorts of concepts, aggregative with distributive, which may, on occasions, conflict. Aggregative concepts like the maximisation of advantage, the common good, the general welfare, the public interest, and so on are concerned with a total benefit, and not at all with the way in which such benefits are distributed. On the other hand, distributive concepts like justice, fairness, equality and equity are concerned with the apportioning or balancing of benefits rather than the totalling of benefits. Similar considerations apply in the case of impositions, where justice is concerned with a balancing of impositions, and utility with the totalling of impositions. What is least disadvantageous is not necessarily the most just.

Kleinig's example is important, for it demonstrates that the desert-retributivist school[8] is willing to sacrifice some "good" to a particular

---

[7] J. KLEINIG, PUNISHMENTS AND DESERT 79–80 (1973). For similar points, see Hospers, *supra* note 4 at 35; J. RAWLS, A THEORY OF JUSTICE (1969).

[8] A recent article, Kellogg, *From Retribution to "Desert", The Evolution of Criminal Punishment*, 15 CRIMINOLOGY 179 (1977), has argued that the commensurate desert philosophy is not retributivist at all, as that sense is historically understood, but has as its main aim equality and fairness in punishment disposition. Kellogg's thesis provides an important insight, for the older school of retributivism never had to actually implement the notion and was therefore never faced, directly, with the implications of punishing the crime rather than the criminal. Yet, as Kleinig has demonstrated, desert and retribution carry with them the principle of equality, because they are as concerned with distributive justice as they are with justice alone. See also Mundle, *Punishment and Deceit*, in H. ACTON, THE PHILOSOPHY OF PUNISHMENT 65, 71–75, (1969); Zalman, *supra* note 6 at 931.

It is therefore not surprising, nor inconsistent with the base notion of retribution,

person or to society in general in order to obtain distributive justice for those directly affected. It is clearly a moral, not a pragmatic, stand.

The second weakness with the utilitarian theory, as a theory of criminal punishment, is that it seems scarcely concerned with the gravity of the offender's criminal act, except as it may provide justification for state intervention generally. The crux of this philosophy is the offender's future actions, and the future actions of others, not their past actions. Thus, for example, it has often been argued against the utilitarian viewpoint that it would permit punishment of an innocent offender if general deterrence would ensue.[9] While most philosophers have now rejected this argument as unfair to the utilitarians,[10] the point is still valid: the orientation of the utilitarians is the future; the past offense of the criminal is relevant only insofar as it indicates either (1) the possibility of his future rehabilitation; (2) his possible future dangerousness; or (3) the kinds of persons who would, in the future, be deterred if he were punished.

Whether one agrees with these goals as justifying a system of confinement or not is beyond the scope of this book; but it seems eminently clear that the essence of the criminal sanction is the amount of moral blame it carries. Any system that ignores this requirement of blame cannot be accurately called a system of criminal punishment. The United States Supreme Court has indirectly agreed that the purpose of a criminal sanction is blameworthiness and that utilitarian goals, even if proper, cannot be used to justify the imposition of a *criminal* penalty. In *Robinson* v. *California*[11] the Court was faced with the constitutionality of a state statute making it a crime for a person to be addicted to certain drugs. In invalidating that statute, the Court, in

---

that much of this book, and much of the writing on implementing desert generally, is concerned with equality of punishment as a prime—perhaps the prime—goal of sentencing. It might well be, therefore, that we could dub the school the equal punishment school rather than the desert school.

Strict limitation on discretion is the major procedural method of assuring equality of sentencing and, hence, distributive justice, and much of the concern of this volume is with methods by which discretion that will, or may, result in inequality of punishment may be restricted. Far from being nonretributivist, however, the true desert proponent will be as interested in assuring that the criminal law return to (or perhaps, more accurately, fully adopt for the first time) the implications of mens rea and moral culpability as essential to imposition of any criminal sanction. Retribution stresses the moral culpability—the evil mind—of the transgressor, for it is only in that moral culpability that the predicate for criminal liability lies.

[9] See Armstrong, *The Retributivist Hits Back,* in H. ACTON, THE PHILOSOPHY OF PUNISHMENT 138, 152 (1969); Mabbett, *Punishment,* in *id.,* 39, 44.

[10] H.L.A. HART, PUNISHMENT AND RESPONSIBILITY (1968).

[11] 370 U.S. 660 (1962).

dictum, said that there would be no constitutional difficulty if the state merely wished to hospitalize the individual for a period of time until cured (the utilitarian aim), but that it could not attach to that individual a criminal sanction as well. Since both hospitalization and criminal punishment involve confinement, it is clear that the Court was not differentiating between the two systems on the basis of loss of freedom. Therefore, some other difference has to explain the Court's decision. That difference is blame—stigma. No one blames a person who has a disease when he is placed in a hospital to be cured; but society, and the criminal law, do blame a person who has committed a criminal act.

The utilitarian school ignores the centrality of blame in any viable system of criminal punishment. Criminal sanctions are imposed upon offenders because they have committed a morally reprehensible act and, therefore, are subject to blame. Moral repugnance to the actor in a criminal situation is the only justifiable basis for distinguishing the criminal law from other kinds of legal actions (such as tort claims) against persons who injure, and the purposes of criminal law should be served by our penal sanctions.[12] It is this ascription of moral blame that differentiates the criminal sanction from other legal penalities. If sentencing serves primarily a retributive function, we will reaffirm in a strong and direct manner the community's mores and its right to enforce those mores, within wide limits, upon all the members of society.

Recognition of the role that blame must play in any valid sentencing scheme requires what the utilitarian school rejects—a central focus on the *act* the offender committed and the moral culpability with which he committed it. Furthermore, equality of sentence, in the sense of equal duration of punishment, is then required for similar acts, since the amount of blame is the same; to blame one offender less for precisely the same level of blameworthy conduct is to blame the other more. Finally, because blame is the key to criminal sentencing, we must mete it out scrupulously and meticulously, assuring that the right amount of blame is given to the offense; in short, we have a requirement of proportionality of the sanction to the offense, because the blame must be based upon the act and not upon the actor. When the key is moral blameworthiness, every equally morally blameworthy

---

[12] Sir James Fitzhugh Stephens recognized this, but was wrong when he declared that "it is morally right to hate criminals. . . ." J. STEPHENS, II A HISTORY OF THE CRIMINAL LAW OF ENGLAND 81 (1883). If punishment is to be retribution, and not vengeance, it must be carried out dispassionately. Kant, Hegel, and other founders of the retributivist school are in accord on this. Hospers, *supra* note 4 at 22.

offender must be punished equally severely or the basis of the punishment is lost. We must therefore turn to the question of how we determine the "seriousness" and "blameworthiness" of the offense.

SERIOUSNESS

If the purpose of the criminal sanction is to apportion blame—and punishment—according to the seriousness of the offense, how does one determine seriousness? Von Hirsch has suggested that seriousness has two components—the culpability of the offender and the harm done.[13] We shall explore these concepts seriatim.

The Culpability of the Offender

Since the late sixteenth century at least, the criminal law has said that it differentiates criminal defendants on the basis of their culpability as demonstrated by the mental state—mens rea—with which they committed the crime. Thus, homicide "malice prepense," officially distinguished from other homicides since at least 1391,[14] became in 1547 the only nonclergyable homicide offense; homicide by "chance medly"—what (roughly) we would now call manslaughter—was differentiated by the law because a difference was perceived in the blameworthiness of those who actually planned and intended to kill and those who killed on the spur of the moment.

Defining the requisite mental state, of course, is not an easy task; yet the Model Penal Code has attempted to bring, from the muddle of case law in the nineteenth and twentieth centuries, a consensus of understanding that enormously assists the process: the code distinguishes between acts "purposely," "knowingly," "recklessly," or "negligently" perpetrated[15] and imposes different punishments upon the same result, dependent upon the mental state.[16]

---

[13] VON HIRSCH, DOING JUSTICE (1976). But see Bedau, *supra* note 5 at 65.

[14] 16 Rich. II 380.

[15] M.P.C. §2.02 (1962).

[16] One might expect that, with over two centuries of dogged attempts by the judiciary, and with the concerted efforts of groups such as the American Law Institute, agreement would be near, at least on the basic levels of culpability.

Recently, the House of Lords demonstrated that agreement may be close. In the *Hyam* case [Hyam v. Director of Public Pros., (1975) A.C. 55], the House distinguished between persons who (1) intend to (a) kill, (b) inflict serious bodily harm, (c) subject a person to a high risk of death, or (d) subject a person to a high risk of serious bodily harm; and (2) those who, while knowing that the risks alluded to are present, do not in fact intend that the victims will be subjected to them. In many ways, this is similar to the division which the ALI draws between "purposely" and "recklessly" acting, although the category of "knowing" in the ALI's model might encompass some actors in the second category.

Why it has taken so long for the common law to grope its way even to a tentative agreement and definition of *mens rea* is far too complex a question to explore here,[17] but some tentative answers may be suggested.

First, the difficulty of proving at trial a particular mens rea led courts to establish various "legal fictions," which allowed the fact finder to ignore the defendant's actual state of mind and to ask, essentially, what state of mind the average person would have had had that person committed the act. The fiction of "constructive malice" and the "presumption" that one intended the "natural consequences of one's acts" also undercut the requirement of actual subjective liability. Utilitarian notions of deterrence, particularly as articulated by Justice Holmes,[18] added to the diminishment of the requirement of actual mens rea. Indeed, some argued that by the beginning of this century, true subjective *mens rea* had become irrelevant to disposition of criminal cases.[19]

Second, the criminal law was tainted in this century by the addition of numerous "strict liability" offenses, in which, at least in theory, the defendant could be punished[20] vicariously and/or without any actual mental state at all.[21]

---

[17] For a stunning attempt to do so, see G. FLETCHER, RETHINKING CRIMINAL LAW (1978).

[18] O.W. HOLMES, THE COMMON LAW (1881).

[19] Levitt, *Origin of the Doctrine of Mens Rea*, 17 ILL. L. REV. 117 (1918).

[20] The degree of punishment, however, was sometimes limited. Thus, in Commonwealth v. Koczwara, 307 Pa. 575, 155, A.2d 825 (1959), the court upheld a "strict liability" statute for selling liquor to a minor, but only if there was no possible incarceration. Others, such as Sayre, *Public Welfare Offenses,* 33 COLUM. L. REV. 55 (1933), argued that this should be a requirement if criminal liability was to be imposed either vicariously or without regard to *mens rea*. To a large extent, of course, if one removes the possibility of loss of freedom and removes blame as a critical ingredient of the act, it is no longer theoretically a criminal act; to call it criminal may be both misleading and inaccurate.

[21] The advent of the industrial revolution has resulted in innumerable prohibitions relating to health, safety, and welfare, in most of which there is no requirement of *mens rea*. Only a few United States Supreme Court cases deal directly with this issue. In United States v. Balint, 258 U.S. 250 (1922), for example, the court said that knowledge—usually a requirement of *mens rea*—was not required for tax violations regarding drug sales. The actual holding of the case, however, was that the government need not allege in the indictment that the defendants knew the item was morphine; this holding would be consistent with a later determination that either (1) the defendant had the burden of proof that he did not know; or (2) if the defendant raised the issue, the government would then have to prove knowledge beyond a reasonable doubt. An analogy could be drawn here to insanity, since the government need not allege sanity in the indictment, but may be required to prove sanity beyond a reasonable doubt if adequately raised by the defendant. A recent case, United States v. Park, 421 U.S. 658 (1975), can also be read as suggesting that violations of health codes can be based on strict liability, but closer reading of the Court's opinion demonstrates that at least negligence is required before guilt can be imputed. Finally, the Court has clearly indicated that in

Third, the two schools of thought—subjective and objective criminal liability—often reached the same result, therefore suggesting that rigorous analysis of the reasons for the result was unnecessary. Thus, for example, one could support the defense of insanity on the utilitarian basis that other mentally ill persons are not to be deterred by punishment[22] or on the grounds that the mentally ill offender is not morally culpable and therefore not deserving of punishment. Self-defense could be supported on the utilitarian ground that punishment would not deter self-preservation (*viz.* Justice Holmes' famous aphorism that "detached reflection cannot be demanded in the presence of an uplifted knife"[23]) or on the basis that the defendant did not intend to kill, but merely to escape, and, therefore should be treated as at least excused and, perhaps, justified.[24] (The more sophisticated utilitarian argument against allowing such defenses—that some might fake the defense if available[25]—is less clear, except that the counterutilitarian argument that the populace would not tolerate a system of laws that punished nonmorally culpable people appears to have weight here.)

There are, of course, numerous areas where the two schools clash. Thus, in the self-defense example, the law today is that a person who kills honestly believing that he is in imminent danger has a defense only if the belief was a reasonable one—an unreasonable mistake as to the danger is not a defense. This objective standard is clearly utilitarian, since the retributivist would argue that the actor who honestly believes that there is a danger is not morally culpable (unless one takes the position that it is morally culpable to live and take life, rather than not take life and die). Similarly, the criminal law today generally is that no mistake or ignorance of the criminal law is a defense, no matter how reasonable. Thus, a defendant who seeks the advice of three lawyers before acting upon a course of conduct will still be criminally liable if it turns out that the lawyers were wrong.[26]

---

some cases, notably the "infamous crimes of the common law," it would be unconstitutional to dispense with a *mens rea* requirement. That too, was dictum. Morrissette v. United States, 342 U.S. 246 (1952). Nevertheless, it does seem clear that, at least in most states, there are numerous "statutory public offenses" that dispense with the requirement of *mens rea* entirely.

[22] But see Hart, *supra* note 10.

[23] Brown v. United States, 256 U.S. 335, 343 (1921).

[24] The difference between justification and excuse, critical to an appreciation of the criminal law, is too broad to examine here. Again, see Fletcher, *supra* note 17. See also Austin, *A Plea for Excuses*, in PHILOSOPHY OF LAW 316 (J. Feinberg and H. Gross, ed., 1975).

[25] See Greenawalt, *"Uncontrollable" Actions and the Eighth Amendment: Implications of Powell v. Texas*, 69 COLUM. L. REV. 927 (1969).

[26] Staley v. State, 87 Neb. 539, 131 N.W. 1028 (1911). There are a few cases contra,

Again, a retributivist would argue that the offender is morally non-culpable: he has not only not sought to breach the social compact, but has affirmatively sought not to breach it.

These factors—the growth of the objective school of criminal law, the expansion of presumptions, and the overlap of results that utility and retribution often achieve—have deflected much of the discussion of substantive criminal law, particularly that dealing with *mens rea,* from the central focus of blame.[27]

If, however, we now establish a sentencing system in which blame is essential, we will be required to reexamine much of our criminal law and to make the hard decisions that in the past, we have all too often evaded.[28] This will be no easy task. Whether the taking of bread by a starving person should be treated as theft has split legal authorities (not to mention ethicists) for centuries; but to convict and stigmatize that person as a thief, only to place him on suspended, unsupervised probation and to bid him Godspeed, is defensible only, if at all, upon utilitarian grounds. To that extent at least, these issues require further examination by those who seek to devise a new sentencing framework based on blame. But at least if we announce that that is the predicate of our system, perhaps the issue will be more directly addressed.

This, however, does not end the discussion. The degree of blame has thus far been said to be reflected in the existence of *mens rea*—very specifically defined states of mind. But why should the concern of the criminal law, and of those who seek to impose blame, end there? Why should not other characteristics of the defendent, such as his background, the stresses under which he acted, and the purpose (motive) for which the act was done all contribute to a determination of his blameworthiness? After all, we do, in a normal moral discourse, consider such factors. Does not a sentencing system based upon blameworthiness require individualization, not as a method of predict-

---

e.g., Long v. State, 65 A.2d 489 (Del., 1949), and the Model Penal Code greatly expands the defense. It does not, however, allow advice of counsel as a defense.

[27] Indeed, many attacks on the utilitarian positions were themselves framed in utilitarian terms. Thus, mistake of law based on advice of officials was urged as a defense because it would encourage people to know the law; the argument that the offender who did not, in fact, know the act was not blameworthy was mentioned, if at all, in a footnote toward the end of the discussion.

[28] See, e.g., Regina v. Dudley and Stevens, 14 Q.B. 273 (1884), where the court held two seamen who had canabilized another while they were adrift in a lifeboat for twenty-one days liable for murder, but urged, in the opinion, an executive pardon, which they knew would be forthcoming. See Note, *In Warm Blood: Some Historical and Procedural Aspects of Regina v. Dudley and Stephens*, 34 U. CHI. L. REV. 387 (1967). Thus, the court was able both to announce a harsh verdict (the criminal law condemns this act) and to know that it would have no effect.

ing future behavior, but in order to accurately determine the deserved punishment?[29]

One pragmatic answer is that the search for character has not worked well thus far: unbridled judicial discretion intended to count such factors has led to unbridled judicial disparity. Different judges view the same facts about a defendant's past differently; one may consider that a young, black, urban dweller who has committed several crimes has already suffered and, therefore, that his deserts should be lessened so as not to unfairly enhance his suffering, while another may view those same facts as indicative of a character unworthy of amelioration. The assessment is simply too subjective.

A second pragmatic answer is that the information upon which such judgments are to be made—even if all judges were to agree on their importance and impact—is simply too unreliable to allow decisions as to freedom or blame.[30] Furthermore, to consider such factors, even if the evidence were reliable, would be to allow undue state prying into what should be private facts.[31]

Some less pragmatic responses are also available. The first—a "definitional stop"[32] really—is the core retributivist[33] argument that the act includes the offender's *mens rea* and that, therefore, the *mens rea* is a public fact, unlike the other private items upon which the individualizer school would focus its approach.

A second argument is that in establishing a sentencing system, we are not necessarily justified in simply translating normal moral discourse into the system. It may be true, finally, that only God can impose an accurate moral judgment on any person[34] and that to ask judges or any other official tribunal to make that final judgment,

---

[29] Several writers, without any explanation, have so asserted. See Feinberg, *Introduction*, in PUNISHMENT (J. Feinberg and H. Gross, eds., 1975); Ezorsky, *Introduction*, in PHILOSOPHICAL PERSPECTIVES ON PUNISHMENT xxvi (G. Ezorsky, ed., 1972); Orrick, *Legal Issues in Structuring Sentencing Discretion*, 4 NEW ENG. J. ON PRIS. L. 327 (1978). This position has been taken to an extreme by Gardner, *The Renaissance of Retribution—An Examination of Doing Justice*, 1976 WIS. L. REV. 781. Gardner argues that the criminal law should allow every aspect of the defendant's background to be introduced at trial and the jury be virtually uninstructed on *mens rea*, left simply to judge whether it is just to hold the defendant criminally responsible. Of course, jury nullification allows the jury to ask the latter question, but does not require the introduction of evidence of the offender's entire life. Von Hirsch, in DOING JUSTICE, raises the issue of justice in an allegedly unjust society, but does not pursue it. See ch. 17.

[30] Coffee, *The Future of Sentencing Reform*, 73 MICH. L. REV. 1361 (1975) (hereafter cited as Coffee I).

[31] For example, even if a defendant's religious devotion indicated the need for less punishment, we might not wish to allow the state to make such inquiries.

[32] Cf. Hart, *supra* note 10.

[33] And some other philosophers as well. See Austin, *supra* note 24.

[34] Kleinig, *supra* note 7 at 76.

even assuming that we have all relevant information, is simply arrogant or worse. Is a person who kicks cats more blameworthy for the murder that he has committed than a person who is nice to children? While we, as individuals, may attempt to make those judgments for our own individual actions, we may not wish—or trust—the state to make those same judgments particularly since the effects of state action are so much more drastic than those of private action. Some questions of morality, after all, are too fine to leave to the state.

A final response to the suggestion that retributivists must individualize because blame is a complex matter is that such individualization stresses factors beyond the present control of the defendant, and blames (or praises) him for irrelevant matters. Defendants cannot change their past behavior or character and are therefore made liable (or more liable) by events now beyond their control. *Mens rea* is different, since it is within the ability of each defendant, whatever his past, to control his present mental state and therefore to avoid criminal acts in the present.[35] An analogy to grading of students' exams is apt (though the *mens rea* may be different). To give a student an *A* or *F* on a *C* paper because the paper wasn't characteristic would clearly be unfair and unequal.

This may mean that, in some cases, we do in fact punish unequal defendants equally, if by unequal we refer to the entire background of the defendant. If this is so, however, it is still more desirable than our present system, which distributes punishment at random; it is also more equal than that system since it focuses on knowable facts that are clearly and unequivocally in the control of the defendant. Now the point made earlier on Jon Kleinig's observations concerning distributive justice is critical: if, in order to achieve equality of distribution, we must lose some benefits to one offender (or even to most), that loss is justified by a notion of fairness and justice to all offenders.[36] If, to achieve relative equality based upon the most obvious facts known to

[35] This may appear to beg the question in the case of persons who are allegedly "crime prone." If there were strong evidence that such persons exist and that they have little control over their mental state (e.g., are easily provoked), there might be an analog to insanity (e.g., kleptomaniacs). But thus far such evidence has not been clearly presented.

[36] Coffee, in a recent article of immense interest and intensity, suggests a similar analysis by reference to "Pareto's curve" as applied to the optimal punishment scheme. Coffee, *The Repressed Issues of Sentencing: Accountability, Predictability and Equality in the Era of the Sentencing Commission*, 66 GEO. L.J. 975 (1978) (hereafter cited as Coffee II). While I find Coffee's approach far too mechanical (assuming that the mathematics could ever be accomplished, which I doubt), the notion that punishment should be equally distributed to offenders even if most end up suffering a bit more is important. Thus, to vary Kleinig's notion, if there were nine units of punishment, we could distribute them 9, 0, 0, thus affording two defendants no punishment at all—this would be the greatest good to the greatest number. But distributive justice requires 3, 3, 3, even though two offenders will now suffer more.

us (the offense and the defendant's *mens rea*), we must omit some facts that, if known to us, and "properly" weighed might reduce some offenders' punishments but retain the others' at the same level, the need for equality, both as a philosophical principal and as a pragmatic guide for action, requires us to omit those facts.

The Harm Done

Prima facie, the "harm done" is easily determined: the defendant killed, stole, destroyed, looted, coerced. But, when the *mens rea* element is added, and particularly if the *mens rea* is seen as an integral part of the act, the question is not so easy.

Most persons, I suspect, would treat a car theft as less serious than a murder, because the harm actually accomplished is less in the first instance—the car is replaceable, potentially insurable, and hence its loss partially reversible; its loss does not effect such a dramatic change in the lives of the affected victims. But whether, within a specific crime definition, a focus on the harm actually caused is desirable, or even philosophically defensible, is a more difficult question. Thus, for example, many penal codes impose significantly different punishments upon a person who stabs another with a deadly weapon depending on whether, for example, the victim lives or dies: the focus is on the harm actually done.[37] But in many cases, the effectuation of the harm may be beyond the control of the offender: wind may blow out the arsonist's fire or cause the speeding bullet to miss its target; the proximity—totally fortuitous—of a hospital or a skilled physician may save the life of a victim who in all other circumstances would die. Similarly, a thief who robs a till has committed larceny. Usually, if not always, it is a matter of fortuity whether the crime is grand or petty larceny. Assuming that the offender had the same *mens rea*, there appears to be little reason to differentiate punishment based upon these fortuitous lessenings of the harm intended.[38] As Jon Kleinig has cogently argued, in a probing analysis of the link between crime and punishment[39]:

---

[37] Allen, *Retribution in a Modern Penal Law*, 25 BUFF. L. REV. 1 (1975).

[38] This is even more apparent in the case of the "eggshell plaintiff" in tort law. If *A* intentionally, but lightly, kicks *B* in the knee and *B*'s leg becomes inflamed to the point that it is ultimately lost to him, *A* must pay for the entire loss, although totally unforeseeable and clearly unintended. Vosberg v. Putney, 80 Wis. 523, 50 N.W. 403 (1891). A similar result in criminal law, however, would be monstrous. The difference, it is suggested, is that tort law is concerned with compensating the injured, innocent plaintiff, while criminal law focuses on the blameworthiness of the defendant.

[39] Kleinig, *supra* note 7 at 131–32. Another eloquent statement on this issue is H. MORRIS, ON GUILT AND INNOCENCE 1–31 (1976). The present law, of course, could be justified on utilitarian grounds—that to punish attempted and consummated crimes equally could lead offenders to be sure that their attempts are successful. But this reasoning is weak, since no person who attempts a crime expects or anticipates that it will not succeed.

But there is one other kind of case which needs to be considered as well—the fact that we punish attempted crimes more leniently than those which are successful. If we are justified in doing this, it might be thought to indicate fairly clearly that utilitarian considerations ought to predominate in penalty-fixing, even if within limits imposed by desert considerations. One way in which we might be tempted to accommodate these cases would be to deny that attempted crimes were as evil as successful crimes. Related as wrongdoing is, not merely to motives and intentions, but also to harm, the wrong which fails to cause any harm will not be as heinous as the one which succeeds. But it is not clear that harm and wrongfulness can always be as simply related as this. The extent of harm may be some guide to wrongfulness in cases of negligence, but does the same relation hold when harm is actually *intended?* Is the man who fails to murder someone, simply because he is a bad shot or his weapon jams, any better than the person who succeeds? It might then appear that when harm is intended, the intentions or motives take priority over any results or consequences of the act in contributing to seriousness. This is still not completely satisfactory, because we do not always allow that a man's good intentions absolve him from guilt for acts which are harmful: the father who kills the child (whose conception he tried to avoid) to spare it from the jungle of life. The relation between intention and harm in the assessment of moral gravity is therefore a complex one.

The common law of crimes has historically punished attempts less severely. Indeed, in early common law, the perpetrator who attempted a crime, but in fact inflicted no criminally recognizable harm, was totally exculpated. In the thirteenth century, Bracton declared: "For where is the crime, if no harm has been done?"[40] For reasons totally unconnected with a philosophical inquiry into this state of affairs, the law moved slowly toward punishing attempted criminality first as a misdemeanor, then as a felony in some cases. The Model Penal Code, the latest reassessment of the criminal law, has urged that, for most crimes, the successful and unsuccessful attempt to be punished equally, particularly where the failure to achieve the criminal result was beyond the control of the offender.[41]

For this reason, *Doing Justice* talked about the harm "done or risked." But it failed to discuss systematically the issue raised by Professor Allen—whether the principle of "aggravated harm" (that

---

[40] See also Robinson, *A Theory of Justification: Societal Harm as a Prerequisite for Criminal Liability*, 23 U.C.L.A. L. REV. 266 (1975).

[41] A.L.I., M.P.C. §5.06(a). This does not apply to the highest level of felony, however, such as those where the penalty for the actually consummated crime could be death. The code has substantial problems in terms of "blame," however, since it draws the "attempt" net far too widely and allows conviction even though the defendant is caught at a very early stage and has not come near consummating the offense.

is, differentiating the successful attempt from the unsuccessful one)—should be totally abolished in the criminal law. A sensitive reassessment of the sentencing scheme should probe this question before establishing a rank ordering of offenses.[42]

A further problem is the question of what harms we will recognize at all and to what extent. The paradigms, of course, are easy: death as the most serious physical harm, destruction of property as the most obvious property harm. But this is insufficient. Arguably, the major harm incurred in many crimes is not physical at all, but psychological; rape seems to be an eminent example. Mugging may result only in the loss of a few dollars and no physical harm at all; but it may, through fear, also immobilize a city dweller or, even worse, cause him to move from the city. The loss of property occasioned by burglary is generally insurable; the loss of the sense of security in one's own home, even if the victim was not present during the burglary, is not so readily assuaged.

One possible solution to this last problem is to posit that the psychological harm that is caused by an offense is, generally, the same no matter how that offense is consummated. Thus, any offense that involves, for example, the "reckless creation of a risk of death" might be assumed to carry with it a "normal" psychological burden, both upon the victim and upon society in general, that would then translate into a static sentence for that offense. But it would still take great skill to properly define the precise harm inflicted.

The difficulties are even greater in those offenses where there is no single victim such as abuses of office, sales of pornography, and trade in heroin. Such a reevaluation might lead us to conclude that in some instances, there is no definable harm and, therefore, no real crime (the so-called victimless crime). Or we might conclude that some injuries are so vague and amorphous (the injury inflicted by the sale of pornography) that we cannot seriously consider that harm in a scale of criminal offenses.

The task is not an easy one. But by focusing on the type of harm done, rather than simply accepting common law or statutory definitions of crime, analysis may be made both clearer and more explicable.

Another issue that would have to be dealt with is whether foreseeable harms should be included as a part of the definition of the risk outlined in the crime. The most difficult aspect here would be determining to what extent, if at all, offenders should be held responsible for the responses of their victims, which actually caused the ultimate

---

[42] The question of how to define the crimes "attempted" or "consummated" is left to Chapter 3.

harm. Thus, *A* rapes *B*, who then commits suicide because of the disgrace she feels[43]; *A* robs *B*, who shoots at *A*, but kills *C*, an innocent bystander; *A* robs *B* but *C*, a police officer, shoots at *A* and kills *B*, or *D*, a bystander.[44] These, and many more examples, raise serious questions of causation and the extent to which it should be imported whole from the tort law to the criminal law. After a quarter century of flirting with incorporating the doctrine wholesale, the Pennsylvania Supreme Court determined, in 1970,[45] to reject entirely the notion that felony-murder liability could be imposed on a felon because of the reaction of either the victim or other actor. This, however, may not solve the problem, since the question is still one of whether the defendant has created the risk in such a way that he should be justly held responsible if the risk eventuates, as in *Stephenson*.

In short, a system of punishment that focuses on the offense and seeks to apportion blame on the basis of the harm that the offender consummated or attempted and on the basis of the intent with which he acted is more likely both to achieve equality of punishments and to be more manageable. By focusing on relatively objective, public facts that are relatively easily knowable (or at least inferable), we may avoid both the unfairness of seeking to weigh intangibles and the inequalities that stem from subjective judgments of individual triers and sentencers.

But equality of punishment, while a necessary condition of a fair system, is not a sufficient condition. A life sentence for every jaywalker, while equal, would not be fair; fairness requires another dimension—proportionality.

BEYOND EQUALITY—THE NEED FOR PROPORTIONALITY

Proportionality of punishment fits two ways in a retributivist sentencing scheme. To punish an armed robber and a thief with the same punishment has two effects: (1) it unfairly increases the amount of moral stigma and condemnation imposed upon the thief (assuming armed robbery is a more serious offense); and (2) it unfairly reduces the amount of moral stigma and condemnation imposed upon the armed robber.

Von Hirsch and Hanrahan have put the position nicely[46]:

---

[43] Stephenson v. State, 205 Ind. 141, 179 N.E. 633 (1932).
[44] Commonwealth v. Almeida, 362 Pa. 596, 68 A.2d 595 (1949).
[45] Commonwealth ex rel. Smith v. Meyer, 438 Pa. 218, 216 A.2d 554 (1970).
[46] A. von Hirsch and K. Hanrahan, Abolish Parole? 18 (typewritten version, 2d draft). As with the principle of moral culpability as a necessary predicate for punishment,

The commensurate-deserts principle imposes [two] kinds of constraints on the severity of penalties. First, it imposes a rank-ordering of penalties. Punishments must be arranged so that their relative severity corresponds with the comparative seriousness of offenses. . . . Second, the principle limits the absolute magnitude of punishments. A penalty scale . . . must also maintain a reasonable proportion between the quantum of punishment and the gravity of the crimes involved. The scale should not be so much inflated that less-than-serious offenses receive painful sanctions. . . . Nor should the entire scale be so much deflated that the gravest offenses received only slight punishments.

It is clear, however, that neither current practice nor current theory of sentencing focuses on proportionality. The indeterminate sentence is, by definition, not concerned with the offense but with the offender; any relation of the actual sentence to the severity of the offense should be totally coincidental. In practice, the mountain of dismal information on disparity of sentences demonstrates that what some judges deem proportionate others do not. Thus, proposals for sentencing guidelines or other methods of restricting judicial discretion that rely on or accept as desirable current practice ignore the requirement of proportionality.[47]

The requirement that penalties be proportionate to the offense has been said to be the Achilles' heel of a desert model of sentencing for two

---

the notion of proportionality could, in most instances, be supported even by those who reject desert and favor utilitarian grounds: people would not stand for a code that treated jaywalkers and murderers alike and would rebel at the legal system. Therefore, to preserve obedience to the system, there must be, at least in general, a proportionate scale of punishments.

[47] L. WILKINS, D. GOTTFREDSON, and J. KRESS, SENTENCING GUIDELINES: STRUCTURING JUDICIAL DISCRETION (1976), studied actual sentencing practices of judges in several jurisdictions and then concluded that most sentences could be predicted on the basis of sentencing guidelines. Thus, the guidelines were really statistical tabulations and made no qualitative judgments about the desirability of the figures. For example, the guidelines might show that a person convicted of armed robbery, with two prior offenses, would typically be sentenced, on the average, to x months. Since x was an average or median sentence, the range of sentences (disparity among judges) could be very wide indeed. With the statistical techniques used by Wilkins et al., however, the number of factors considered relevant (and hence the skewing effect) was substantially reduced. New Jersey has recently put into effect statewide sentencing guidelines, again empirically derived from past sentencing practices, but with some forty-eight factors to be considered per offense. This makes Mulligan's stew of the notion of proportionality. See also Coffee II, *supra* note 36. Suggestions to use, in a system of fixed sentences, the "actual time served" suffer from some of the same difficulty, but less clearly so if the alleged function of the parole board—to equalize disparate sentences—occurs. See Chapter 8. To the extent that this does not occur, however, the only justification is that actual time served provides a starting point and indicates what now appears to be the maximum sentences deemed necessary today. See Chapter 3. There is also the argument that using that figure will best assure that prison populations will not dramatically increase. See Chapter 7.

reasons: (1) there is no rational method of determining the exact sentence that is proportionate to a particular crime; and (2) because of that, a sentencing scheme could be proportionate internally, but disproportionate externally, yet subject to no meaningful criticism because the baselines for the system are too arbitrary. The second of these criticisms will be explored in Chapter 3. Here, we turn to the first criticism.

The thrust of the critique is simple[48]:

> No man, no scientist, no legislator, no judge, has ever been able to indicate any absolute standard, which would enable us to say that equity demands a definite punishment for a definite crime. . . . If it is agreed that patricide is the gravest crime, we meet [*sic*] out the heaviest sentence, death or imprisonment for life, and then we can agree on a descending scale of crime and on a parallel scale of punishments. But the problem begins right with the first stone of the structure. . . . Which is the greatest penalty proportional to the crime of patricide? Neither science, nor legislation, nor moral consciousness, can offer an absolute standard. Some say: The greatest penalty is death. Others say: No, imprisonment for life. . . . And if imprisonment for a time is to be the highest penalty, how many years shall it last—thirty, or twenty-five, or ten?

This has led some to argue that

> Decisions about . . . desert are likely to be more subjective, more individualized, more particularistic and thus less amenable to review [than decisions based on utilitarian aims] . . . . The lack of good measures of . . . desert serves to mask the failure of those standards to conceal their cases of misclassification, to disguise the degree of which they distribute punishment randomly . . . the amount of injustice that results from the use of desert and deterrence as sentencing standards is unknown, if not unknowable.[49]

These observations are clearly correct if precise measurements are necessary to justify a desert model. But retributivists from Hegel on have noted that precise proportionality, while theoretically essential to a system of justice, cannot be achieved under any system and, therefore, that "rough" proportionality will suffice.[50]

Pincoffs has summarized the position:

> If the aim is the more modest one that there should be a reasonable proportion between what a man has done and what he suffers for it, the

---

[48] E. Ferri, The Positive School of Criminology 12–13 (1901).

[49] Heinz, Heinz, Senderowitz, and Vance, *Sentencing by Parole Board: An Evaluation*, 67 J. Crim. L. & Crim. 1, 28 (1978). See also Bedau, *supra* note 5 at 64–66.

[50] G. Hegel, The Philosophy of Right 71 (trans. E. Knox, 1952).

difficulties may prove more tractable. It may just be that while there are advantages in fine judgments concerning punishment, judgments of desert cannot be finely determined . . . it may be that desert appraisals . . . must sometimes rest on less than satisfactory evidence.[51] Moreover, the problem of the inaccuracy of mathematics is not unique to the desert model; as Golding has observed, "The real problem for the deterrence theorist . . . [is] how and how much to punish: what kinds and what amounts are necessary to reduce the incident of crime in the desired degree, whatever that is."[52]

In short, the argument that desert theorists must show that the proposed punishment is exactly proportionate to the offense for which it is imposed is a straw man; perhaps von Hirsch should have spoken of "Roughly Doing Justice Equally."[53]

One more issue on proportionality remains, however. We have rejected the suggestion that punishment should be varied upon the background of the offender, as opposed to the *mens rea* with which he committed the act, on the grounds that these judgments were simply too fine to make and that they were not part of the act. But if individualization on the basis of such factors is not permissible in determining the extent of blame to be imposed, might other factors be relevant in determining the amount or type of punishment? One basis on which retributivism has based punishment is the amount of harm inflicted suggesting that the punishment should, at least metaphorically, balance that harm. Suppose, however, that one month in jail is deemed proportionate to return to the offender roughly the amount of harm he has inflicted both on the victim and on society, but that this

---

[51] Pincoffs, *Are Questions of Desert Decidable?*, in J. CEDERBLOM and W. BLIZEK, JUSTICE AND PUNISHMENT 75, 85 (1977). Accord: Mundle, *supra* note 8 at 65, 73; Golding, *Criminal Sentencing—Some Philosophical Consideration*, in Cederblom and Blizek, *supra* at 89, 104. Jon Kleinig has examined the question in depth in PUNISHMENT AND DESERT (1973).

[52] Golding, *supra* note 51 at 96.

[53] This lack of precision, and the concern that desert may come to mean extravagantly long sentences, has led Coffee to suggest another approach to establishing a sentencing scheme. Taking Rawls' argument that legislation, to be just, should be drawn in a "veil of ignorance," he posits that legislators would rationally adopt a scheme which would protect the "worst off group," since they would not know whether they belong to that group. Coffee then suggests that that system is mathematically calculable and can be achieved without recourse to what he dubs the "mysterious assumption" that it is desirable to punish those who commit crimes because they deserve it. This short summary is unfair to Coffee's point, and his article should be visited thoroughly. See Coffee II, *supra* note 36. Aside from the obvious practical problems, which Coffee does not really address, there is at least one difficulty—granted that Rawls' legislators are actuated by self-interest (a desire not to have Draconian punishments that they themselves might suffer one day), it still requires a sense of rationality that, if present, would seem to lead to a rational desert, proportional sentencing scheme.

particular offender demonstrates some particular vulnerability to the punishment—he is claustrophobic, or about to die, or his family will starve if he is removed from caring for them. Must we then insist on the punishment, or does it, in view of these individualizing factors, become disproportionate?

The first two cases have some similarities. In each, the fact asserted is known—and the effect upon the offender is known—to a degree of such certainty that we can call it a fact. The second sentence becomes, effectively, a life sentence, and we know it; the first becomes a sentence to a month of torture, and we know it. These are not cases such as that posed by John Dean, who argued against imprisonment on the grounds that he would be raped there.[54] Had we known, even with reasonable certainty, that that was inevitable, then the argument might have been more compelling, but that was not the case. In short, to the extent that clearly known facts about the offender's particular susceptibility would make the punishment more serious or more severe than the sentence anticipates, some adjustment might be possible.

The third illustration may assist. It is sometimes argued that by sending the defendant to prison, the criminal system is making the defendant's family starve. This, however, is clearly wrong: if anyone is making them starve, it is the defendant, not the law. Moreover, this is a prediction subject to numerous inaccuracies. Further, there will be alternate methods of alleviating the pain dependants suffer. Finally, if we were to accept such a notion, we would surely have to determine the same facts as regards the victim—how many children he left behind, what financial arrangements were made, and so forth. These purely fortuitous facts would then be squeezed into the notion of proportionality—and the entire approach would be nullified.

The first two examples, then, are predictions, but of the way in which natural forces would operate upon the defendant (given a high enough probability of rape, however, this might also be viewed as a natural force). The third does not deal directly with such forces and hence is not, or was not, beyond the power of the defendant, and/or the state, to change. The possibility of mitigation is also relevant to distinguishing between the first two cases: in the first, sentence to an open prison might solve the problem; in the second, nothing the state can do can alter the situation.[55]

[54] See United States v. Tolias, 548 F.2d 277 (9th Cir. 1977).

[55] This does not, of course, exhaust the questions raised by these hypothetical problems. Still another twist might be suggested: if, instead of dealing solely in "years of imprisonment," we talked of the proportion of the sentence in terms of "punishment units" and had some (rough) measure of these units, the system might become very complex indeed. For example, we might say that one year of confinement in a maximum

MIXED SYSTEMS OF PUNISHMENT

The examples given in the last few paragraphs would cause no major difficulty for some who consider themselves desert theorists but whom Ezorsky labels "teleological retributivists"[56]—persons who mix retributive with utilitarian goals. There are at least two schools of these thinkers: (1) those who see desert as a requirement for eligibility for punishment, but then would allow utilitarian goals to dictate the method, duration, and such of punishment; and (2) those who agree with the first position, but further agree that desert and proportionality should establish the maximum penalties available for a particular crime, yet would allow utilitarian notions to permit reductions from the maximum.

The first school is really no school. Prior to the mid-1950s, the retributivist fight with the utilitarian was over whether criminal activity must be demonstrated by the state to justify any kind of punishment. Retributivists feared that the notion of the medical treatment model would (if it had not already) lead to the abrogation of the notion of *actus reus* as a *sine qua non* for state intervention. Perhaps typical of this school, although one of the major fighters against the notion that beneficence alone would justify deprivation of liberty,[57] is C.S. Lewis, who conceded that "All I plead for is the *prior* condition of ill desert; loss of liberty justified on retributive grounds before we begin considering the other facts. After that, as you please."[58] Lewis, and others, were attacking the concern that the utilitarian school would, if necessary, justify the punishment of an innocent person. But if that ever was a real concern, it was ended when Hart[59] and Rawls[60] adopted the

---

security institution, where liberties and privileges are very restricted, is "worth" two years in a minimum security institution. To the extent—but only to the extent—that we say that "the" punishment is deprivation of the opportunity to live in the free world, that problem does not arise. And perhaps our "punishment" calipers are not fine enough to consider these other factors. In theory, however, we may be required to attempt to measure them.

[56] Ezorsky, *supra* note 29.

[57] "To be taken without consent from my home and friends; to lose my liberty; to undergo all those assaults on my personality which modern psychotherapy knows how to deliver; to be re-made after some new pattern of 'normality' hatched in a Viennese laboratory to which I never professed allegiance; to know that this process will never end until either my captors have succeeded or I have grown wise enough to cheat them with apparent success—who cares whether this is called Punishment or not? That it includes most of the elements for which any punishment is feared—shame, exile, bondage, and years eaten by the locust—is obvious. Only enormous, ill-desert could justify it; but ill-desert is the very conception which the Humanitarian theory has thrown overboard." Lewis, *The Humanitarian Theory of Punishment*, 6 Res Judicatae 224 (1953).

[58] C.S. Lewis, *On Punishment: A Reply*, 6 Res Judicatae 519, 522 (1954).

[59] Hart, *supra* note 10.

[60] Rawls, *Two Concepts of Rules*, 44 The Philosophical Review 1 (1955).

dichotomy of the "General Justifying Aim" and the "General Distributive Aim" of the criminal law and agreed that limiting distribution of actual punishment to those who had in fact violated the law would not undermine the utilitarian argument that the purpose of the criminal law was deterrence. Both Hart and Rawls also agreed that some principle—possibly desert—limited the maximum amount of punishment that could be imposed, even if this retarded utilitarian aims. Others, such as Packer,[61] argued that once the criminal had broken the law, there were no side restraints on the amount of punishment that could be imposed (assuming, of course, utilitarian rationale).

The second mixed school urges desert both as a principle of distribution and as a maximizing restraint, but would allow utilitarian aims to supplement these goals. Each of these writers begins with the premise that desert is the main criterion of punishment, but that other factors may be considered. Thus, von Hirsch would allow considerations of incapacitation and deterrence to raise the presumptive sentence, so long as the actual sentence imposed did not exceed what would be allowed by desert even absent incapacitation and deterrence. On the other side are those who, like Norval Morris,[62] argue that a key goal of any system of justice is to diminish suffering and that if desert would call for "needless" suffering, the sentencer should exercise "parsimony." Armstrong captures this notion when he observes that while desert justifies punishment, one is not obliged to punish.[63]

This short description of possible variations on the pure desert theme illustrates that questions of the desirability of precise (or even roughly precise) proportionality still divide even those who take an essentially desert orientation. Few of these writers, however, have directly confronted the issues of distributive justice raised by Jon Kleinig. At the very least, more exploration of the precise parameters of desert will be necessary before a resolution of these issues will be achieved.

SUMMARY

The criminal sanction is not merely part of a continuum of possible social responses to undesired conduct. It is a separate and unique procedure to express blame upon the actor. Consequently, the focus of a criminal sanctioning system must be the blameworthiness of the conduct; utilitarian approaches to criminal punishment do not take blame

---

[61] H. Packer, The Limits of the Criminal Sanction (1968).
[62] N. Morris, The Future of Imprisonment (1974).
[63] Armstrong, *supra* note 9 at 138, 155. See also Hospers, *supra* note 4 at 21, 22–24.

seriously and therefore degrade the criminal process to simply another method of social control.

Blameworthiness is not easy to define, but it would appear that a manageable approach would be to consider (1) the harm actually inflicted (or attempted) and (2) the mental state (culpability; *mens rea*) of the offender. Each of these will pose difficulties to any analyst, whether desert-oriented or not. Should psychological harm either to the victim or to society in general be considered in assessing the "harm" caused? If so, by what measure? If not, how is sanctioning "public crimes" to be justified? What harms are "caused" by a specific act? Can these harms be measured empirically, by attempting to determine what effects burglary really has in the real world?

As to culpability, what factors should be considered in determining the *mens rea* of the offender? Are there mental states other than intent, purpose, and recklessness that should be weighed? What of motive, or individual pressures, such as poverty and necessity? And to what extent, even if we do consider these factors in normal moral discourse, should we allow the state to inquire into their presence or absence?

Finally, a desert model requires that the punishment be proportionate to the offense that the actor committed. But there is no method by which this proportionality can *a priori* be determined. Moreover, the same problem of individualizing punishment may arise here—Should we consider the vulnerability of the actor to certain types of punishment while determining which punishment is proportionate to the offense?

This chapter has sought to raise these questions and to suggest tentative answers to at least some of them. But much more work will need to be done before there are even adequate, much less acceptable, answers to them. The reintroduction of desert to the dialogue concerning criminal punishment, however, has brought these questions of justice to the forefront, rather than allowing them to remain hidden behind a utilitarian smokescreen. If the current debate over desert does nothing more, it will have contributed significantly to the evolution of our understanding of what it means to say that something is criminal.

Chapter 3

The Taxonomy of
Sentencing Equality

We have thus far established the following principles:

1. The Goal of Equality. Persons who have committed similarly serious offenses should be blamed, and punished, similarly. Any differences in sentence should be accounted for by differences in the way in which the crime itself was perpetrated.
2. The Goal of Proportionality. Sentences in all instances should be proportionate to the seriousness of the offense.

How do we go about establishing such a system of sentencing? How should it be described? There are two parameters—defining the offense and defining the punishments available.

DEFINING THE OFFENSE

Encyclopedias and Telephone Books

One way to define the offense is to be as particular as possible in including all relevant data in the definitions. The Twentieth Century Fund, in its report, *Fair and Certain Punishment*, redefined sample offenses by breaking them into degrees. Thus, the report delineated the following categories of armed robbery:[1]

Armed robbery in the first degree is the forcible taking of property from the person of another by the use of a loaded gun, where the offender discharges the gun with intent to injure or kill another person.

[1] TWENTIETH CENTURY FUND, Fair and Certain Punishment 37 (1976).

Armed robbery in the second degree is the forcible taking of property from the person of another by the use of a deadly weapon other than a loaded gun, where the offender uses that weapon with intent to seriously injure or kill another person.

Armed robbery in the third degree is the forcible taking of property from the person of another by the use of a loaded gun where the offender discharges the gun under circumstances in which the likelihood of personal injury is high.

Armed robbery in the fourth degree is the forcible taking of property from the person of another by the display of or threat to use a loaded gun.

Armed robbery in the fifth degree is the forcible taking of property from the person of another by the use or attempted use of a deadly weapon other than a loaded gun under circumstances in which the likelihood of personal injury is high.

Armed robbery in the sixth degree is the forcible taking of property from the person of another by the display of or threat to use a deadly weapon other than a loaded gun.

A second, very similar, approach is taken by the Washington Parole Board, which defines a crime generically and then adds increments of punishment if certain facts are present. Thus, for example, the category of "sexual molestation" carries a basic sentence of twelve months. If there was intercourse, additional months are added. Similarly, if the victim was vulnerable, more months may be added. And if the victim was vulnerable specifically by age,[2] still more months may be added, depending on the precise age of the victim. Using these variables (there are others stated by the Board), the crimes may be said to include:

Sexual molestation
Sexual molestation of a twelve year old
Sexual molestation and intercourse by force
Sexual molestation and intercourse by force of a twelve year old

Each of these offenses, defined by the "base" crime and its aggravating factors, carries a different sentence.

Clearly, these provisions are attempting to deal with the problem which Professor Zimring accurately described: "Any system of punishment that attaches a single sanction to a particular offense must define offenses with a morally persuasive precision that present laws do not possess."[3] Even assuming that there is a difference between a

[2] See Chapter 6.
[3] F. Zimring, Making the Punishment Fit the Crime: A Consumer's Guide to Sentencing Reform. [Occasional papers from the University of Chicago (1977).]

"loaded gun" and other "deadly weapons" (and there may not be, in an elevator, for example)—it is surely dubious whether the use of a gun as opposed to a knife truly represents a different level of culpability.[4] If the employment of any deadly weapon is a factor to be considered in determining culpability, should the age or vulnerability of the victim also matter? Assault by a fourteen-year-old on a six-year-old may be more culpable than a fight with another fourteen-year-old, even if the same physical harm (e.g., broken nose) is done.

Mystifyingly, *Fair and Certain Punishment* lists various "aggravating and mitigating circumstances" that may be employed by the sentencing tribunal in varying from the presumptive sentence (these factors are considered in Chapter 6). Why is the use of a loaded gun so different from those other factors that it actually makes a difference in the definition of the crime (under the *Fair and Certain Punishment* scheme), while other factors are only to be considered in the judge's discretion? This book does not say.

Thus, the "telephone book" epithet with which this scheme is greeted may in fact be appropriate—by grading each offense in terms of innumerable variable specific facts, the legislative drafter may evolve "armed robbery in the 143rd degree: taking property by force from a person in a wheelchair, in daylight, while other persons are present, without the use of a loaded gun, deadly weapon, or other instrument which could under any circumstances, cause death, serious bodily injury, or fright."[5]

Classification

At almost the other end of the spectrum is the current movement toward consolidation of definitions of criminal acts, a movement spurred by the almost total failure of previous criminal legislation to define with any precision the relative seriousness of specific offenses. Through a century of haphazard legislation, there has evolved a

---

[4] There may, of course, be concrete differences in danger, but these are irrelevant unless the actor both perceived these differences and chose the weapon accordingly.

[5] The encyclopedic approach has also been criticized because it allegedly puts too much discretion in the prosecutor's hands. If, the argument goes, the difference between first and second degree robbery is the presence of a loaded gun, the prosecutor will plea bargain over whether he will allege (or prove) that the gun was loaded. Or whether the defendant had the gun at all. In short, the critique posits that by being so specific, the approach enhances plea bargaining.

I find the argument unconvincing, even if true. Although we will discuss plea bargaining more fully in Chapter 9, the fact is that any system is vulnerable to plea bargaining. The attempt of a new sentencing system to specify the various levels of risk and harm that the criminal law should consider, would, if successful, be worth the risk that it would be manipulated. Moreover, as indicated in Chapter 9, if the sentencing structure is properly implemented, this risk will diminish. That is not to say that plea bargaining will be abolished, but only that the deficiency alleged to be present in the encyclopedic model could be corrected or at least limited.

plethora of crimes and a plethora of inconsistent indicia of the seriousness of the offense. New criminal legislation is enacted without any
conscious attempt to relate that crime to those then existing on the
statute books. The consequence has been a crazy quilt of crimes and
punishments.

These systems have been internally inconsistent and occasionally
bizarre. Thus, Peter Low, in attempting to categorize existing federal
legislation, found that the Federal Code had fifty-five different
maximum penalty combinations.[6] Louis Schwartz, director of the National Commission on reform on Federal Criminal Laws, declared that
Congress had differentiated one-hundred or more categories of offenses,[7] and Herbert Wechsler, father of the Model Penal Code, found
nineteen different prison maxima in Pennsylvania's sentencing legislation.[8]

Recent reform movements have responded to this unfettered diversity of classification of offense and sanctions by classifying offenses in a
relatively small number of classes, with equivalent punishments for
each offense in the same class. Most recent state legislation, following
the lead of the Model Penal Code, has adopted this approach, with the
number of different classes varying between five and ten.

This movement toward classes of offenses obviously premises that,
while different offenses have different elements and even invade different societal interests, they can be classified in terms of equal seriousness deserving of roughly equal punishment. This system clearly
avoids the dilemmas posed by the telephone book attempt to classify
every minute detail of every criminal act. But in so doing, it may fail to
stress the differences that in fact may occur during a specific crime
(i.e., the level of harm actually inflicted or risked). Moreover, the
theory behind the specific classification may be unclear. Thus, in the
Model Penal Code, burglary of a dwelling and causing a fire with the
purpose of destroying a building or of collecting the insurance are both
second degree offenses. Virtually all offenses against public adminis-
tration, including bribery of public officials or jurors, are offenses of the
third degree, as are terroristic threats, polygamy, reckless burning or
exploding, and some sexual abuses. It is likely that the drafters of the
Code understood the grading system as reflecting some underlying
philosophy, but the Code does not express that reflection, thus leaving
the reader to grope toward the unarticulated rationale which the Code

---

[6] MEMORANDUM TO NATIONAL COMMISSION ON REFORM OF THE CRIMINAL CODE (1968).

[7] NATIONAL COMMISSION ON REFORM OF FEDERAL CRIMINAL LAWS, STUDY DRAFT xxiii
(1970).

[8] Wechsler, *Sentencing, Corrections and the Model Penal Code*, 109 W. PA. L. REV.
465, 476 (1961).

used in establishing its groupings, and ranking arson for insurance as more serious than bribery.

Defining the Offense By The Interest Jeopardized

What these schemes, particularly the encyclopedic approach, have in common is that they are trying to articulate, in as specific a form as possible, the risk of actual physical harm caused by the offender; if actual physical harm had been caused (or attempted—see Chapter 2), the offender could and should have been charged with that harm. But these terms do not demarcate between the harm caused and the risk created. Thus, for example, while one who discharges a firearm may well inflict more physical injury than one who uses a knife, this is not inevitably so—the gun discharger may shoot into the ceiling to command attention, while the knife user selects his victim's body as his target. Similarly, possession of a firearm or a deadly weapon or dangerous instrument may reflect a willingness to use the item, or it may not. Certainly there is no actual harm that is inflicted by the mere possession of the knife or gun, and the potential inference about culpability that may be drawn may be exceptionally tenuous; it could be argued, for example, that a criminal who possesses, but refuses to use, a knife to effect escape is less morally blameworthy than one who never possessed such a knife—and thus never weighed the uses—in the first place.

The problem arises from the fact that we continue to use common law terminology in our criminal codes. Perhaps, in the fourteenth and fifteenth centuries, when burglary was narrowly defined as the breaking into a dwelling house at night, with the intent to commit a felony, everyone understood that the harm involved was *at least* the psychological uncertainty felt by the home owner and, more likely, the threat to life which was likely to occur since the inhabitants of the house were likely to be present. Today, however, when statutory "burglary" may include breaking into a telephone booth and stealing the contents of the coin receiver, the term "burglary" does not readily involve those same harms, actual or potential. The same is true of arson and, less clearly, of other crimes once narrowly defined by common law but now expansively broadened by modern codes.

I propose, therefore, that we consider jettisoning the common law definitions of crime and that we concentrate instead on the interests involved or jeopardized *as the crime was carried out.*[9] A new sentencing

[9] Such an approach also rejects the suggestion in *Doing Justice* that we develop punishments by determining the harm "characteristically" inflicted by a particular criminal act. That suggestion also founders on the acceptance of common law definitions.

scheme, that is, should define crime in terms of the interests that were in fact injured or threatened, without regard to whether the result actually occurred; differentiations could rest upon the culpability—the mens rea—of the defendant. For example, crimes of the first degree could be defined as "Crimes in which death or serious bodily harm was purposely inflicted or attempted." This category would include all patterns of conduct in which the defendant exhibited the requisite *mens rea* and act: both what is now first degree murder and what the Twentieth Century Fund calls "first degree armed robbery" would fit within this category. The fact that property was lost in the process would be treated, if at all, only as an aggravating or mitigating factor; the critical point would be the most serious aspect of the defendant's entire course of conduct.[10]

Thus, if we were defining crimes against the person (leaving aside the psychological harm for a moment), it might look something like this:

1. Death knowingly or purposely attempted or consummated;
2. Serious personal injury knowingly or purposely attempted or consummated;
3. Risk of death knowingly created, but death not intended;
4. Risk of serious personal injury knowingly or purposely created, but not desired;
5. Risk of death recklessly created;
6. Risk of serious personal injury recklessly created;

---

[10] The deserts model has difficulties in dealing with the multiple offender. Similarly, the definition of "a" criminal act, subject under other theories of criminal liability to great flexibility and distortion, should create for the just deserts theorist a substantial dilemma. The theoretical problem is clear: if defendant *#1* commits crime *A,* and defendant *#2* commits either two *A*'s, or crimes *A* and *B*, defendant *#2* should be more severely punished than defendant *#1*. If that does not happen, then either defendant *#1* is receiving a sentence disproportionately severe to the offense he has committed or defendant *#2* is receiving a sentence disproportionately lenient to his blameworthiness, or both. Neither is acceptable under a vigorous equality model.

Unhappily, because of the lack of precision of language, it is simply not possible to determine whether one crime or two (or more) has occurred. Difficulties arise with multiple acts all intended to achieve one final result—for example, six embezzlements to obtain $100,000, and so forth. The test of the "single criminal transection" is an impotent, but charming, attempt to define our way out of this dilemma.

The reason the test is important, however, is that acts can be sliced so thin, divided into so many innumerable subacts, that it is simply not possible to create a language that will artfully and rigorously tell us how to define each act. Here, Professor Zimring's observations on the limits of language are equally on point. Is waving a gun in the presence of forty people in a bank forty assaults? Or one? Do the assault(s) "merge" into the bank robbery? Why? Et cetera. These problems are probably incapable of ultimate solution; we may simply have to accept an arbitrary formula for dealing with such enigmas and rest there.

7. Personal injury knowingly or purposely attempted or consummated;
8. Risk of personal injury knowingly created, but not desired;
9. Personal injury recklessly inflicted;
10. Risk of personal injury recklessly created.

A similar list could be established for property crimes. Offenses that involve public safety, but no direct property or personal injury (bribery, corruption, drug abuse, pornography), would have to be very carefully weighed. But by defining the crime in terms of interest affected, rather than by the method by which the interest was affected, we may more closely articulate what we are really doing and avoid the need for many "aggravating and mitigating factors" at the same time.

RANKING THE OFFENSES

Two approaches to a definition of seriousness are possible—empirical and intuitive. The empirical approach could emulate the research conducted by Professor Marvin Wolfgang, and others, who asked respondent groups to rank order a large number of rather specific offenses and crime circumstances. Intriguingly, the rank ordering given by relatively disparate respondent groups was strikingly similar: without guidance from the researchers on what serious meant, the respondents had reached an apparent consensus on the meaning of the term and used that unarticulated definition to channel their ranking determinations.[11]

The results of the Wolfgang study should not be surprising: as a general rule, respondents ranked offenses against the person higher

---

[11] T. SELLIN and M. WOLFGANG, THE MEASUREMENT OF DELINQUENCY (1964). See also Rossi et al., *The Seriousness of Crimes: Normative Structure and Individual Differences*, 39 AMERICAN SOCIOLOGICAL REVIEW 224 (1974); Wellford and Wiatrowski, *On the Measurement of Delinquency*, 66 JOURNAL OF CRIMINAL LAW AND CRIMINOLOGY 175 (1975); Thomas, Cage, and Foster, *Public Opinion on Criminal Law and Legal Sanctions: An Examination of Two Conceptual Models*, 67 JOURNAL OF CRIMINAL LAW AND CRIMINOLOGY 110 (1976); Sechrest, *Comparisons of Inmates' and Staff's Judgments of the Severity of Offenses*, 6 JOURNAL OF RESEARCH IN CRIME AND DELINQUENCY 41 (1976); Figlio, *The Seriousness of Offenses: An Evaluation of Offenders and Non-Offenders*, 66 JOURNAL OF CRIMINAL LAW AND CRIMINOLOGY 189 (1975); Rose and Prell, *Does the Punishment Fit the Crime? A Study in Social Validation*, 61 AMERICAN JOURNAL OF SOCIOLOGY 247 (1955); Riedel, *Perceived Circumstances, Inferences of Intent and Judgments of Offense Seriousness*, 66 JOURNAL OF CRIMINAL LAW AND CRIMINOLOGY 201 (1975); Kutchinsky, *The Legal Consequences: A Survey of Research on Knowledge and Opinion About Law*, in KNOWLEDGE AND OPINION ABOUT LAW 101 (A. PODGORESKI, W. KAUPEN, J. VANHOUTTE, P. VINKE, and B. KUTCHINSKY, eds. 1973).

(and therefore more serious) on the scale than most offenses against property and those offenses that involved serious harm to the person higher than those personal offenses that did not.

Nevertheless, such an empirical study is of limited value. While it reflects a general consensus among various groups in our society as to which offenses are more serious, it does not assist the policymaker in determining why that is so—namely, what serious means, in fact, to those respondents. This might not prove an insuperable barrier if the deviser of the new sentencing scale were charged with simply replicating the ranking of offenses and their subsequent categorization. But there are at least two difficulties with such a mirroring concept of devising the new sentencing scale: (1) some public perceptions of seriousness vary over time (for example, marijuana or selective service offenses); and (2) in some instances, the public perception might be inconsistent with a sound concept of seriousness. There is, of course, the further problem of defining—and accurately sampling—the appropriate public.

Yet the alternate method of proceeding is to reduce the sample to a specially defined group—for example, in the case of statutes, legislators; in the case of sentencing guidelines,[12] judges—who may not be representative of the entire community's sense of seriousness.[13] This would be what I call the intuitive approach—whatever the body, including the sentencing commission discussed in Chapter 4, there would be no hard basis on which to rank the offenses, however defined.

Neither approach is satisfactory, and neither will afford a perfect ranking of the offenses according to their seriousness. Yet some general, rough sense of ranking, implicit in the findings of Wolfgang, suggests that neither method would necessarily be invalid.

DETERMINING THE PUNISHMENT

Once the offenses are listed according to their rank of seriousness, the difficulty of providing appropriate penalties begins. Here, there are several questions: (1) determining the "intervals" among the offenses; and (2) ascertaining the types and durations of punishments proportionate to each offense. The latter issue itself has several subissues: (a) the form of sentencing scheme and the discretion allowed the sentencer; and (b) the types of punishment allowed each offense.

[12] See *infra*, pp. 60–61.
[13] Indeed, we could hypothesize that this is one reason we continue to tolerate jury nullification.

The Interval Problem

Even assuming that, somehow, we arrive at a ranking of offenses, that ranking alone does not tell us the degree of difference among the offenses. Bedau has put it this way:[14]

> Even if we can agree that a malicious killer is morally and legally more culpable than an accidental killer, how are we to answer the question, "How much more culpable is he—twice as culpable? ten times? seven and one-half times?" . . . Granted that murder is more harmful than rape, how much worse is it in terms of harm to the victim (or to society)? Twice as harmful? Ten times as harmful? . . . There is no way of telling, e.g., whether an offense that falls on the mid-point of the culpability scale and the bottom of the harmfulness scale is exactly as grave or half as grave, or twice as grave, as an offense that falls on the mid-point of the harmfulness scale but at the bottom of the culpability scale. Culpability and harmfulness seem not even as like each other as the proverbial apples and oranges. . . .

This critique, however, is overdone. Perhaps, as a strictly philosophical matter, it would be desirable, even imperative, to draw such a precise balance of the two vectors. But real life neither allows nor requires such precision. As we have already seen, proportionality is itself a rough concept, and in the real world, rough proportionality is all that can be either expected or required.[15]

The final resolution of this question requires an "anchoring"[16]—a determination of the highest and lowest possible punishments for the worst and least important of offenses. Where shall we look for this anchorage?

Maximum Permissible Sentences

Once again, when confronted with seeking numbers or even types of sentences to impose in a proportionate sentencing system, we are forced to acknowledge that there is no right figure for any offense, no matter how defined. But there are certain guidelines that should assist us in at least assaying this task:

1. Imprisonment should be the punishment of last resort;
2. Duration of imprisonment, or of nonincarcerative sanctions, should

---

[14] Bedau, *Concessions to Retribution in Punishment* in J. CEDERBLOM and W. BLIZEK, JUSTICE AND PUNISHMENT 51, 64 (1977).

[15] See pp. 27–30, *supra*.

[16] See Cederblom, *Introduction*, in J. CEDERBLOM and W. BLIZEK, JUSTICE AND PUNISHMENT 7 (1977). See also J. KLEINIG, PUNISHMENT AND DESERT 116 (1973).

be short so as to minimize the pain inflicted, since unnecessary pain is to be avoided.

Imprisonment as the Punishment of Last Resort. This notion is hardly new, nor is it unique to retributionist theory. Prison is painful; the deprivation of liberty itself, without any further punishment, is severe. Particularly in countries where liberty is highly prized the pains of imprisonment are perhaps even more severely felt than elsewhere.

Because of its deprivations, and because it is such an extreme punishment, prison should be reserved for the most serious offenses, so that the pain involved will be commensurate with the pain the offender inflicted on the victim. Even then, the duration of confinement should be relatively short. Our sentences—and our actual time served—are generally much longer than most other countries.

This position may surprise many who think of a desert model as a derivative of the "throw away the key" approach to punishment. But as the earlier sections of the book have tried to indicate, this is a misperception: desert requires proportionality, but not vindictiveness, in sentencing. Clearly, some crimes will require the ultimate pains of imprisonment, at least until we discover some new forms of severe, long-term punishment. (Physical changes, such as lobotomies, would be severe and would have long-term effects, but would not be as acceptable on a number of other grounds.) Retribution is not revenge; it desires proportionate suffering, not disproportionate torture. In view of the real pains that imprisonment, even in the most humane of prisons, entails, it is perfectly consistent to support minimum incarceration. As one writer recently put it: "No natural order requires that imprisonment be the only punishment that criminals fear and whose infliction gives society a sense of vindication."[17]

In the past decade, the American Bar Association, the National Council on Crime and Delinquency, and the National Advisory Com-

[17] Krattenmaker, Book Review, 66 Geo. L. J. 1317, 1322 (1978).

Indeed, it is possible to argue that, given the conditions extant in virtually every prison today—rape, violence, etc.—that imprisonment is too harsh for any offense. But that argument is for another day; here, the assumption is that, for the foreseeable future, imprisonment will remain as one method of punishment.

While we often speak of prison as a last resort, the fact is that we imprison more people, per capita, than any other Western country. Recent figures show that our prisons and jails hold 244 people for every 100,000 of population—ten times the rate in The Netherlands, six times the rate in Sweden, and even three times the rate in Britain. The *status quo* response to those figures, of course, is that we are a different society—innately more violent, and far more heterogeneous (and hence more likely both to generate and implement hatreds, either in a bigoted way or otherwise). But these explanations, even if allowable to some extent, simply cannot justify a rate three times, much less twenty times, that of other civilized countries.

mission on Criminal Justice Standards and Goals have all suggested that except for the most heinous offenses, the average sentence should be no longer than five years. Since all these recommendations assumed a system of parole and good time, this would translate into actual time served of approximately eighteen months as a maximum sentence for the worst crimes, except in cases of truly outrageous crimes, such as murder, rape, and perhaps one or two others. Taking these recommendations as a guide, we can say that person-to-person crimes, which do not, and were not intended to, end in serious personal injury or death, should have maximum actual time served of eighteen months. From this, a scale of proportionate punishments to other offenses, ranging both up and down in seriousness, should be possible.

One need not, of course, accept the ABA-NCCD-NAC position. *Doing Justice*[18] suggested a maximum of three years for all but the most serious crimes and would rarely allow a sentence of more than five. Since that book envisioned far less discretionary release and reduction mechanisms, it could be suggested that it is close, in fact, to the ABA-NCCD-NAC recommendations. Finally, the average time actually served today, for all offenses, would further corroborate that the ABA-NCCD-NAC position was sensible: it has been estimated that the average time served for all offenses in 1975, prior to first release on parole, was twenty and a half months.[19]

In addition to any humanitarian reasons for seeking relatively low sentences for most crimes, there are pragmatic ones: the greater the severity of possible sentences (and hence of time to be served), the less certain they are to be applied. Processes of jury nullification, plea bargaining, judicial manipulation of fact-finding, and so forth will so distort the process that it will become the same standardless system we now have. If that does not happen, prison populations may in fact increase beyond any possible capacity of the institutions. For these

[18] A. VON HIRSCH, DOING JUSTICE (1976).

[19] ABT ASSOCIATES, I PRISON POPULATION AND POLICY CHOICES, 165 (1977). There are many reasons for not accepting average time served today as *the* base on which to draw a new sentencing scheme. One important reason is that these figures do not take into account persons on probation. For example, using hypothetical figures, assume 50 percent of all burglars are put on six months probation while the average time served in prison is two years. This means that the average time of punishment for all burglars is actually fifteen months; the average time served figure is skewed by nine months because it only talks about durations in prison. Since probation is used in very high frequencies for some crimes, the average time served figure is likely to be actually very small. Indeed, if the average probationer actually serves only one-half of the time imposed before being granted release by the court, the time would correspondingly decrease. Nevertheless, these figures are important indications that the times suggested by ABA et al. are not unrealistic. For the argument that sentences should not, and perhaps cannot, reflect present actual time served, see Chapter 7.

reasons, high potential sentences are undesirable, whether or not one believes them to be in fact proportionate to the offense.

Mandatory Minimum and Nonincarcerative Sanctions: Crossovers.

What has already been said about the need for equality in sentencing choice and the need for consistency in punishments clearly suggests that for most crimes, the type of proportionate punishment will be either imprisonment or nonimprisonment; in short, where imprisonment is a potential sanction, nonimprisonment should not be, and vice versa.[20] To sanction one offender with eighteen months' imprisonment, while giving another offender who has committed the same offense twelve months of nonincarcerative punishment, would so distort the scale that equality of sentences, as well as proportionality, would be in serious jeopardy. Where the law calls at all for imprisonment as a sanction, in the equality model, a nonincarcerative punishment would be tolerable only in the rarest of circumstances. Similarly, where the normal sentence would be nonincarcerative, only in the most extreme case would imprisonment for any duration be warranted. Obviously, to the extent that nonincarcerative sanctions become punitive (see the following section), this gap between incarceration and nonincarceration becomes narrower; but even in the best of cases, the chasm between liberty, however conditioned, and imprisonment is so wide that it would be difficult to bridge. The equality model, therefore, frequently requires that most criticized of penal measures—the mandatory minimum.

Virtually no legislative action in the sentencing arena has been more universally condemned than the mandatory minimum sentence. The American Bar Association, the National Advisory Commission, NCCD, and numerous others have banned even its mention from civilized circles. Of recent model proposals, only the Model Penal Code allowed mandatory minimums, and even this was true only if the offender was sentenced to prison; in virtually all cases, the judge could opt for probation instead.

Yet most of the reasons advanced against the mandatory minimum sentence are rehabilitative in nature—primarily, that defendants should not be sentenced equally when their prospects for rehabilitation are different.[21]

---

[20] A more sophisticated analysis might suggest that we could measure punishment in points and that, for example, two years on probation might be the equivalent in points of four months actually in prison. See Chapter 2, pp. 31–32, *supra*. This discussion assumes that not to be the case, at least for the near future.

[21] The other major argument against mandatory minimum sentences is that they induce plea bargaining, since the defendant knows that he must avoid being convicted of

This, then, suggests the answer to what is otherwise a devastating attack on the desert model—that if probation, or some other nonincarcerative sanction, were allowed as an alternative to a relatively fixed, nondiscretionary durational term of imprisonment, the notion that like offenses should be treated alike would be demolished. Instead, the answer would be: if imprisonment is required to meet the demands of just desert, nonimprisonment is not allowed, except in the most extreme cases; if nonimprisonment is a sanction commensurate with the gravity of the offense, only the most severe situation would condone a term of imprisonment.

The Other Side: Nonincarceration

Whether or not one accepts the precise figures as to prison sentences suggested above, it is clear that if the ABA-NCCD-NAC approach is accepted, there will be a need for increased use of nonincarcerative sanctions. Yet under a desert model, these sentences of nonincarceration must not be, and must not be viewed as, nonpunishment. Both in theory and practice nonincarcerative sanctions must be punitive; if they are not, there will be a loss of proportionality between those who receive imprisonment and those who do not, and there will be a loss of public support when those who have committed offenses are essentially released to the community without punishment.

Probationers should be put to community service, or required to live in halfway houses, make restitution to their victims, or accept other similar conditions on their liberty. Yet unlike today's probation conditions, which are based on the notion that the probation officer must

---

crime Z, which carries a specific minimum sentence; therefore, he will always plea to charge Y, which does not. This point will be explored in Chapter 9; but here we can say that (1) if all sentences are mandatory in the sense that if imprisonment is called for, probation cannot be given; and (2) if crimes or crime classes are properly defined, this problem will be lessened. It will not be eliminated—but it may be drastically reduced.

Yet another argument against the mandatory minimum is that if too widespread, prison populations will be greatly expanded. Even in the context of present sentencing practices, this has been shown to be untrue. In the context of an entire new scheme of sentencing, the effect on prison population should be considered before the sentences are promulgated. (For further discussion of this point, see Chapter 7.)

In a careful study by the Federal Judicial Center, An Evaluation of the Probable Impact of Selected Proposals for Imposing Mandatory Minimum Sentences in the Federal Courts (1977), the basic findings were that, except for opiate cases and bank robbery cases, current federal proposals for mandatory minimum sentences in a number of different offenses would only tangentially actually affect the amount of time currently served by offenders convicted of those offenses. The conclusion was reached essentially that in many of the crimes, there would be no difference at all. There would be some 400 higher sentences and time actually served in terms of mandatory minimum. Nevertheless, the general conclusion is that on the whole the changes in the law would affect the practice relatively little.

have constant power over the probationer to assure that he does not recidivate, the conditions in a desert model probation would be painful, but would not invade the offender's privacy. Conditions that require the assent of a probation officer to marry, get a driver's license, leave the state, and so forth, would be unnecessary and inconsistent with the desert model; fortunately, an increasing number of states are discarding these conditions in any event. Instead, the conditions of a desert model probation would require the probationer to perform some affirmative act, perhaps utilitarian, but in any event arduous and punitive. Creativity and ingenuity by the agency that sets the possible penalties are clearly necessary here.

There are some difficulties here. As Krattenmaker suggests, it is possible that some "community service" might be beneficial to the offender in any one of several ways: (1) it might involve the use of a skill that this offender already had, thus making it less like punishment and more like his typical job (e.g., requiring a convicted lawyer to work for the legal aid society for six months or to represent certain interests that may not often be represented); (2) some such tasks might involve the accretion of skills, so that the offender is not really being "punished" as such.[22] The problem is one both in the abstract, and in practice, when these offenders are compared to offenders who do not receive such beneficial assignments.

This is not a problem for the teleological retributivist.[23] Moreover, the analogy might well be drawn to the prisoner who takes advantage of programs of rehabilitation inside the prison.[24] But there is a difference, since one offender is effectively being ordered to undertake a program that may rehabilitate him, while another is being required to participate in a program that is highly unlikely to do so. Still, the basic sanction is the same—deprivation of autonomy (if not full liberty) for some fixed period of time. That there are fallout benefits should not unduly concern us.

In short, nonincarceration, as a viable program of sanction, should be a readily available sentence. The imagination of the standard setters should mold new and vigorous notions of sanctions and of nonincarcerative punishment. So long as the sentence of nonincarceration is equally distributed to all persons who have committed offenses of the same seriousness, the movement toward equality and proportion is not offended.

[22] Krattenmaker, *supra* note 19 at 1325.
[23] See Chapter 2, pp. 32–34, *supra*.
[24] See Chapter 7, *infra*.

THE MECHANICS OF SENTENCING

The final issue of sentencing structure is the punishment to be imposed for the specific offense. In an indeterminate sentencing scheme, the critical decision to be made by the judge is the type of punishment (whether the defendant will be incarcerated at all); the duration of the punishment is effectively left to other agencies. In a determinate sentencing system, however, the sentencer should decide both the specific type and the effective duration of punishment.

Our concern here is the discretion (or lack of it) the sentencing tribunal has in selecting the determinate sentence. Many who object to determinate (or flat) sentencing do so believing that all discretion will be removed from sentencing judges: we will have "sentencing by computer."[25] Yet nothing in the notion of determinate sentencing requires that. Each of the following, for example, is a determinate sentence scheme:

1. The legislature says that armed robbery shall be punished by three years' imprisonment and that each judge must impose a sentence of three years.
2. The legislature says that each armed robber must be punished by a determinate sentence between three and ten years. A judge is given full discretion to elect the precise sentence (e.g., five, seven), but it must be a single, fixed term of years rather than an open-ended, indeterminate sentence (e.g., "three to five" years).

Each of these is a determinate sentence model—yet only the first, which I shall call "point" sentencing, removes all discretion from the judge. In this system, once the level of criminality has been ascertained and placed in its proper (legislative) cubbyhole, and the defendant has been convicted, the judge becomes superfluous.[26]

[25] For one who supports "computer sentencing," see G. MUELLER, SENTENCING: PROCESS AND PURPOSE (1977).

[26] This, of course, ignores the discretionary nature of the judge's fact-finding authority—even if there is a jury. But in a world where 85–90 percent of all criminal defendants plead guilty, the facts are essentially stipulated. Of course, a judge may—and should—ignore such a stipulation if it does not accurately reflect the actual circumstances of the crime. A defendant who clearly committed armed robbery, for example, will often plead to robbery if the arming increases the sentence. The judge should, as a matter of desert theory, ignore the plea, since it is unjust both to other robbers and to other armed robbers that this defendant is being treated as less blameworthy than he deserves. But the pressure for judges to go along with a plea bargain is enormous. Just recently, however, California—consistent with the basic thesis here that justice is only done if the offender is punished for what he actually did—amended its new sentencing

But the second system—which I will call "range" sentencing—is also determinate, yet retains a great deal of judicial discretion, depending upon the breadth of the range (obviously three to ten is a very broad range).

Which of these is the more desirable is answerable only by returning to first principles: aside from the current general attempt to restrict judicial discretion in sentencing, there is the mandate of the equality philosophy that each crime receive a sentence that is (1) proportionate to its seriousness; (2) based primarily upon the offense, with little if any variation for the offender; and (3) part of a system of punishments that is itself internally proportionate.

"Range" Sentences and Overlaps

Broad range sentencing—allowing the judge to select any determinate sentence between three and ten years—would fail to meet these objectives in two ways. First, there is the obvious possibility of disparity between persons who have committed the same crime: one armed robber might receive a sentence of three years, while another could receive a sanction three times as long. If the crimes are acceptably defined, so that they reflect a level of general moral culpability, such disparity would be unwarranted. (If the crimes are not sufficiently precise, of course, the difference in sentences might be warranted, but then the code would suffer from other weaknesses.)

The second weakness is the potential overlap of sentences for crimes of differing moral culpability. Suppose, for example, that armed robbery were punishable by three to ten years, burglary punishable by two to five years, and forgery by one to four years. This would mean that some forgers or burglars could receive sentences greater than that imposed upon an armed robber. While it may be possible to think of some burglaries (or even forgeries, although that is difficult) that could deserve more punishment and blameworthiness than an armed robbery, the likelihood that unwarranted discrepancy will occur frequently is so great that it cannot be allowed. It would seen, therefore, that the ranges would have to be narrowed, so that the overlaps with sentences for other crimes of a less serious nature are either minimized or removed entirely.[27]

---

law to allow the judge to "enhance" the sentence on the basis of certain proven facts, even if the prosecutor (pursuant to a plea) did not seek such an enhancement. While there are problems of procedural due process in such a system, these are manageable; and the defendant is sentenced for what he "really" did—assuming, again, that we are reasonably secure in the precision with which "enhancing" facts are defined. Plea bargaining is discussed more fully in Chapter 9.

[27] It is a nice question whether an equality model properly constituted should allow any sentencing overlap between the various classes of crimes. Professor Zimring might

Given a relatively narrow range of sentences for each defined offense, it would be possible to simply allow the judge to roam through
the range at will. Thus, for example, assuming a range of two to four
years for armed robbery, the sentencing judge could be informed that
any determinate sentence selected from within that range would be
valid.[28] Particularly if the judge were assisted, as well, by a set of
"mitigating and aggravating circumstances" (see Chapter 6) by which
the sentence could be placed at the higher or lower end of the range,
this would seem to be both workable and defensible. Thus, a judge
about to sentence an armed robber who found three aggravating circumstances present, would tend to sentence in the upper part of the
range (three and one-half to four years), while a judge who found
mitigating circumstances present would tend to sentence in the lower
part of the range (two to two and one-half years).

The desirability of making judges accountable, however, may require further prescriptive devices. One such device is the presumptive
sentence, a mechanism suggested by the Twentieth Century Fund,
Professor Fogel, and Professor von Hirsch and now adopted in Indiana,
New Jersey, and California.[29] Rather than allow the judge to select any
sentence within the established range, without further justification,
presumptive sentencing premises that somewhere within the range

---

argue, for example, that it is simply impossible to be sufficiently precise to be sure that
the worst forgery is less morally culpable than the best robbery. Even if this is true,
however, the need for overlap is not apparent. If there is to be justice on the one side,
because there is no overlap, it could be argued that by creating overlap, the potential for
even more injustice is not only created, but assured. On the whole, the better policy is to
recognize that even though we are not capable of adequately defining the interests
jeopardized in every criminal situation, we should forbid overlap and then leave it to
evolution of criteria, through appellate review and other mechanisms, to take up the
slack. Of course, if the suggested five year maximum is accepted, it simply may not be
possible to totally avoid overlap, even if a large percentage of offenses receive nonincarcerative sentences. At that point, the standard setter should avoid overlap in the more
serious offenses, allowing overlap in the less serious, on the grounds that the differences
between the less serious offenses are likely to be less than those of the more serious. See
Coffee, *The Repressed Issues of Sentencing: Accountability, Predictability and Equality
in the Era of the Sentencing Commission*, 66 GEO. L. J. 975 (1978).

This, however, assumes that the focus is solely on the offense; if other characteristics
such as the past criminal record of the defendant are considered (see Chapter 5), there
will have to be some overlap, since there will not be sufficient distinct durations available. Thus, if past convictions are relevant considerations, a first time armed robber
might receive a shorter sentence than a fourth time forger. This becomes consistent with
the desert model since while the harm done by the robber is greater, his culpability is
less; therefore, the seriousness of his crime (harm plus culpability) is less. As Chapter 5
will indicate, I cannot agree that consideration of past offenses is consistent with a just
deserts rationale; nevertheless, this is how the system would be rationalized.

[28] By "valid," I mean sustainable on appellate review. See pp. 53–55, *infra*.

[29] See Chapter 10. As the material there shows, however, the other restrictions urged
in this book (narrowness of range, shortening of sentences) have been accepted only by
California. Even there, the 1978 amendments have broadened the ranges unduly.

should be the sentence that should be imposed upon the typical crime and that variations from that sentence should be allowed—even within the range—only on the basis of articulated, written reasons.[30] Thus, while retaining judicial discretion in sentencing, the presumptive approach strictly restrains that discretion, requiring the sentencing judge to express, subject to appellate review, his or her reasons for deviating, even within the range, from the prescribed sentence. In other words, the judge must indicate what makes this particular crime different from the typical crime.

Presumptive sentencing is not unique to a desert model. It could fit an indeterminate system with wide judicial and correctional discretion, a definite system with judicial discretion, or the flat sentence system with narrow judicial discretion. But it fits most comfortably with the last.

Important—though perhaps not critical—to this scheme is the notion of "aggravating and mitigating factors," which would allow variation from the presumptive sentence. The particulars of these factors, as well as analysis of proposed or enacted criteria, will be left to Chapter 6. Here, however, one point needs to be underscored: both *Doing Justice* and *Fair and Certain Punishment* agree that the function of aggravating and mitigating circumstances is to allow variations within the sentencing range, not to permit the judge to go outside the range to the full extent of the legislation.[31] Much recently passed or pending legislation would use these factors to allow a judge to go outside the range, up (or down) to the highest (or lowest) legislative punishments permissible, leaving the judge free within the range without any constraints. This essentially reintroduces the possibility of widespread disparity, particularly since every enactment, after listing a series of aggravating and mitigating factors, provides the wild card of "any other factor deemed appropriate."

Of all the legislation either enacted or proposed, California's new sentencing law most closely resembles the presumptive sentence model. Although not explicitly so declaring, the California legislation prior to the 1978 amendments established four classes of crimes pun-

---

[30] Written reasons should be required even where the presumptive sentence is imposed, to discourage judges who would seek to avoid the "reasons" requirement by mechanically imposing the presumptive sentence.

[31] A. VON HIRSCH, *supra* note 18 at 99ff; TWENTIETH CENTURY FUND, *supra* note 1 at 21. As will be explained in Chapter 4, legislative maxima set the final outer limits for punishment beyond which a sentencing judge could never reach. But if sentencing guidelines are established by a sentencing commission or other agency, they might well not touch every point in the legislative scheme. Thus, if crime Z carried a legislative maximum of three years, the sentencing guidelines' range might well be twelve–twenty-four months. Particularly if the jurisdiction has recidivist statutes (see Chapter 5), the upper range of the legislative maxima must be reserved for them.

ishable by prison confinement and establishes for each a presumptive sentence: for the highest (class *A*) the presumptive sentence is six years; for *B*, four years; for *C*, three years; and for *D*, two years. The judge may, on the basis of aggravating or mitigating factors, increase or decrease by one year (the decrease for class *D* is eight months). Although there are some minor problems with so-called enhancement provisions, which allow the judge to increase the base term by a specified number of years, the California system is both in spirit and in letter the nearest to presumptive sentencing, as explicated here, now in operation. That legislation, as well as all other presently enacted legislation, is described in Chapter 10.

"Point" Sentencing

Point sentencing is basically the only sentencing device compatible with the encyclopedic notion of defining seriousness, in which each crime is narrowly and specifically defined so as to incorporate all legislatively endorsed aggravating and mitigating circumstances. To allow variations of sentences for each of those very narrowly defined crimes would almost certainly violate the notion that crimes of different seriousness should be punished differently. For example, if, in the *Fair and Certain Punishment* descriptions related earlier, first degree armed robbery were punishable by four to six years and second degree by three to five years, the carefully drawn differences between first and second degree robbery could disappear in the sentencing process. A person who used a dangerous weapon but not a loaded gun might receive a sentence of five years, while one who committed the legislatively more serious offense of first degree armed robbery (use of a loaded gun) might receive a four year sentence. This overlap would reintroduce disparity not only among offenders, but among offenses— precisely the disparity that an equality sentencing model intends to erase.

THE NEED FOR SENTENCE REVIEW

Thus far, we have established the following propositions:

1. Sentencing alternatives should be proportionate to the seriousness of the offense, as defined by the social interest endangered and by the *mens rea* of the defendant.
2. The sentencing scheme should articulate the presumptive sentence, as well as the upper and lower ranges of sentences that would be allowed where there were aggravating and mitigating circumstances.

3. The range of sentences should be narrow, and cross-type sentences (probation versus incarceration) should be proscribed. Overlaps should be minimized.
4. Nonincarcerative punishments should be favored, but these punishments should be designed to be punitive in nature.

How are these prescriptions to be enforced upon the myriad of trial judges, even within a single jurisdiction, who may react adversely to the entire notion?[32] The obvious solution is review of the sentences actually imposed, to determine whether they have been properly fixed within the terms established by the agency that promulgated the rules on sentencing.

That, however, is far from easy. Although appellate federal courts once had the power to review sentences,[33] they have eschewed that power for nearly eighty years. Just four years ago, the United States Supreme Court, in stinging dictum, denounced any notion of appellate review of sentences in the federal system,[34] even though the American Bar Association, among others, has come out strongly for appellate review of sentences.[35]

Even assuming, however, that legislation established appellate review, the standard of review is critical. Without probing here the depths of such a subject, it can be said that a presumptive sentence should be presumed correct, while a nonpresumptive sentence should be presumed incorrect.

Both the defendant and the prosecutor should have the right to appeal. Although there is an argument that prosecutorial appeal is either undesirable, unconstitutional, or both, many states now allow such appeal, and it has been endorsed by the ABA Standards Relating to Appellate Review.[36] In a system whose prime aim is equality and consistency of sentencing, the goal of equality should outweigh the individual defendant's right to secure a bonus by appearing before a judge who may generally sentence more lightly than other judges; the goal of equality may in fact require harsher sentences upon some

---

[32] Adverse reaction is not necessarily to be limited to judges. Defense counsel and prosecutors, who see their ability to plea bargain limited, may also feel constrained to object to the process.

[33] Act of March 3, 1879, ch. 176, §1, 20 Stat. 354; United States v. Wynn, 11 F. 57 (C.C.E.D. Mo. 1882); Bates v. United States, 10 F. 92 (C.C.N.D. Ill. 1881).

[34] Dorszynski v. United States, 418 U.S. 424 (1974).

[35] AMERICAN BAR ASSOCIATION, STANDARDS RELATING TO APPELLATE REVIEW OF SENTENCES (1968).

[36] See Dunsky, *The Constitutionality of Increasing Sentences on Appellate Review,* 69 J. CRIM. L. AND CRIM. 19 (1978).

offenders, but if prosecutorial appeal is not allowed, the need for consistency will be weakened substantially.[37]

Appellate review of sentences has not worked well thus far in this country.[38] It is not clear whether it will work well with a new equality model. It could easily be undermined by appellate tribunals that simply abdicate their responsibility, or it could be undermined by substantial plea bargaining. Arguably, with specific guidelines for sentencing, with specific ranges into which sentences should normally fall, and with a requirement of written reasons for every sentence this past history will not prove prologue. But it is clear that, at least until judges have become sufficiently familiar and (hopefully) comfortable with the

---

[37] The statute should preclude potential vindictiveness on the part of the prosecutor. See Appendix A, sec. 13(d), for an attempt to do this by varying the times during which the two sides may appeal.

[38] Note, *Appellate Review of Primary Sentencing Decisions; A Connecticut Case Study,* 69 YALE L.J. 1453 (1960). Perhaps the most exhaustive analysis of appellate review in action has been Zeisel and Diamond, *Sentence Review in Massachusetts and Connecticut* (LEAA, forthcoming). An offshoot of that study, Samuelson, *Sentence Review and Sentence Disparity: A Case Study of the Connecticut Sentence Review Division,* 10 CONN. L. REV. 5 (1977), concluded that the Connecticut process of appellate review of sentences had been virtually worthless and recommended, in effect, that the Sentence Review Division, the agency established for appellate review, instead become a sentencing commission, promulgating sentencing rules, with guidelines for judges. Not surprisingly, the Connecticut experience demonstrated the typical problems of sentencing: both sentencing courts and the SRD seemed uncertain as to which purpose of sentencing should receive priority; the conflicts between the purposes were never resolved by the legislature; and the SRD, composed of trial judges temporarily assigned, were loathe to reverse on the basis of unreasonableness a sentence pronounced by a fellow trial judge. Furthermore, the SRD looked only at the sentence before it and, with rare exceptions, consistently refused to consider comparable sentences, thus making its prime job—the reduction of disparity—impossible to accomplish.

The report also found that the key reason for disparate sentences was plea bargaining—both the trial judge and the SRD refused to overturn a sentence that had been bargained. This, then, led Samuelson to suggest plea-bargaining guidelines as well; this issue is discussed *infra,* in Chapter 9.

Strangely, the SRD never seemed to recognize either its role in reducing disparity or the parole board's role in that same process. Ms. Samuelson gives several examples (a relatively small number initially) of instances where sentences were reduced upon appeal. In a number of these cases, the reduction was of the maximum, not the minimum, sentence, a virtually meaningless reduction with the presence of parole. Thus, for example, in one case, the defendant had received a six to twenty-five year sentence for narcotics sale; this was reduced to six to ten; in another case, the board reduced a ten to sixty-five year sentence to ten to thirty-seven. The removal of twenty-eight years from the maximum sentence could only be symbolic; no prison system in the country would expect to hold a defendant either thirty-seven or sixty-five years. Thus, even where appellate review worked, it was realistically ineffective. That Ms. Samuelson ultimately calls not for a reform of the review process, but rather for a total change of structure and role for the SRD, effectively reproducing the role of a sentencing commission, may indicate why that path, rather than appellate review, must be the primary route to achieve uniformity in sentencing.

desert model, it may well suffer the same fate that jeopardized parole in the early 1900s—judicial animosity run riot. At least some precaution, however tenuous, should be taken against that possibility. Appellate review of some sort seems necessary.

SUMMARY

A presumptive sentencing scheme limits judicial discretion to relatively narrow ranges of sentencing choices, based primarily (I believe exclusively) on the seriousness of the offense. This requires exploration of what we mean by the seriousness of the offense. I have argued here that, in theory, the best possible mode of defining seriousness is to consider, within the same definition of a crime, not only the harm actually done, but also that which is threatened, qualified only by the mental state of the offender. Thus, rather than robbery, burglary, assault, and so forth, our definitions of offenses should be changed to intentionally causing or risking bodily injury, property loss, and the like, thus making attempts coterminous with successful completion of a particular offense and focusing more carefully on the culpability of the offender rather than on the results of his conduct. Consistent with the deserts model, however, the culpability factor must be limited to the act actually done and not include the predicted further behavior of the offender. Efforts to define each presently recognized crime, with all possible variations built into the sentencing scheme, would result in a cumbersome, self-defeating encyclopedic approach to sentencing, which would either be so abused as to reintroduce sentencing disparity or so closely followed as to make proportionate punishments a nullity.

 *Chapter 4*

Setting the Guidelines: Of Sentencing Commissions and Others

If the sentencing reforms of which we have thus far spoken are to occur, the process will require both great attention to detail in the promulgation of the sentencing parameters and a continuing monitoring of the process, including collection of data, analysis of deviations, suggestions for changes, and so forth. Who is to perform this task?

THE LEGISLATURE

The obvious agency is the legislature. Legislatures have historically asserted their hegemony over sentencing decisions, and the judiciary has by and large acquiesced in this assertion. Moreover, to the extent that the deserts approach to sentencing is based on the response of moral outrage to the crime, it would seem that the agency closest to the community's sense of moral outrage—its duly elected representatives—should be the proper agency to perform this task.

Many of the critics of von Hirsch's book have assumed that the model requires legislative sentencing,[1] fearful that legislators will seek to ensure their reelection by enacting Draconian provisions; they have therefore argued against any model which would deeply involve the legislature with sentencing reform.

Even a casual glance at the statutes that have already been passed

[1] Among those making this mistake are Zimring, *Making the Punishment Fit the Crime: A Consumers' Guide to Sentencing Reform* 6 HASTINGS CENTER REPORT 13 (December 1976); and the Model Sentencing and Correction Act of the National Conference of Commissioners on Uniform State Laws (2d draft, July 1978), p. 129 (hereafter MSCA).

in some states (discussed in Chapter 10) will demonstrate the acuity of those who mistrust legislative sentencing. Legislation that allows sentences of twenty to fifty years or thirty to sixty years is simply beyond the pale of any concept of proportionality, which as we have already seen is one central point of the deserts theory. Moreover, it surely is contrary to any notion of narrow ranges constructed to restrict judicial discretion.

But it may be unfair to saddle the deserts movement with responsibility for those monstrosities. Such sentences almost inevitably would have arisen anyway; the trend toward conservative and harsh sentences was already underway prior to the publication of von Hirsch's book. Therefore, the pragmatic objection of critics that legislatures, awakened to the sentencing system, will react with vengeance, is valid criticism neither of the model nor of the proponents of the model. Furthermore, von Hirsch's critics have failed to note that he recognized this problem and suggested an alternative solution: "Another alternative is to have an administrative agency prescribe the standards . . . ."[2]

Several reasons argue that the legislature is not the proper agency for performing the detailed work required to establish a proportionate, equality-based sentencing system. First, legislators are far too busy to pay close attention to the complexities and intricacies that are involved in establishing a scale of proportionate penalties for hundreds of different crimes. Either the scale will become ludicrous or the differences in crimes and culpability will become meaningless; legislators simply do not have the time to argue and debate carefully over such matters. Legislatures have in the past recognized this and, after stating the ultimate parameters, have left the fulfillment of those parameters to other agencies, such as judges and parole boards. Thus, the proposition argued here would not divest the legislature of power that it has previously exercised; it would instead simply shift to another agency the power that legislatures have previously delegated.

Second, legislatures are generally the proper bodies to do many things in our democratic society because they are the elected representatives of the majority. But in some instances that very representativeness seriously raises questions about their qualifications to deal with certain topics. Any legislation that arguably infringes upon the basic rights of a minority is to be viewed with suspicion. The criminal element in our society is such a minority—a minority that the majority wishes (properly) to punish. Furthermore, at least under present law in most states, persons who are convicted of crimes will, at least for the duration of their confinement and in many cases for the rest of their lives, be deprived of a number of meaningful civil rights, including the

[2] A. VON HIRSCH, DOING JUSTICE 103–104 (1976).

right to vote. When legislators therefore legislate against a group of persons who are about to become disenfranchised, there is simply too much possibility that the legislation will be unrealistically and unfairly harsh.

Third, legislatures change memberships, sometimes quickly, sometimes dramatically. Sentencing decisions should not be readily subject to quick manipulation by changing majorities, whether they be more liberal or more conservative. There is a need for stability in sentencing policy. Indeed, in several states in which the legislatures have established sentences initially, hordes of bills have been introduced in the immediately succeeding sessions to alter, either up or down, specific sentences for specific crimes. That kind of facile alteration is undesirable.

Finally, the new sentencing approach should be constantly monitored. The legislature itself simply cannot do this, and we cannot expect a legislative committee to sit as oversight committee collecting the enormous amounts of data that would be necessary to do a proper job. Thus, just as it has delegated in so many other instances, the legislature should delegate the task of devising and revising the guidelines, as well as of monitoring the system.

Still, the legislature should hold the ultimate (effectively, review) power over the actions of the agency to which it delegates initial power to design the system of sentencing. Further, it should do precisely what it has done in the indeterminate sentencing scheme—set the maximum parameters beyond which the agency to which this power was delegated could not go in establishing the guidelines themselves. Whether it should describe in detail the guiding principles of sentencing and the philosophy by which that agency is to measure its actions is less clear. Many of the bills pending in the legislatures, including S. 1437 concerning the federal system, gave quite free range to the standard-setting agency. On the other hand, if the purposes and principles of sentencing are to be articulated by anyone, it should be by the legislature. The suggested statute in Appendix A adopts this course, urging the legislature to define as closely as possible the precepts and policies by which sentencing patterns should be developed. Thus, the legislature should do what it can best do and leave the detailed implementation to a delegated body, complete with full-time experts and staff.

THE JUDICIARY

The judiciary seems just as obvious a body to establish sentencing policy as the legislature. Indeed, one could argue that the judiciary is a more likely receptacle for this power, since it already sentences and thus has experience with the difficulties of assessing punishment. In fact, in some states, the judiciary has already undertaken this task. In Vermont; Denver, Colorado; and Essex County, New Jersey; for example, trial courts participated in a two year project, sponsored by LEAA, under which detailed studies were made of past sentencing practices. The result of this project was a matrix by which the project researchers were able to predict over 80 percent of the sentences that any judge would impose in a given case.[3]

This study, carried out under the direction of Professors Leslie Wilkins and Don Gottfredson, essentially replicated a similar study of the workings of the United States Parole Board. It was intended to demonstrate to judges that while they believed that every sentencing decision was unique, in fact their sentencing determinations were based upon a small number of variable factors that, when properly analyzed, could be seen to be in constant use by virtually all the judges in a given court system.

The Wilkins-Gottfredson study compels judges to rethink their sentencing practices and suggests the matrix system as a guide for later sentencing determinations. A judge seeking to sentence an armed robber with certain characteristics, for example, could look to the matrix system to determine what sentence that defendant would receive, on the average, from the judges in that jurisdiction. Hopefully, informed by that data, the judge would then rethink his or her own sentencing decision to consider whether there was sufficient justification to vary from that average sentence, thereby reducing disparity.[4]

It would appear possible, therefore, for the courts—or the administrative branch of the supreme court in a state—to gather the kind of information generated in the Wilkins study and then to announce to all the judges in that jurisdiction the establishment of sentencing guidelines, in whatever form, that should govern future sentencing decisions. Indeed, in late 1978 New Jersey did precisely that and several other states are considering similar action.

The difficulty with such a program, however, should be obvious. Sentencing patterns revealed by such a study may be filled with patterns of discrimination or of rank arbitrariness. To enshrine such discrimination, through a mandatory matrix or guideline system,

---

[3] L. WILKINS, D. GOTTFREDSON, and J. KRESS, SENTENCING GUIDELINES: STRUCTURING JUDICIAL DISCRETION (1976).

[4] The study, while only descriptive, gives the clear impression that, in the second phase of the project, the matrixes were to be given some presumptive weight. One court using these matrixes, however, has specifically denied that the matrix has any prescriptive force. Instead, it is said to be used only as a piece of information, as any other piece of information might be employed. State v. Whitehead (Essex County, N.J. Super Ct. May 10, 1978).

throughout the state, without any substantive evaluation of their desirability, would be untenable; "what is" is not necessarily "what should be." Moreover, current sentencing practice is based upon an amalgam of all the purported purposes of sentencing—desert, rehabilitation, deterrence, incapacitation—as seen through the eyes of each individual judge. For a new method of sentencing, based upon a careful analysis and adherence to one of those purposes, desert, to be based upon sentences developed without any such theoretical framework would be self-defeating.

Nevertheless, a process could be established by which the judiciary would gather data, analyze them for substance, and then promulgate sentencing guidelines based on desert, using this information as it was relevant. Many of the deficiencies mentioned with regard to the legislature would be ameliorated, if not totally avoided. The judiciary, for example, is substantially distant from the pressure of day-to-day public passion. Its membership does not change as rapidly as the legislature's might. It is a relatively small, relatively coherent group and is generally under a centralized authority that could enforce its rules upon its membership.[5]

There are, however, still difficulties. It has been argued, for example, that judges, much like legislators, having sentenced in terms of false time for so long, will find it difficult in the long run to seriously consider terms and sentences that are true time and that the results of the judicially established sentencing guidelines will be excessively long sentences, disproportionate not only to the offense, but to what in fact has been the practice in the state to that time. The argument is not fully persuasive; indeed, many judges, aware of the impact of parole and good time, now sentence to real time by discovering how large the inflation must be on a sentence in order for the defendant to serve the time the judge thinks proper. Thus, a judge may sentence a defendant to nine years, fully expecting that he will serve only two; indeed, it is not uncommon for correctional administrators to relate instances of judges calling them and asking how long a sentence must be imposed in order to assure actual service of the punishment that the judge actually deems appropriate. For such judges, a switch to real time might not be as conceptually difficult as the argument suggests.[6] Still, there is a danger that not all judges will in fact be so aware.

[5] The MSCA, *supra* note 1, gives another reason. There may be states in which sentencing power is exclusively in the hands of the judiciary, and participation by others would be, or seem to be, unconstitutional. For those states, the MSCA suggests an advisory board of nonjudges to deliberate with the actual board of judges in establishing sentencing matrixes.

[6] A variation of this theme has recently occurred with the adoption by the United States Parole Commission of parole release guidelines very similar to those sentencing

Moreover, membership in the agency that establishes sentencing policy should be representative of the entire state population. The judiciary—predominantly white, predominantly male, predominantly middle aged—is not sufficiently representative; it is an insular body, which could not claim such representativeness. (While this is not true of the legislature, the other arguments against legislative action still stand.)

THE SENTENCING COMMISSION

A third—and the most salutary—possibility is to establish a new agency, whose independence from any of the branches of government will be likely to create meaningful regulation—a sentencing commission. The originator of the concept of a sentencing commission, though with somewhat different duties, appears to have been Judge Marvin Frankel:[7]

> The proposed commission would be a permanent agency responsible for (1) the study of sentencing, corrections, and parole; (2) the formulation of laws and rules to which the studies pointed; and (3) *the actual enactment of rules* subject to traditional checks by Congress and the courts. The third is emphasized, not because of a claim to novelty, but because it is thought to be especially important if the commission is to be an effective instrument of reform rather than a storage place.

Because it promulgates rules and regulations on a very public issue, the commission should be composed of highly diverse persons across the spectrum of criminal justice activities. Minnesota has already

---

guidelines discussed here. In Addonizio v. United States, 573 F. 2d 147 (3d Cir. 1978), for example, the sentencing judge initially imposed a sentence of ten years. After Addonizio had served four and one-half years and had been denied parole twice, he sought relief from the trial judge. The trial judge acknowledged that Addonizio was being retained by the parole board longer than he, the trial judge, intended and granted relief. The Third Circuit, in a major opinion, upheld the action. The case illustrates the observation that judges often now sentence, or attempt to sentence, in terms of real time. Yet, obviously, the inability of judges to assure that that time—and only that amount of time—will be served leads to serious difficulties for the defendant, like Addonizio, who finds himself incarcerated for a longer period that the judge intended. The paradox is forced because of our current desire to impose misleadingly long false time sentences, in the hope that the parole mechanism will reduce them to realistic punishments. This is not, however, unique to the parole mechanism, as the discussion in Chapter 7, concerning good time, will demonstrate. For example, Illinois' new sentencing statute imposes what appear to be excessively long sentences; but since the defendant is likely to earn "day-to-day" good time, the actual duration will be half of what the judge imposes. These dishonesties should not be perpetuated in a new sentencing scheme. Indeed, this is one glaring weakness in the Model Sentencing and Corrections Act. See Chapter 7 for a further discussion.

   [7] M. Frankel, Criminal Sentences 119 (1973). (Emphasis in original.)

enacted legislation calling for a sentencing commission; the legislative mandate requires that judges, prosecutors, defense counsel, corrections personnel, and the lay public sit on the commission, thus making the body truly representative. Illinois, Pennsylvania and the Model Sentencing and Corrections Act provide for similar diversity.[8]

Indeed, Professor Zalman has suggested that there be at least one designee from the legislative branch, the prosecutor's office, and the judiciary and that each branch have a veto power on the commission.[9] I disagree; on the other hand, perhaps a provision requiring two-thirds of the commission, rather than a mere majority, to agree to specific sentencing guidelines would be useful to assure that the guidelines and policy statements have the support of a substantial majority of the commission.

The commission should be an independent agency. Appointments to the commission can be achieved in a number of ways, but perhaps the best method is that adopted by Minnesota, which provides for some specific persons (the Director of Corrections, the Chief Justice) or their designees, as well as some more generic types, the latter to be designated by the governor, with the advice and consent of the legislature (or one house). Another device, not necessarily undesirable, is to allot to each branch the appointment of a specific number of persons to the commission. Each such appointing authority should assure that the commission does not become a satrapy for persons who cannot find patronage jobs elsewhere; particularly since this agency, unlike others, will not afford easy transferability to the private sector (Who in the private sector can use an expert on sentencing?), the jobs are likely to be somewhat permanent, which is desirable. Still, that permanency urges the appointment of persons with a broad view of the criminal justice system rather than mere advocates with a potential bias.

The sentencing commission's first task would be to collect data on sentences presently imposed and actual time presently served in the jurisdiction. Using this data as a base, which would also have some informational value as to which crimes are considered serious by actors in the criminal justice system in the jurisdiction, the sentencing commission should consider, in relative isolation from outside pressures, the difficult and perplexing questions of substance dealt with elsewhere in this book—whether first offenders should be treated more leniently than repeat offenders; what are proper aggravating and mitigating circumstances; how one defines and ranks crimes according to their seriousness; and so forth.

The next step is problematic. The commission could report to the

---

[8] MSCA, *supra* note 1, §3–110. See Chapter 10.
[9] Zalman, *A Commission Model of Sentencing*, 53 NOTRE DAME LAWYER 266 (1978).

legislature and basically cease functioning. The legislature would then employ the report as it saw fit. But this would simply reinvent the problems already outlined in the section on the legislature. Much more desirable is the path formulated in some legislation—the commission would promulgate a proposed system of sentences, ranging from the in-out (probation versus incarceration) decision to the duration (length of incarceration) decision, for each class of crime. Public hearings would then follow, as with any other administrative rulemaking, and the commission would then promulgate actual sentencing guidelines.[10]

There is still, however, a need for legislative participation. It is highly unlikely, after all, that legislators will renounce their final authority to decide on the policy issues raised by presumptive sentencing and incorporated into a sentencing model by the commission. The legislature, however, should in the initial legislation, agree that it will not tamper with individual parts of the complex program established by the commission and should either adopt or renounce the commission's work in toto. In the latter case, the commission could be instructed to return with a new system of sentencing. Two considerations suggest this approach: (1) the concern that, for a given crime, the legislature might be too influenced by fleeting concerns of the electorate; and (2) the concern that tampering with a carefully constructed system of sentencing would skew the proportionality concept of the entire model.

Thus, the division of labor might well look like this: the legislature would declare, initially, that the maximum possible sentence that could be established by the sentencing commission for Class A offenses would be ten years. The commission would then promulgate a set of rules, which would establish a presumptive sentence of, say, three years, but allow a sentencing judge to increase the sentence to four years, in the presence of aggravating factors, or to decrease the sentence to two years, in the presence of mitigating factors.[11]

Once the commission's rules are legislatively adopted (or allowed to take effect in the absence of legislative veto), the commission would collect data concerning sentences imposed under the rules and deter-

---

[10] All such actions, and future proposal changes in the guidelines, should be subject to the State Administrative Procedure Act. See Coffee, *The Repressed Issues on Sentencing: Accountability, Predictability, and Equality in the Era of the Sentencing Commission*, 66 GEO. L.J. 998ff (1978).

[11] One point should be made here. It is not necessary, in my view, that the commission actually provide for a possible sentence for every point on the legislative range of minimum-maximum. Thus, for example, if the legislature were to say that the commission could not authorize a sentence below three years or above ten years, the commission would be within its power to establish a set of guidelines in which the presumptive sentence was five, the mitigated sentence four, and the aggravated sentence seven.

mine, on a yearly basis at first and on a less frequent basis thereafter, whether any changes should be proposed to the legislature.

The first sentencing commission will have to tread softly, but firmly. As Professor Michael Tonry has put it:[12]

> The sentencing commission will be perched on the edge of an abyss; some of the abyss's contents are known or foreseeable and others are not. Given the complexity, novelty, and scope of the commission-guidelines idea, the complex political-ideological-intellectual-bureaucratic-institutional context in which the commission must operate, the fragility of the guidelines concept in the face of judicial truculence, and a healthy human skepticism about the abyss, *the commission will be well advised to move in small steps, with caution* (emphasis added).

The commission should deal with both the in-out (probation versus incarceration) decision and the duration decision. Some of the reasons for this are suggested in Chapter 8. Additionally, there is some danger that membership on the sentencing commission, especially in its initial years, will not be seen as a prize to be coveted. Particularly if a sitting judge has to either resign or in some other way divorce himself from the bench, at least while on the commission, it may be difficult to obtain the services of highly competent persons to fill such slots. If potential members of the sentencing commission were informed that their sole function would be to decide the in-out issue—which crimes or groups of crimes should be given probation as opposed to incarceration—but that they were not to confront the durational issue, it is probable that many desirable persons would be even less willing to serve than if the commission had full power to deal with both in-out and durational questions.

SUMMARY

Legislatures are simply not able to maintain the day-to-day monitoring of the newly established sentencing scheme and should not be

---

[12] Tonry, Sentencing Guidelines and Sentencing Commissions—An Assessment of the Sentencing Reform Proposition in Criminal Code Reform Act of 1977. (Unpublished)

Recently, Professor von Hirsch and Katharan Hanrahan have suggested that parole boards, devoid of their present functions, could perform the sentencing commission function, at least as to duration of confinement. A. von Hirsch and K. Hanrahan, The Question of Parole: Retention, Reform, or Abolition (1979). One of the minor difficulties with such a proposal is that it establishes a new governmental agency (the sentencing commission) for establishing rules as to the in-out (incarceration-probation) decision while retaining another agency whose job is thereby reduced. Minnesota rejected just such a proposal before establishing one sentencing commission to set both in-out and duration guidelines. For further discussion of this position, see Chapter 8.

expected to do so. Moreover, for other reasons, including changing membership, closeness to the public passions, and lack of expertise, the legislature should not be the body to establish the exact sentences, or range of sentences, for crimes. Instead, its job should be to define the crimes substantively and to set limits, high and low, in which the agency must work to establish its guidelines.

The new agency, a sentencing commission, should be widely representative of all actors in the criminal justice process, including prisoners, and of the public as well. It should constantly monitor the compliance by judges with the established guidelines, on both the in-out decision and the durational decision and should report periodically to the legislature concerning its findings.

Chapter 5

First Offenders and Recidivists

THE DEBATE

Many difficult and perplexing questions of seriousness would have to be faced by a sentencing commission in devising a schedule of punishments: unsuccessful versus successful attempts, risk versus result, etc. Each of these topics deserves a full discussion by itself. Here, however, I will limit my discussion to one which seems to have particularly divided desert writers—whether under a just deserts rationale the first offender may be treated differently from the repeater. The part of *Doing Justice* that raised more debate about the theoretical consistency of the work than any other single aspect[1] was the report's position that first offenders could, consistent with a rationale that stressed parity among offenders, be treated more leniently than repeat offenders or, to put it another way, that repeat offenders deserve more punishment than first offenders.[2]

---

[1] See, e.g., the views of Joseph Goldstein in A. VON HIRSCH, DOING JUSTICE 172–74 (1976). See also Harris, *Disquisition on the Need for a New Model for Criminal Sanctioning Systems*, 77 W. VA. L. REV. 263 (1974); Scheller, Book Review, 67 J. CRIM. L. & CRIM. 356 (1976).

[2] This may appear to be, and certainly would be attacked by Professor von Hirsch as being, an unfair way to state the issue. Instead of viewing this as treating the repeat offender more harshly than he deserves, von Hirsch argues that the first offender may be treated more leniently—with more parsimony—than he otherwise deserves. Therefore, the sentence imposed upon the recidivist is not higher than the norm; it is assumed that the norm is set for repeat offenders. That, it strikes me, is a strange way of articulating a normal sentence. Moreover, I do not believe it really changes the problem of rationalizing the differences in sentences.

At first blush, this seems so incongruous with the rest of the desert theory that the burden to justify it must shift to its proponents. After all, the harm imposed by the offense is the same in each instance; the injury inflicted both on the individual victim and, perhaps less clearly, on society appears to be the same. Moreover, the placement of first offenders into a special category appears simply to open the door for more ambiguous and dubious characteristics to appear in sentencing decisions.

The argument made in *Doing Justice* was basically one of notice—that the repeat offender was more morally culpable and, therefore, more deserving of blame, because the first sentence an offender received brought home to him the notion that the law meant business and that its directives were indeed intended to reach him for his personal control and reprobation. Therefore, the argument proceeded, a first offender is less morally culpable than a second or repeat offender, because he has never received personal censure through the notice afforded by a criminal sanction. Once given this notice, the offender who repeats is then demonstrating a resolve to act in the face, and in clear defiance, of authority.

There are both theoretic and pragmatic problems to this position. First, defiance alone cannot, in a moral system, be the predicate of liability or of increased liability.[3] Von Hirsch admits that, and so there is no dispute on that issue.[4] Second, there is no inherent reason why it is necessary, for purposes of notice or even moral censure as such, that the person be convicted. Arrest, pre-trial incarceration, trial, and so forth would certainly bring home to the defendant that the law meant business, and a juvenile "conviction" would surely carry some measure of moral censure.[5] Moreover, failure to convict because of some reason extraneous to the offenders' culpability should certainly have no effect upon the notice aspect. (It might, of course, have some effect on the deterrence of the offender, who has been given notice that, while the system is serious, it can make mistakes; but it should have no effect upon notice of the seriousness with which offenses are treated.) Yet von

[3] Contempt of a court order is not mere defiance in the sense of the case now under consideration and is therefore inapposite.

[4] Professor Fletcher's criticism of *Doing Justice* ignores von Hirsch's refusal to rely on defiance, and is therefore at least facially misleading. G. FLETCHER, RETHINKING CRIMINAL LAW 460–66 (1978). On the other hand, particularly given some theorists' persistence in justifying different treatment to first offenders, discussed *infra* in the text, Professor Fletcher may in fact have hit the right chord—that notwithstanding the protestations, the real basis for the different treatment is defiance.

[5] Of course, release without conviction might indicate to a guilty person that the law is all bark and no bite. But conviction followed by unsupervised probation, suspended sentence, or a ludicrously short term of confinement might well carry the same message, so that conviction alone is not necessarily a sufficient condition.

Hirsch clearly rejected anything less than a prior adult, criminal conviction as sufficient notice to justify increased punishment. The conviction's almost supernatural powers were left unexplained.

Further, if the notice argument was correct, another problem arose: did one have to be given notice that the law "meant business" as to the specific kind of crime or just in general?[6] That is, could repeat offender statutes be limited to offenders who repeated the same (or at least a similar) crime? *Doing Justice* evaded the question, saying simply that the notice argument "loses some of its force if the current offense is sufficiently dissimilar from the prior ones."[7] Why that was so was not explained, nor is it self-apparent.

Most existing habitual offender laws do not even consider this question: the commission of any second (or third, or subsequent) felony, without regard to the nature and seriousness of the first felony, will result in additional punishment. But recent legislation or legislative proposals do attempt to deal with this. Thus, Connecticut's proposal had an intricate mathematical precision by which the prior offenses were scored: a class C misdemeanor was worth one to four points in considering increased punishment, while a class B felony was "worth" twenty points.[8] A few other states have similarly tried to differentiate the amount of increased punishment on the basis of the prior offense; indeed, some have attempted to vary the present sentence on the basis of both the present offense and the past offense. These attempts are surely more consistent with a commensurate deserts approach, assuming that prior convictions are to be counted at all, than are the blunderbuss laws we now find on the books.

Doing Justice also suggested an affirmative argument for dealing with repeaters more harshly, but it is no more convincing. Arguing by analogy to the arena of sports, the book suggested that we often "retire the trophy" after it has been won consistently by one competitor. This, the argument went, is done because he is said to deserve that special honor. If we recognize repetition in sports as a basis for action, we could, consistently, recognize it in crime (albeit with a different result).

The analogy, however, does not hold. First, the sports analogy concerns only skill; if the same person won the trophy five times by luck (each other competitor broke a leg), it is hardly likely that the trophy

---

[6] Von Hirsch, *supra* note 1 at 86.

[7] *Ibid.* This is only true—if at all—if the new offense is more serious than the prior offense. If the first offense, for example, were rape, merely the notice aspect would obtain for a second offense of, for example, shoplifting. So even von Hirsch's concession was too broad. Von Hirsch appeared, later, to change his view slightly on this. In a book review, Hofstra L. Rev. (in press), he has acknowledged that the seriousness of the prior crimes would be relevant.

[8] See Chapter 10.

would be retired. Punishment, on the other hand, requires ascription of moral blame—a far different currency.

Second, even assuming that the winner has in fact beaten his competitors several successive times, without enormous bad luck to those competitors, it is nevertheless true that each victory is comparative, not absolute: a bad horse in a very bad year may win the Triple Crown, while the better horse in a very good year may fail to win even one jewel. The same is not true of moral character.

Finally, to the extent that the retirement is truly earned, it is because we see the winner as having more "something" (skill, artistry, etc.) than the mere trophy suggests. For repeat offenders, this something could only be persistence or defiance—neither of which would justify punishment.

These, and other, criticisms led von Hirsch to reject arguments made in *Doing Justice* for punishing the second offender more seriously, but not his position that the second offender should be punished more seriously. He then argued that the second offender is "more morally culpable" because he has demonstrated a "character trait"— persistent disregard of others' rights.[9] Von Hirsch argued that if this is part of the defendant's character, he is more morally blameworthy for having done the act a second time and, therefore, is properly exposed to more punishment.

But this cannot be right either. First of all, a taxonomy of indication of disregard for human rights cannot clearly be enunciated or adopted by deserts theorists. Does a person who, for the first time, blows up an airplane, demonstrate less disrespect for human rights than the forger who repeats bad checks or, for that matter, even the contract killer who, for hire and calculatedly, kills two people at two separate times? "Disregard for human rights" cannot be so easily calculated.

But more than that, the argument of character clearly raises the specter of bringing into the sentencing process all of that soft data upon which sentencing judges have relied for the last hundred years—the defendant's religion, his past employment, his relations with his spouse, his childhood history, whether he loves animals, and so forth. The many problems with allowing such information to be considered by a sentencing court have already been explored in Chapter 2 and will not be repeated here.[10]

---

[9] See A. VON HIRSCH AND K. HANRAHAN, THE QUESTION OF PAROLE: RETENTION, REFORM, OR ABOLITION (1979). Von Hirsch says that he really means to ask whether the defendant's crime was "in character" rather than whether his character is good or bad. I find the difference not persuasive.

[10] For a brilliant analysis of the inadequacy—and inaccuracy—of the data now used in presentence reports, see Coffee, *Future of Sentencing Reform: Emerging Legal Issues*

Still a third argument to justify lighter treatment of first offenders has now been articulated—"partial tolerance." The notion essentially analogizes adult punishment to our treatment of juvenile offenders and posits that we allow them lighter punishments than we impose on an adult because we say their character has not yet fully been developed. Similarly, the argument goes, we should accord first offender adults partial tolerance because it may be that they, too, have not learned sufficiently of the seriousness of their acts.

The echoes of von Hirsch's first two arguments in this new approach are not, I believe, coincidental. The analogy to learning is clearly a twist on the notice argument; the analogy to character is simply the second argument recast. Still, the argument is attractive, and it nicely limits the amount of increased punishment we can mete out to repeat offenders: since the partial tolerance is only temporary, once the temporaneity has disappeared, we punish by full desert—but no more than full desert—for the crime. In short, the argument clearly is for parsimony for first offenders, not for increased punishment for repeat offenders.

But the argument will still not down. It is true that we treat juveniles with tolerance in tort law, but that, I submit, is not because they are minors, but because they are beginners, and we must accept beginners and their concomitant lack of judgment in order to obtain an eventual social good—professionals. No such social good will obtain in criminal practices. Moreover, to the extent that we do deal less severely with juvenile criminality, an explanation at least as cogent is that the juvenile's *mens rea* is less, because his appreciation of the harm inflicted is less. A ten year old who kills a playmate, even with intent, simply does not appreciate the finality of the harm he inflicts; therefore, the punishment should be far less severe.[11]

If these arguments against differential treatment are valid, why this bulldog tenacity by a leading proponent of commensurate deserts to a principle that is both dubious on its own merits and seriously inconsistent with the deserts model, at least as perceived by most deserts supporters? Why is there always this nagging desire to punish repeat offenders more severely?

---

in the *Individualization of Justice*, 73 MICH. L. REV. 13614 (1975). And see Coffee, *The Repressed Issues of Sentencing: Accountability, Predictability, and Equality in the Era of the Sentencing Commission*, 66 GEO. L.J. 975 (1978).

[11] This would suggest, of course, that the seventeen year old who kills or robs should be treated as severely as the adult, and we are now coming to that conclusion in our system. We are also coming to that conclusion in tort, with the development, generally tacit, of a mature minor theory of tort and contract. See Singer, *Consent of the Unfree: Behavior Modification and Medical Experimentation in the Closed Institution*, 1 J. LAW AND HUM. BEH. 101, 144–48 (1977).

The answer, I think, is that we simply feel that there is a difference. As David Rudenstine has put it, although prior offenses should not theoretically be considered in a desert model:[12]

> In fact, everybody I know who's an adherent to the punishment model makes priors relevant. They justify it by simply throwing up their arms in frustration and saying, "I don't know what the rationale is, but it strikes me as ludicrous not to pay attention to the fact that this person did the same act once or twice before, or did a different act and was before the same court."

What bothers us, I believe, is that in ordinary discourse, we do sometimes look to such factors, and our normal reaction is to allow the state to consider such factors in sentencing. But for all the reasons given earlier—that sentencing by the state is *not* "ordinary moral discourse" by individuals—this innate reaction should be rejected.

There is also the obvious pragmatic argument against repeat offender laws—they give far too much discretion to prosecutors. Indeed, there is a great deal of evidence that the only use to which habitual offender statutes are now put is plea bargaining.[13] In a recent case from Nebraska, a defendant demonstrated statistically that the prosecutor actually sought prosecution under the habitual offender statute in only 3 percent of the cases and actually only obtained the implementation of that statute in 1 percent of the cases in which the statute was applicable. In the other 99 percent of the cases, it was used strictly as a plea bargaining technique.[14] Whatever we wish to do with plea bargaining, either now or in the future, it is totally undesirable to give the prosecutor a potent weapon of this nature when it will have absolutely no effect at all upon the sentence and when, even if it had an effect, the evidence is overwhelming that habitual offender statutes are abused and abusive. A theory that purports to take a new approach and a new look at sentencing in general should not endorse such a mechanism.

Finally, habitual offender statutes are anathema to virtually every concept of least drastic alternative we have. The parade of horribles is commonplace. A person who passes three checks on three separate days in the course of a week may be separately charged, separately convicted, separately sentenced, and become an habitual offender incarcerated for life, even though for every other week in his life he has

---

[12] Remarks in COMMUNITY SERVICE SOCIETY, PROCEEDINGS OF THE COMMITTEE ON CRIMINAL AND JUVENILE JUSTICE, CONFERENCE ON DETERMINATE SENTENCING FOR JUVENILES 8 (1978).

[13] See Bordenkircher v. Hayes, 434 U.S. 357 (1978).

[14] Martin v. Paratt, 412 F. Supp. 544 (D. Neb. 1976), *aff'd* 549 F.2d 50 (8th Cir. 1977).

been a law-abiding citizen. A recent case from West Virginia involved an offender, convicted of a minor check forgery, who had previously been convicted of two felonies, one of which was so minor that it was hardly noticeable at all, the other of which was rather substantial; he was sentenced to life on the basis of the new check forgery some ten years after his last crime. The United States Court of Appeals for the Fourth Circuit held the statute as applied unconstitutional.[15] Habitual offender statutes are simply not worth the candle.[16]

THE PRAGMATIC COMPROMISE

If, however, this analysis is rejected and repeaters are treated differently, the remaining problems to be addressed are: (1) should (a) all past offenses count for increases, (b) only those past offenses like the present offense, or (c) only a selected category of offenses (e.g., all violent felonies); (2) how many times should the penalty be increased (i.e., should every past offense, even the fortieth, increase the punishment incrementally, or should we, for whatever reason, stop at a specific number); (3) how much should the increase, both incremental and total, be; and (4) how much incremental increase should be allowed prior to the stop point?

[15] Hart v. Coiner, 483 F.2d 136 (4th Cir. 1973). *Accord*, Rummel v. Estelle, 568 F.2d 1193 (5th Cir. 1978); Thacker v. Garrison, 445 F. Supp. 376 (W.D.N.C. 1978).

[16] One of the fascinating materials in the Model Sentencing and Corrections Act of the National Conference of Commissioners on Uniform State Laws (2d draft, July 1978), is a table, derived from LEAA, SOURCEBOOK OF CRIMINAL JUSTICE STATISTICS, Table 6.53, at 485 (1974), which shows that, aside from the possible use of habitual offender statutes, repeat offenders do not in fact serve much more time than first offenders.

Crime	Median Term (in years) Prior to Parole (1965–70)	
	Prior Record	*No Prior Record*
Homicide	4.7	5.0
Manslaughter	1.9	1.7
Armed Robbery	2.0	2.4
Aggravated Assault	1.3	1.2
Burglary	1.4	1.2
Theft or Larceny	1.1	1.0
Vehicle Theft	1.2	1.0
Check Fraud	1.3	1.0
Other Fraud	1.0	0.9
Forcible Rape	4.4	3.7
Other Sex Offenses	2.2	2.0
Narcotics Offenses	1.8	1.3

(This, of course, is no longer true for the federal system, which expressly bases much of its salient factor score on past record.)

The first question has already been discussed and need not be resurrected here. The second and third questions are answered reasonably easily by desert analysis: since the focus of any sanction should be on the present offense, any increases allowed for offenses should be modest. The kinds of statutes that are now on the books and that allow life imprisonment on the basis of third or fourth offense would be prohibited.[17]

The answer to the fourth question is somewhat implicit in the requirement of modest increases generally. But there is a subsidiary question: Should the increases be arithmetic or skewed? Since the basic reason for allowing such increases would be utilitarian, we must turn to utilitarianism for the answer. There are three possibilities: (1) to increase the punishment equally for each new offense; (2) to increase more harshly for the second offense, but less harshly for succeeding offenses; or (3) to increase the punishment slightly for the second offense, but more harshly for the third offense. The first seems to be neutral between the utilitarian aims of incapacitation and deterrence. The second stresses specific deterrence, since it seeks to stop the offender from returning to a life of crime. The third stresses incapacitation—substantially increased punishment for someone who simply will not stop and therefore appears to be more likely to repeat criminal activity if released.

Without further discussion here, suffice to say that, in light of the general ambiguity about deterrence in general, much less in terms of the efficacy of threatened increased punishment for a second offense, the more understandable is the third position. Moreover, in terms of mitigating the pain imposed on offenders, it gives offenders "two bites at the apple" before they are subject to substantially increased penalties. For these reasons, the proposed statute in Appendix A adopts the third approach in an optional provision for those states which believe a recidivist statute to be desirable for utilitarian purposes, or to be consistent with desert principles.

[17] Similarly, increases of great magnitude would be banned. Indiana, for example, provides for a potential increase of thirty years for a repeat offender. California, again, is much more modest, providing for an increase of up to three years for every prior incarceration (not merely conviction). For a general discussion of the recent legislation, including this point, see Chapter 10.

Chapter 6

Aggravating and Mitigating Circumstances

After determining the structure of the sentencing scheme itself and the presumptive sentences to be imposed for various offenses or types of offenses, the sentencing commission must define factors allowing variations from the presumptive sentence—so-called aggravating and mitigating circumstances. Of course, if the commission adopts the encyclopedic approach to sentencing, then the need for aggravating and mitigating factors is much less pressing, since the offense definitions themselves will seek to account for all relevant factors. But if we accept the wisdom of Professor Zimring's point that we will simply never have sufficiently precise language to accommodate the tangible but tenuous distinctions that differentiate levels of moral conduct, then the need for such factors becomes apparent.

It should be reemphasized here that in the ideal presumptive sentence mode, these factors would allow the sentencing judge to vary from the presumptive sentence, but not to go outside the range. Thus, for example, if the legislative maximum on armed robbery was five years, but the commission had established a presumptive sentence of three years, with a possible six month increase in the presence of aggravating circumstances, the most that the judge could impose would be three and one-half years, not five. Some states, having established a sentencing range through legislation or administrative mechanism, have adopted a hybrid that decimates the concept: within the range, the judge has full discretion without need to refer to any facts ("free range sentencing"); if he finds one aggravating or mitigating circumstance, he may avoid the range entirely and go up to the legislative maximum.[1]

This effectively returns to the judge, through the back door, all the discretion that was theoretically limited by the regulations. This also occurs when the legislation articulates aggravating and mitigating circumstances that are complementary and, between them, cover all possible circumstances. Thus, for example, if an aggravating circumstance is that the defendant has a prior record of criminal activity and a mitigating factor is that the defendant has led a law-abiding life, the judge has been reinvested, through this mechanism, with all the discretion he had previously under the indeterminate scheme. I call this the "Catch-22" syndrome.

Yet a third way of rediscovering judicial discretion is to make the ranges so wide as to avoid the need for the judge to go outside the range. Thus, for example, Indiana has a presumptive sentence of thirty years for Class A offenses, with a range of twenty to fifty; a judge may vary from the presumptive sentence by the finding of a single mitigating or aggravating factor. Since the most important datum in determining sentence should be the offense, aggravation and mitigation should only play within narrow ranges, since they only intensify or lessen the core harm that has been done; they change it not in type, but only in degree. Thus, from lowest (mitigated) sentence through highest (aggravated), the sentencing range must be narrow; allowing substantial deviation from the range would eventually allow the deviations to swallow the rule.

Before turning our attention to specific factors, we should reestablish criteria by which to determine whether they are compatible with a commensurate deserts model. That model concerns itself with the offense the defendant has committed: considerations of rehabilitation, deterrence, or incapacitation are illicit or at least highly-suspect under such a system. Thus, the factors allowable should be focused on the crime and the method in which it was committed; extraneous factors, focusing on the defendant's past or future conduct, are inadmissible under the model.[2] With that background, then, let us approach the issue of aggravating and mitigating circumstances.

Many proposals, including those already enacted by some states, list a bewildering number of aggravating or mitigating circumstances. California, for example, denotes seventeen aggravating and fourteen mitigating circumstances; Alaska lists thirteen aggravating factors

---

[1] Ironically, this assumes, correctly, a difficult point—that the range need not be coterminous with the legislative minimum and maximum.

[2] Subject, of course, to the debate discussed in Chapter 5: see also Chapter 2.

and twelve mitigating ones. Arizona, on the other-hand, is relatively specific in what external facts may be considered, but then muddies the water by declaring that "Any other factor which the court may deem appropriate may be employed by the sentencing judge." (Indiana and the Model Sentencing and Corrections Act have the same escape clause.) To the extent that the ranges are narrow (they are in California, but are not in Arizona) and that the judge must, in all events, sentence within the range, this may appear innocuous. But if the ranges are wide, or if the judge may, upon finding such factors, totally ignore the range, the system does not achieve the equality of sentences posited as our goal.

The following sections analyze the aggravating and mitigating factors as specified in the following sources:

1. Enacted or proposed legislation or administrative rules:
   Alaska H.B. No. 661 (4/13/78) (cited as Alaska).
   Arizona, House Bill 2054, Chapter 142 (1977) (cited as Arizona).
   California Judicial Council, Cal. Rules of Court, Rules 401–453 (1977) (cited as California).
   Illinois, 38 Ill. Code §§ 1005-5-3.1 and 3.2 (1977).
   Indiana Code, §35-8-1A-7 (1977).
   Oregon Administrative Rules, Board of Parole, chapter 254 (1977) (Exhibit D) (cited as Oregon).
2. Proposed models, such as the Model Penal Code (MPC),[3] the Model Sentencing and Corrections Act (MSCA),[4] and other similar suggestions.
3. *Fair and Certain Punishment.*[5]
4. *Doing Justice.*[6]

This sample is hardly exhaustive. Nevertheless, these sources are representative of most attempts at listing such factors, at least in notion if not specific wording. If there are especially important variations in states not explicitly covered, they will be mentioned.

As each factor is listed, there will be an indication of the source or sources from which the material is taken. Variations in wording will be noted. For the sake of analysis, the factors are divided into three groups: (1) those dealing with the defendant's precrime conduct; (2)

---

[3] AMERICAN LAW INSTITUTE, MODEL PENAL CODE, PROPOSED OFFICIAL DRAFT (1962).
[4] NATIONAL CONFERENCE OF COMMISSIONERS ON UNIFORM STATE LAWS, MODEL SENTENCING AND CORRECTIONS ACT, ADOPTED AUGUST 1978 (hereafter cited as MSCA).
[5] TWENTIETH CENTURY FUND, FAIR AND CERTAIN PUNISHMENT (1976).
[6] A. VON HIRSCH, DOING JUSTICE (1976).

those dealing with the actual commission of the crime; and (3) those dealing with the defendant's postcrime conduct.

FACTORS INVOLVING DEFENDANT'S PRECRIME CONDUCT

Prima facie, all such factors are invalid under the desert model, which focuses exclusively on the seriousness of the offense, not the defendant's prior character or conduct. Nevertheless, some such factors may be relevant; at the very least, it should prove both useful, pragmatically, and instructive, theoretically, to consider whether such factors can be utilized harmoniously with the desert concept.

Prior Record and Second Successive Crime

The issue of prior record has already been discussed in Chapter 5. However, three states, Alaska, California, and Indiana, provide aggravation if the crime in question was committed while the defendant was otherwise involved in the criminal process.[7] Thus, Indiana and California provide for aggravation if the crime was committed while the defendant was on probation or parole; Alaska appears to aggravate only if the offense was committed while on bail, but Alaska's provision for aggravation for a second felony may cover the parole crime.

The deterrence genesis of these provisions is clear; nevertheless, if one were to adopt recidivism as a basis for increased sentence, surely this approach is more sensible than that which creates an unstructured discretion present in the past record section. If von Hirsch's notice argument applies anywhere, it would apply to an offender who commits a second offense while on bail for a charged offense. And surely this would be more probative of his character than a mere record of "criminal activity." Alaska's provision, however, is unclear on this point, since it appears that there is no requirement that the defendant ever be found guilty on the first, bailed offense. Thus, if the defendant is falsely arrested for crime *A* and is bailed and while on bail actually commits crime *B*, he appears to fall within the Alaska provision even if he never committed crime *A*. This weakness could be avoided with a simple amendment to the statute.

Prior Conduct on Conditional Liberty

While the fact that the offense was committed while on probation or parole might, in some instances, at least arguably justify increasing

---

[7] This is distinct from, and possibly additional to, whether the defendant has a prior record.

the sentence, nothing supports the two provisions in California's list of aggravating and mitigating factors that "The defendant's prior performance on probation or parole was (unsatisfactory) (good)."[8] There is no apparent reason why the defendant's prior conduct while on probation or parole should be related to his new sentence, since that probation or parole was completed "successfully"—i.e., noncriminally.

FACTORS CONNECTED WITH THE ACTUAL OFFENSE

The vast majority of aggravating and mitigating factors enunciated by the various jurisdictions and proposals under consideration deal with the offense itself and its method of commission. Since commensurate deserts is concerned with the moral culpability of the offender, and since moral culpability is reflected more precisely by the manner of perpetration than by any other facts except the crime itself, it would seem initially that at least some of these factors might well be harmonious with a deserts model. Nevertheless, many of the factors listed by these statutes are not compatible with the deserts model.

The Defendant's Mental Status

A number of the mitigating circumstances elaborated by the various provisions are concerned with the mental state of the offender and actually reflect a disenchantment with the present substantive criminal law. Thus, many states provide mitigation if the offender acted under "provocation,"[9] "duress,"[10] or "necessity."[11]

[8] The MSCA, *supra* note 4, has a similar provision, §3-109(8).

[9] a. Except in the case of (specific kinds of assault) the victim provoked the crime to a significant degree (Alaska).

b. In a conviction for assault . . . the defendant acted with serious provocation from the victim (Alaska).

c. The defendant acted upon a strong provocation (Model Penal Code; Illinois; MSCA).

d. The victim, or victims, provoked the crime to a significant degree by their conduct (*Fair and Certain Punishment*; Oregon).

e. The crime was committed because of an unusual circumstance, such as great provocation, which is unlikely to recur (California).

f. The victim was an initiator, willing participant, aggressor, or provoker of the incident (California).

g. The victim of the defendant's criminal conduct induced or facilitated its commission (Model Penal Code and Illinois; Indiana adds, as well, "provoked").

[10] a. The defendant committed the crime under some degree of duress, coercion, or compulsion insufficient to constitute a complete defense but which significantly affected his conduct (Alaska; *Fair and Certain Punishment*).

b. There were substantial grounds tending to excuse or justify the defendant's criminal conduct, though failing to establish a defense (Indiana; Model Penal Code; Illinois; MSCA).

None of these provisions is surprising. The common law historically has been reluctant to acknowledge excusing conditions.[12] Thus, a person actually driven to homicide by taunts or jeers will be guilty of murder, since words alone will never reduce the crime to manslaughter no matter how emotionally distraught the defendant actually was.[13] Duress will never be a defense to homicide[14] and may well not be a defense to other crimes. Necessity—generally restricted as a defense to situations where natural forces converge on the defendant—is similarly not a defense to some homicides,[15] and there is a general requirement that the gain obtained by the crime outweigh the loss it inflicts.

The truth is, of course, that we have never really reconciled our own concerns about such situations. We do not want to see Dudley and Stevens hanged, for we understand the gruesome situation in which they were placed; yet not to convict, once prosecuted, or not prosecute, once discovered,[16] seems somehow equally to jar our moral sense. We therefore instruct the criminal law to convict and then allow another part of the system to surreptitiously provide mercy.

The common law position is in stark contrast to most Continental systems, at least in its rationale—the common law insists that in a crime committed under provocation, duress, or necessity, the *mens rea* required for the offense is present and that such exculpatory, or even reducing, defenses are primarily granted out of mercy for the defen-

---

c. The defendant participated in the crime under circumstances of coercion or duress, or his conduct was partially excusable for some other reason not amounting to a defense (California).

d. The defendant was under unusual or substantial duress, although not such as to constitute a defense . . . (Arizona).

[11] a. The defendant was motivated by a desire to provide necessities for his family or himself (California; *Fair and Certain Punishment*; MSCA).

b. The defendant was motivated to commit the offense solely by an overwhelming compulsion to provide for emergency necessities for his immediate family (Alaska).

[12] For recent discussions, see Fletcher, *The Individualization of Excusing Conditions*, 47 S. Cal. L. Rev. 1269 (1974); Note, *Justification and Excuse in the Judaic and Common Law: The Exculpation of a Defendant Charged with Homicide*, 52 N.Y.U.L. Rev. 599 (1977).

[13] A classic, recent case is R. v. Bedder [1954] 1 W.L.R. 1119 (1954) 2 All E.R. 801. A few cases have drawn an "informational words" exception to this notion, but it is rare. See, State v. Flory, 40 Wyo. 184, 276 P. 458 (1929); Toler v. State, 152 Tenn. 1, 260 S.W. 134 (1924).

[14] W. Lafave and A. Scott, Criminal Law 374 (1972). But see M.P.C. §2.09.

[15] The landmark case is R. v. Dudley and Stephens, 14 Q.B.D. 273 (1884) where defendants killed and cannibalized a young boy in order to sustain themselves in a life raft adrift for twenty days in the Atlantic Ocean. They were found guilty of murder, although the court strongly urged a pardon, which was forthcoming.

[16] Discovery of these situations, of course, may be difficult. In *Dudley and Stephens*, for example, no one would have known what happened in the lifeboat except that both defendants immediately told their story upon rescue. One can only guess at the motivations that caused such confessions.

dant's plight. This seems clearly wrong—or at least overstated. Suppose *A* discovers her spouse *B* in bed with *C*. If *A* kills *B* or *C* immediately, the common law posits that *A*'s *mens rea* was intent to kill, but mercy will be afforded. If *A* waits several hours and then kills *B* or *C*, the common law characterizes the *mens rea* similarly as intent. Clearly, however, the mental states *are* different. The Continent recognizes that the impact of truly extreme situations so affects the mental state of the defendant that he cannot truly be said to have the requisite intent for the act.[17]

Dissatisfaction with the common law's harsh view of culpability has led in recent years to erosion of the rules and, ultimately, to substantial rejection of those notions by the Model Penal Code. Thus, for example, the code provides a reduction to manslaughter of any homicide committed while the defendant was laboring under an "extreme mental and emotional disturbance."[18] Even this standard, which might recognize some cases of words as provocation, was limited by adding the objective notion that the jury should still ask itself whether a person, like the defendant, would have been reasonably moved to act as he did. The notion of the objective standard of liability, proselytized by Holmes,[19] dies hard indeed.

The mitigating provisions in question here are obvious attempts to provide some amelioration of the harsh common law standards. To attempt to alter the substantive criminal law in the sentencing criteria, however, is both duplicitous and undesirable. If, as a society, we are now willing to recognize that *mens rea* is absent when an offender in fact is so provoked that he loses control or honestly (but unreasonably) fears danger, we should say so through our substantive criminal law. To provide, in our criminal law, that subjective perception and mental state are not relevant and then slide them in through the back door of sentencing is both bad law and bad policy—bad law because it fails to acknowledge that it is inconsistent with the criminal law's requirement of actual *mens rea*, bad policy because it makes the substantive criminal law appear harsher and more Draconian than it really is, perpetuates the bad law when the sentencer interprets the provision differently than his colleagues, and leads the citizenry to lose respect for the law.

Still, the provisions may be defensible on Professor Zimring's basis—no matter how carefully constructed the notion of *mens rea*, or excuse or justification, may become, there will still be some room for

---

[17] Fletcher is the most recent writer to bring this analysis to the common law. See Fletcher, *supra* note 12; and G. FLETCHER, RETHINKING CRIMINAL LAW (1978).

[18] MPC, sec. 210.3.

[19] O.W. HOLMES, JR., THE COMMON LAW (1881).

play within the joints: we cannot be sure that we have covered all the morally acceptable cases of exculpation. That being the case, a small amount of judicial discretion, appropriately limited, may be desirable. This, of course, suggests a clash between the jury—which refused to nullify, apparently on the basis that community judgment would not tolerate this conduct—and the judge, who decides that some community tolerance is required. At the least, reasonable persons could differ about the desirability of providing some such escape hatch, even if the substantive criminal law were changed.

Of somewhat different cloth are those provisions that attempt, again surreptitiously, to change the common law of insanity by providing for mitigation if the defendant was suffering from "diminished capacity."[20] Again, the legislative motivation for these provisions is understandable, particularly since such a mental state may often not be exculpatory under the substantive law, but simply reduce the crime of conviction. Nevertheless, there is a difference between these provisions and those discussed earlier. In those states where diminished capacity is considered at trial, the jury is not asked to consider the defendant's act in relation to the "reasonable person"; the only issue is whether *this defendant* lacked full capacity. That question is different from the provocation-duress-necessity question; there, the defendant is clearly normal, and the jury is likely to ask not only if this defendant was provoked, but also whether they would have so acted under the circumstances. The objective standards, that is, cannot be totally erased from the standard by which the jury will judge the defendant. Therefore, it is possible that a jury that finds, even under a highly liberalized standard of subjective culpability, that the defendant was provoked, may nevertheless convict because they view his acts as unreasonable; in short, the jury may nullify a subjective standard of culpability, thus making judicial amelioration slightly more tolerable. In the diminished capacity case, however, the jury will not so act. The defendant is saying he is not one of them; if the jury agrees, it will say so—it will not feel compelled thereafter to measure him against the "objective" norm.[21] Thus, the justification for allowing the court a second chance to slightly alter the fact finder's conclusion is missing.

Again, so that there is no misunderstanding, let me be clear: di-

---

[20] a. The defendant was suffering from a mental or physical condition that significantly reduced his culpability for the offense (MSCA and *Fair and Certain Punishment*; same for California, except that it uses "crime" for "offense").

b. The defendant's capacity to appreciate the wrongfulness of his conduct or to conform his conduct to the requirement of law was significantly impaired . . . (Arizona).

[21] They may, of course, consider him dangerous and therefore convict, rather than return an accurate verdict that they fear will release him. But that is a different kind, rather than degree, of question than we are asking here.

minished capacity is doubtlessly relevant to the culpability of the offender, particularly under a desert model. The issue is not the relevance, but whether the jury's determination should be supplemented, or perhaps displaced, by the sentencing judge. The case for allowing such displacement is much weaker here than in the provocation-duress-necessity area.

Similar provisions dealing with the capacity or judgment of the defendant, may be dealt with quickly. Provisions that deal with whether the defendant's sense of morality was overborne by another,[22] or by circumstances,[23] are not defensible, unless it is shown, as some would require, that the offender lacked the capacity to understand the morality of his act, either due to age or to some other factor.[24] Other provisions, some again supplementing the substantive criminal law, are not objectionable on desert grounds, but may have other defects.[25]

---

[22] a. The defendant, because of youth or old age, lacked substantial judgment in committing the crime (*Fair and Certain Punishment*; MSCA).

b. The conduct of an aged defendant was substantially a product of physical or mental infirmities resulting from his age (Alaska).

c. The conduct of a youthful defendant was substantially influenced by another person more mature than the defendant (Alaska).

d. A defendant with no apparent predisposition to do so was induced by others to participate in the crime (California).

e. The defendant had no pressing need for the money taken; he was motivated by thrills or by the desire for luxuries (*Fair and Certain Punishment*).

f. The offense was committed to gratify the defendant's desire for pleasure or excitement (MSCA).

[23] a. The defendant, though technically guilty of the crime, committed the offense under such unusual circumstances that it is unlikely that a sustained intent to violate the law motivated his conduct (*Fair and Certain Punishment*; MSCA).

b. The defendant's criminal conduct was the result of circumstances unlikely to recur (Model Penal Code; Illinois; Indiana). Clearly the provision in (b) is predictive and not acceptable.

[24] The difference in accent in the two Alaska provisions (*supra* note 22b and c) is striking; apparently, the mere lack of judgment that may accompany youth, unlike that which increasing age brings, is insufficient mitigation itself: that a young, immature defendant lacked judgment in committing a crime that he committed alone is irrelevant, at least under this standard, while an aged defendant in the same circumstances has a possible factor of mitigation; unexplained differences such as these pose enigmas on their face and allow law professors to ruminate for hours. In any event, however, it is clear that lack of judgment, which is therefore reflective of real lack of extreme moral culpability, might be a significant factor in a just deserts sentencing model. But it should not be tied to age, since even a middle-aged defendant may have physical or mental infirmities that affect his judgment.

[25] E.g., "Claim of right" provisions (*Fair and Certain Punishment*; California). Claim of right is traditionally recognized as a defense to charges of larceny, and most other property crimes. See Morissette v. United States, 342 U.S. 246 (1952). Where state statutes do not allow such a defense, there is authority that the statute is unconstitutional. See Spiedel v. State, 460 P.2d 77 (Alaska, 1969). If, however, such a defense is neither statutorily recognized nor constitutionally required in a specific state, the moral culpability of the offender is reflected in such a belief and should, therefore, be a relevant mitigating factor.

The Harm Caused or Risked

As already discussed in Chapter 2, few questions of establishing a taxonomy of sentencing—especially one following the deserts philosophy—are more intractable than the question of risk versus result. Whether the unquestionably morally culpable offender on the basis of mercy, parsimony, or just plain luck should receive a benefit, or possibly even escape punishment altogether, because his plan failed due to some thoroughly fortuitous event has been discussed there. Here, the specific provisions that incorporate those issues are listed.

1. The defendant's criminal conduct neither caused nor threatened serious harm (Model Penal Code; Illinois; Indiana; MSCA).
2. The defendant did not contemplate that his criminal conduct would cause or threaten serious harm (Model Penal Code; Illinois; MSCA).
3. The defendant exercised caution to avoid harm to persons or damage to property, or the amounts of money or property taken were deliberately small, or no harm was done or threatened against the victim (California).
4. The amounts of money or property taken were deliberately very small and no harm was done or gratuitously threatened against the victim or victims (*Fair and Certain Punishment*).
5. The amounts of money or property taken were considerable (*Fair and Certain Punishment*).
6. The defendant exercised extreme caution in carrying out the crime (*Fair and Certain Punishment*).
7. The crime involved an attempted or actual taking or damage of great monetary value . . . (California).
8. Amounts of money or property taken, lost, or damaged were deliberately small (Oregon).
9. There was substantial property loss or damage during the episode (Oregon).

Although these provisions talk of either personal or property harm, they have been merged here because of the intriguing method by which they focus on the defendant's *mens rea:* did the defendant try to minimize the harm done, was he impervious, or did he attempt to steal a great deal (or to injure severely)? Intriguingly, there are contradictions. Thus, Oregon and *Fair and Certain Punishment* will mitigate if the defendant deliberately stole little, but does not require deliberation to aggravate if the amount taken was "substantial."

Punishment should not be increased nor decreased based on fortuitous events outside the control of the morally culpable offender, since it is for only those things within his control that he should be charged.

Thus, provisions (1), (5), and (9) are not sufficiently concerned with the actor's mental state. Items (2)–(4) and (6)–(8), on the other hand, do deal with that issue. Among these provisions, surely (2) is the least desirable, since contemplation may be inadequate, and one might charge the criminal defendant who seeks to be deemed less morally blameworthy not merely to "hope" for small injury, but to actively seek it. Whether one should require "extreme caution" (6) or simply "caution," (3) however, is too thin a line to be negotiated.

Cruelty

At least four provisions allow a sentencing judge to consider unnecessary injury as an aggravating factor.[26] This is consistent with a desert model; just as the model itself seeks to proportion the punishment inflicted on the offender to the harm done, it is reasonable to assess the harm inflicted and whether it was necessary to the end sought by the offender.

Hired Crime

Perhaps no offender is more consistently seen as deserving increased punishment as the one who commits crime for hire. His personal involvement is so removed, his detachment so apparently psychopathic, that we cannot comprehend the motivation. Moreover, the defendant seems particularly lacking in moral fiber, a concern that might lead a retributivist to suggest increased punishment. Indicative of this concern with which we view the hired criminal is Wisconsin's recent proposal, which would punish first degree murder with a presumptive sentence of fifteen years, but would create a new crime, murder for hire, with a sentence of twenty-five years—the longest sentence permissible for any crime. Nevertheless, the person who commits what is intuitively a cold and passionless act is little different than any other criminal whose primary aim is pecuniary gain, particularly if the crime itself is one in which the employer's primary motive

[26] a. The crime involved great violence, great bodily harm, threat of great bodily harm, or other acts disclosing a high degree of cruelty, viciousness or callousness, whether or not charged or chargeable as an enhancement under section 2022.7 (California).

    b. The degree of physical harm inflicted on the victim or victims was particularly great (*Fair and Certain Punishment*; MSCA).

    c. The victim or victims were treated with particular cruelty during the perpetration of the crime (*Fair and Certain Punishment*; MSCA, interestingly, omits the word "particular").

    d. The defendant's conduct during the commission of the offense manifested a deliberate cruelty to another person (Alaska).

    e. Especially heinous, cruel, or depraved manner in which the offense was committed (Arizona).

is pecuniary gain. Indeed, one could argue that the employer, rather than the employee, is more morally culpable. But in fact, neither should be differentiated from the typical criminal.[27]

Vulnerable Victims

Perhaps no single type of crime has recently caused more concern than violent crime—or street crime—against the elderly. Several jurisdictions have attempted to pass legislation specifically aimed at crimes against the elderly,[28] but most have failed, primarily because legislatures have recognized that such offenses are simply one example of a more generic type of criminality.

Nevertheless, criminals who knowingly select victims who are incapable of defending themselves are more morally blameworthy than others. Yet all criminals select victims whom they believe, either because of their absence or because of threats against their persons, will be unable to defend themselves. If a provision is to especially single out this mental element of an offense, it should be as precise as possible. Therefore, the provision must focus on the scienter requirement as to the victim's vulnerability. The Alaska provision, therefore, is preferable to others, on the grounds, enunciated elsewhere, that fortuitous events should neither decrease nor increase the defendant's criminal exposure, although the objective standard presented ("should have known") is unacceptable to a desert model.

1. The victim or victims were particularly vulnerable (California; *Fair and Certain Punishment*; MSCA).
2. The victim was sixty-five years of age or otherwise infirm (Indiana).
3. The defendant knew, or reasonably should have known, that the

---

[27] There are three provisions, from two states: (1) The defendant committed the offense pursuant to an agreement that he either pay or be paid for the commission of the offense, and the pecuniary incentive was beyond that inherent in the offense itself (Alaska). (2) The defendant committed the offense as consideration for the receipt, or in the expectation of the receipt, of anything of pecuniary value (Arizona). (3) The defendant procured the commission of the offense by payment, or promise of payment, of anything of pecuniary value (Arizona).

[28] Washington's parole board has avoided the problem of defining elderly but has created a monstrosity of fine line drawing. In its "sexual molestation" grouping (see Chapter 10), the base time is increased if the victim was within specific age categories. The age categories and allowable increases are:

Age of Victim	Permissible Increase
1–5 or 80+	36 months
6–9 or 70–79	30 months
10–12 or 60–69	24 months
13–17 or 50–59	18 months

victim of the offense was particularly vulnerable or incapable of resistance due to advanced age, disability, ill health, or extreme youth, or was for any other reason substantially incapable of exercising normal physical or mental powers of resistance (Alaska).
4. Particularly vulnerable victims, i.e., aged, handicapped, very young (Oregon).

Level of Participation

Many states provide for aggravation or mitigation depending on whether the defendant was the leader of the activity, or in contrast, played a minor or peripheral part.[29] The first issue here is whether we have a "Catch-22" situation. In order to find that we do not, we have to posit three kinds of criminal roles: (1) minor, (2) average, and (3) leaders. Although the early common law differentiated at least two kinds for purposes of punishment—principals and accessories—modern law has compressed that difference. These provisions, then, can be seen as another attempt to change the (new) substantive law.

Moreover, it is difficult to argue that there is a truly minor offender who is an accomplice to the substantive crime. Modern law, which requires that any accomplice have a purpose that the crime occur,[30] recognizes that every accomplice is essential to the commission of the crime (unless criminals are striving to reduce underemployment). The traditional example of the so-called "peripheral" offender—the driver of the getaway car—is off point, since it is at least arguable that the other offenders would not have attempted the crime without the knowledge or belief that there was real escape. Moreover, unless there is a clearer notion of "essential" or "peripheral," where there are multiple principals in the first degree, and each participates equally in the offense, it could be argued that no particular offender was essential to the crime.

---

[29] *Mitigation*: (1) The offense was principally accomplished by another person, and the defendant manifested extreme caution or sincere concern for the safety or well-being of the victim (Alaska). (2) The defendant, although an accomplice, played only a minor role in the commission of the offense (Alaska; MSCA). (3) The defendant was a passive participant or played a minor role in the crime (California). (4) The defendant played a minor role in the crime (*Fair and Certain Punishment*). (5) The degree of the defendant's participation in the crime was minor (Arizona).

Aggravation: (1) The defendant induced others to participate in the commission of the crime or occupied a position of leadership or dominance of other participants in its commission (California). (2) The defendant was the leader of a group of three or more persons who participated in the offense (Alaska). (3) The defendant was the leader of the criminal enterprise (*Fair and Certain Punishment*; MSCA uses "activity" for "enterprise"). (4) The crime involved several perpetrators (*Fair and Certain Punishment*). (5) The crime was committed in the presence of an accomplice (Arizona).

[30] MPC, sec. 2.06.

On the other hand, if the "average" offender is "essential" to the crime, in the sense that his participation is critical to the eventual offense, it may be argued that the leader, the one who initiated the notion of the crime, is more morally culpable and, therefore, deserving of an aggravated punishment. The leader of a criminal enterprise has served as a catalyst for the others; it is more conceivable that the crime would never have occurred without him than that the "average" offender is essential to its perpetration. This, then, could be an aggravating factor in a desert model.

Possession or Use of a Weapon

Four states—California, Alaska, Arizona and Oregon[31]—allow increases in sentences if the defendant was in some way connected to a weapon. This approach, of course, has its counterparts in other states with mandatory minimum sentences for crimes committed with, or while carrying, a firearm.

The problems raised by such criteria can be seen quickly. Even assuming that the criterion is a fair one for increasing sentence, which will be discussed below, there are a number of questions that none of these proposals really fully answer:

1. Should possession alone be sufficient to increase sentence or should there be—at the very least—some demonstration of willingness to employ the item in a way that may, in fact, threaten human life?

2. Is there a difference between a "deadly" weapon and a "dangerous" one? Between a dangerous "weapon" and a dangerous "instrument"?

3. Are there significant differences between persons who "employed," "used," were "armed with," "possessed," and "produced" the item? Does a person who fails to discharge the gun "employ" or "use" it? These ambiguities, even in an otherwise arguably acceptable proposition would raise serious questions. But the issue is whether, under a commensurate deserts notion of aggravation and mitigation, such a standard can remain.

Almost surely, the answer to the first question is that mere possession, or carrying, of a weapon in a manner which did not, in fact, risk life in any way cannot be the basis of increased punishment, since

---

[31] a. The defendant employed a dangerous instrument in furtherance of the offense (Alaska).

b. Use, threatened use, or possession of a deadly weapon or dangerous instrument during the commission of the crime (Arizona).

c. The defendant was armed with or used a weapon . . . (California).

d. Production or use of any weapon during the criminal episode. ("Discharge" of a firearm raises the severity of the offense; therefore, "use" is not "discharge" of a firearm.) (Oregon.)

there was no risk greater than that inherent in the criminal act itself. Thus, the embezzler, or even the robber, who keeps a pen knife in his pocket while committing the crime has not, in fact, increased the risk of injury to persons. The same should be true if he keeps a gun or other "deadly" "weapon" hidden from view and in a position where it cannot and does not harm.

Once the firearm is removed from the coat, however, the tension between risk and result becomes strong indeed. Clearly, unless the weapon has no bullets, injury to persons is risked and possible, if only because the gun may accidentally discharge: at that point, the increased risk, if not accounted for in the definition of the crime (as it should, in fact, always be, as our discussion in Chapter 2 indicated), might be supportable grounds for increasing the sentence. Indeed, the potential differences between "use," "employment," "discharge," and so forth of a "weapon" or "instrument" demonstrates clearly both the difficulty of precisely capturing culpability in a definition of a crime and, additionally, the utility of describing culpability in terms of risk creation, rather than in narrow terms of "use" or "employment."

Abuse of Trust

Strikingly, of the provisions under scrutiny, only Illinois and California have determined that abuses of trust, public or private, may be dealt with as aggravating factors.[32] Again, there are theoretical difficulties—perhaps this should be covered in the substantive law or in the classification of the offenses rather than in the sentencing provisions. On the other hand, to the extent that this is not the case, the offender who abuses a trust is much like one who seeks out a vulnerable victim—because of his superiority, legal or otherwise, he has a built-in immunity from resistance. These, then, should be aggravating factors, but only to the extent that the substantive law does not so provide.

Miscellaneous Factors

A number of jurisdictions allow a potpourri of additional aggravating circumstances. All are utilitarian and merit no discussion.

---

[32] a. The defendant, by the duties of his office or by his position, was obliged to prevent the particular offense committed or to bring the offenders committing it to justice (Illinois).

b. The defendant held public office at the time of the offense, and the offense related to the conduct of that office (Illinois).

c. The defendant utilized his professional reputation or position in the community to commit the offense or to afford him an easier means of committing it (Illinois).

d. The defendant took advantage of a position of trust or confidence to commit the offense (California).

POSTOFFENSE CONDUCT

Several states allow sentencing judges to consider activities of the defendant after actual commission of the crime. These are generally linked to restitution or to cooperation with the police. These factors are highly incompatible with a deserts concept—that the focus of sentencing must be exclusively, or virtually exclusively, upon the crime, not upon the criminal's later reaction to the crime.

Restitution
Mitigating circumstances can include:

1. The defendant made restitution to the victim (California).
2. The defendant has compensated or will compensate the victim of his criminal conduct for the damage or injury that he sustained (Model Penal Code; Illinois; Indiana).
3. Effort to make restitution (Oregon).
4. Before his detection, the defendant compensated or made a good faith effort to compensate the victim or criminal conduct for the damages or injuries the victim sustained (MSCA).
5. Before the defendant knew that his criminal conduct had been discovered, he fully compensated or made a good faith effort to compensate the victim of his criminal conduct for any damage or injury sustained (Alaska).

Of these provisions, Alaska's most clearly focuses on the character of the defendant: all others can be evoked by a criminal captured and convicted who happens to have sufficient funds to compensate. Alaska's standard at least does not allow the defendant to buy mitigation of punishment by feigning what otherwise would be called penitence or remorse.

Aggravating circumstances may include:

1. The defendant, though able to make restitution, has refused to do so (*Fair and Certain Punishment*).
2. Ability to pay fines, restitution or costs and failure to do so (Oregon).

Here again is a good example of the Catch-22 syndrome: Oregon has made it virually certain that the judge could find either an aggravating or a mitigating factor, since the two provisions of Oregon effectively cover all possibilities. At the very least, a provision on restitution failure should be worded as that of *Fair and Certain Punishment*, which makes refusal and not failure the significant factor.

Threatening of Witnesses

Both *Fair and Certain Punishment* and the California Judicial Council's rules make the threatening of witnesses an aggravating factor. Startlingly, *Fair and Certain Punishment* would also aggravate if the defendant "has a history of violence against witnesses," even if no violence is threatened in this instance. California's provision is much broader in terms of the conduct it encompasses, but it does at least require conduct. In both instances, however, the approach is clearly wrong; if the defendant has threatened witnesses or otherwise obstructed justice, he should receive another criminal penalty, arrived at through due process methods, rather than a lesser penalty, arrived at via procedures that provide less than due process at sentencing.

Miscellaneous

Alaska, Oregon, and the MSCA provide mitigation for persons who cooperate with the police; California allows mitigation if "The defendant voluntarily acknowledges wrongdoing prior to arrest or at an early stage of the criminal process." The first is utilitarian; the second rehabilitative.

OTHER PROPOSALS AND STATUTES

California

The foregoing material has concentred on those factors actually designated aggravating and mitigating circumstances by legislation or proposal. In so doing, we have discussed the factors listed by the California Judicial Council in the Court Rules allowed by the California legislation. Of much greater importance, however, are the statutory provisions that in California allow the "enhancement" of a sentence.

The difference is substantially functional: an aggravating factor allows the judge to increase the sentence by no greater differential than one year from the presumptive sentence. An enhancing factor, on the other hand, allows increased sentences for precise periods, up to three years for some factors, as expressly provided in the legislation. These factors, then, are in fact more important than the list of aggravating and mitigating circumstances established by the judicial council.

These factors arguably should have been included in the prior sections because of their function. As already observed in Chapter 3, the initial notion of aggravating and mitigating circumstances was that these factors would allow the judge flexibility, within the range, to decide the sentence. As was also noted there, however, a number of states have misunderstood this function, either willfully or not, and have allowed the judge full unstructured discretion within the range; if a single aggravating or mitigating factor is found to be present, the judge in those jurisdictions may go outside the range completely. California's enhancements perform this same function. The six enhancing factors, and the period of enhancement allowed, are as follows:

1. Armed with a firearm or personally used a deadly or dangerous weapon in the commission or attempted commission of (a felony) (one year enhancement).
2. Personal use of a firearm in the commission of a felony (two year enhancement).
3. Intentionally causing the taking, damage, or destruction of property exceeding $25,000 in value (one year enhancement); (excess of $100,000—two year enhancement).
4. In any case, except homidice, in which the infliction of great bodily injury[33] is not an element of the crime, but in the course of the commission of said crime, and with the intent to inflict such injury (upon persons other than accomplices) (occurs) . . . (three year enhancement).
5. Where the offense is murder, mayhem, voluntary manslaughter, forcible rape, sodomy, oral copulation, kidnapping, lewd acts, or any felony in which the defendant has committed great bodily injury, and the defendant has been incarcerated for a previous conviction of one of these felonies (three year enhancement).
6. A one year enhancement term for every prior felony conviction resulting in incarceration.

Several points should be made about these enhancements. First, even though rather broad, the increased punishments attendant on their presence are strictly limited. Second, the first and second enhancements expressly distinguish between possession and use of a firearm and do not punish "possession of a dangerous weapon" at all. Even if, as suggested above, the possession of any weapon should not be an aggravating factor unless the weapon was used in one way or another, this delineation is much more subtle and cogent than most

[33] The term "great bodily injury" was initially defined by the California code as "prolonged loss of consciousness, severe concussion, protracted loss of any bodily member or organ, protracted impairment of function of any bodily member or organ or bone, a wound or wounds requiring extensive suturing, serious disfigurement, or severe physical pain inflicted by torture." The ambiguity otherwise inherent in the phrase was thus ameliorated. Unfortunately, this specificity was removed by statutory amendment, and the statute now "defines" the term as "a significant or substantial physical injury."

other legislation. The third enhancement, depending on the value of property taken, is, as discussed above, not consistent with a deserts model, except that very high amounts may suggest an additional culpability in terms of planning. Moreover, if "intentionally" requires that the offender know (not merely suspect) the value of the goods taken, then the enhancement is not vulnerable to the criticism that it depends on extraneous, fortuitous factors. The fourth factor, clearly reflective of other states' "cruel, heinous, etc." behavior provisions, is much more carefully drawn than they and hence is at least more likely to be uniformly applied. Of the fifth and sixth enhancements, in addition to the discussion of Chapter 5, the most obvious comment is that they are limited in duration and, additionally, that they depend not only on a conviction, but on a prior actual prison term served, thus suggesting that not even conviction, followed by probation, is sufficient notice of the harshness of prison life, which is clearly hoped to be a deterrent to future criminality.

It is also notable that many of the enhancement provisions have their courterpart in the judicial council's list of aggravating and mitigating factors. Clearly, the defendant cannot have a sentence enhanced and aggravated by the same factor, and both the statute and the council's rules recognize this. Nevertheless, the council instructs the judges to make all pertinent findings, on the basis that if a sentence or an enhancement is struck down, resentencing is not necessary, since the judge's findings will allow a computation of sentence from the record.[34] This is a dubious proposition, but intriguing as a method of attempting to save court time.

Mandatory Minimum Laws

A number of states—many recently—have enacted specific statutes requiring mandatory minimum sentences for some crimes or if some factors are present in some crimes—for example, heroin sale, or use of a firearm. Some of these statutes have their parallel in the aggravating and mitigating factors listed here.

Death Penalty Statutes

Although lists of aggravating and mitigating factors have occurred sporadically in this country—as early as 1851 in Iowa—and are widespread in European countries, they are in fact relatively new in most states in this nation and, until the new legislation, were mostly limited to instances in which the jury is to determine whether to impose the death penalty. Again, several of the factors common to many of the

[34] This may also encourage plea bargaining.

death penalty statutes have their analogs in the lists we have been scrutinizing. But the vast majority of factors in those statutes are, in fact, individualized, as might be expected. Moreover, in 1978, the Supreme Court held that, in a sentencing hearing to determine whether to impose the death penalty, a defendant has a constitutional right to raise any evidence in his behalf he wishes and that state statutes that restrict this right or limiting "mitigating factors" are unconstitutional.[35] The Court was very careful, however, to repeat several times that the death penalty was unique and, therefore, required unique rules as to sentencing.[36] Almost as though it had its eye on the growing move toward restricting judicial discretion, the court made it clear that it expressed no opinion on whether, in a non-death-penalty case, the state could limit the defendant's right to submit any mitigating evidence he wished. The clear implication of the court's opinion, in my own reading, is that a state could do so constitutionally.[37]

SUMMARY

Current legislation, the MPC, the MSCA, and *Fair and Certain Punishment* list a wide variety of different kinds of factors that may be taken into account by a sentencing judge. Aside from the great number, there is substantial variation in the wording of the provisions, which in at least some instances will have a powerful impact on the defendant's vulnerability to increased punishment. These various provisions, like so much legislation in the criminal justice area, has once again developed piecemeal, without any apparent attempt to investigate what other legislatures have done or how other legislatures have worded their provisions. Even in the few instances where this has been done—most notably Illinois' repetition of the Model Penal Code—there are exceptions.

Furthermore, many of the statutory or administrative factors to be considered are really attempts to rewrite the substantive criminal law, a task much better left to the legislature than to individual sentencing

[35] Lockett v. Ohio, U.S., 46 L.W. 4981 (July 3, 1978); Bell v. Ohio, U.S., 23 Cr. L. 3229 (July 3, 1978). See also Richmond v. Cardwell, 450 F. Supp. 519 (D. Ariz. 1978).

[36] "We recognize that, in non-capital cases, the established practice of individualized sentences rests not on Constitutional commands but on public policies enacted into statutes. . . . The need for treating each defendant in a capital case with that degree of respect due the uniqueness of the individual is far more important than in non-capital cases." Lockett v. Ohio, 46 L.W. 4981, 4986 (June 27, 1978). It might in fact be suggested that the Court took these pains because it was aware of the current movement in the states to provide such factors in noncapital cases.

[37] See, however, United States v. Wardlaw, 579 F.2d 932 (1st Cir. 1978).

judges. Defenses of duress, provocation, and the like should be explicitly defined by legislation, which can carefully describe and prescribe the limits of such defenses. The use of the "soft" method of defining mitigating and aggravating circumstances does not meet the legislature's obligation.

Of these forty or more factors, only a handful are compatible with a deserts approach. Obviously, those geared to *mens rea* defenses are compatible with the theory, but are out of place. In addition, only the following can surely be said to be consistent with the notion that the offender is to be punished for what he has done, not for what he is, or for what he may do in the future:

1. The defendant's awareness of the risk involved;
2. Cruelty;
3. Vulnerable victim, known to be such by the defendant;
4. Knowing use—perhaps limited to discharge—of a weapon;
5. Abuse of a position of trust;
6. Leadership role;
7. Attempt to limit the loss.

All other factors do not affect the culpability of the defendant's act and, accordingly, should not be part of the aggravating or mitigating factors present in a deserts code.

Chapter 7

The Prison in a Commensurate Deserts System

Opponents of commensurate deserts sentencing frequently say, and even occasionally believe, that adoption of the system will turn prison into an even more dismal, even more violent institution than it is today. The argument posits that deserts sentencing requires the following changes in prison: (1) the abolition of programs of rehabilitation, since that is contrary to the notion of deserts; (2) the abolition of good time, since continuation of good time would reduce the determinacy of the sentence; (3) an increase in prison population, because there can be no safety valves such as parole release to reduce the population; and (4) as a consequence of these, a more volatile prison, which will lead to increased prison violence, which because of the abolition of good time cannot be adequately punished within the prison walls. Most of these misconceive the process envisioned by the equality model.

PRISON REHABILITATION UNDER A DESERT CONCEPT

Recent data collected by Lipton et al. has raised serious questions about whether rehabilitation programs now in existence in our prisons actually work.[1] While the dispute is hardly settled, it seems reasonable that all would agree that, if this were the case, the prognosis for rehabilitation should not be a basis for sentencing.[2] Desert philosophy

---

[1] D. LIPTON, R. MARTINSON, and J. WILKS, THE EFFECTIVENESS OF CORRECTIONAL TREATMENT (1975) (hereinafter LIPTON).

[2] Alternatively, the call would be for more effective programs. But here the burden

goes further. The philosophical underpinnings of the approach, particularly Kant's categorical imperative, reject the notion that, even if we could predict rehabilitative need and success, we should use that prediction as a basis for the sentencing. Under a commensurate desert model, it is the offender's past conduct, not his or others' future acts, that form the basis for determining the amount of punishment to be imposed.

But the struggle for sentencing equality and desert does not decry the redemption, nor the redeemability, of the human race. It is an attempt to set reasonable limits upon the coercive power of the state, particularly when that power is being used to deprive individuals of their liberty. While the duration of sentence and the type of sanction to be imposed should not vary as a function of the offender's need—or lack of need—for rehabilitation, rehabilitation should remain a goal of the correction system.[3] Indeed, both nonincarcerative sanctions (subject to the discussion in Chapter 3) and prisons themselves should stress the rehabilitative and reintegrative ideal. There should be many more programs in prisons, and there should be many more opportunities for prisoners to participate in programs outside the institutions. Prisoners should be able to work for the minimum wage and thereby to buy their way into programs offered both by the prison or by private industry both in and out of the institution.[4] Prisons should make every effort to offer inmates as many opportunities as they wish or as the state can provide. All these rehabilitative programs are desirable and important; but time in prison should not be determined by program participation or by perceived progress toward rehabilitation. Sanctions imposed and the punishment visited upon offenders should depend upon their crimes.

One major possible reason why the programs which Lipton et al. studied failed is that participation in them was not legitimate. Prisoners attended vocational rehabilitation, occupational therapy, AA, psychotherapy, and so on, not because they really perceived and wanted to change some alleged personal trait or deficiency, but rather because they wished to convince the parole board that they were ready for early release. Such attempts to deceive the board are rampant inside our prison setting; they demoralize both the persons conducting

---

should be placed upon proponents to demonstrate effectiveness before allowing the programs to alter sentencing, even under a utilitarian approach.

[3] Kant himself recognized and agreed to this in CRITIQUE OF PRACTICAL REASON, BOOK I, Ch. I, Sect. VIII, THEOREM IV, REMARK II.

[4] See the MSCA's proposal for a voucher system, by which prisoners may elect any available program and which allows the provider to obtain reimbursement from the state.

the programs and the prisoners. Prisoners are encouraged to manipulate the system, and the parole board is consequently encouraged to look with heavy skepticism, cynicism, and disbelief upon all those who come before it.[5] This cynicism reflects back upon the prison setting itself and increases discontent.

No one knows what the effect upon rehabilitation would be if presumptive, consistent sentencing were instituted. But it is certainly not clear that participation in the programs would either decrease or be less effective. Indeed, it is arguable that the programs might become more effective because those who participate actually wish to do so. As Paul Keve, who has served two different states as commissioner of corrections, has written:[6]

> By reverting to the fixed sentence for adult prisoners, we will not suddenly have the answers to our problems. Dynamic improvements in the treatment program must be instituted in conjunction with the fixed sentence or else it will result in "dead time"—time spent waiting for release without being motivated to improve. But with the fixed sentence we will have a more honest process in which we avoid all temptations to simulate improvement. It will make us provide treatment programs that are of high quality; and it will assure us that inmates who use them will do so from sincere motives because there will be no need to go through the motions in order to impress anybody.

One final point—access to such programs, particularly those with contacts with the outside world such as work or educational release, cannot be discretionary, lest such programs become the coin of discretion in the future desert prison. If we really mean that a person should be given some opportunity prior to ultimate release for education or work release, statutes should provide that every offender has this opportunity. Even utilitarians should agree here, since it has always been anomalous that the worst offenders are forbidden to participate in such programs and hence are thrown out into the street without any

---

[5] Three recent empirical studies of parole boards suggest that this is exactly what occurs. Sacks, *Promises, Performance and Principle: An Empirical Study of Parole Decisionmaking in Connecticut*, 9 CONN. L. REV. 347 (1977); Scott, *The Use of Discretion in Determining the Severity of Punishment for Incarcerated Offenders*, 65 J. CRIM. L. & CRIM. 214 (1974) (a "midwestern state"); Heinz, Heinz, Senderowitz and Vance, *Sentencing by Parole Board: An Evaluation*, 67 J. CRIM. L. & CRIM. 1 (1967). Scott found that of all the factors studied, progress in prison education programs was the only one that did not favorably relate to parole release. Sacks found that the progress was a minor factor, and Heinz found that there was some relation, but did not weight it; indeed, Heinz found that every factor he investigated bore some relation to parole release, which somewhat undercuts this specific finding. Moreover, the United States Parole Commission does not explicitly consider that factor, but only the disciplinary record of the prisoner.

[6] P. KEVE, PRISON LIFE AND HUMAN WORTH 143 (1974).

real preparation, while the best offenders—who arguably need the preparation least—are the ones who benefit by it.[7]

A second problem with the rehabilitative ideal as a method for determining sanction is that, for one reason or another, it must lead to discrimination against certain kinds of groups. In New Jersey, for example, before the case of *State v. Chambers*,[8] there was gross discrimination against female offenders because of the rehabilitative ideal: a state statute (invalidated in *Chambers*) required that sentences for women be longer than those for men convicted of the same offense so that there would be greater opportunity for women to be rehabilitated.[9] A similar abuse is that persons committing nonviolent offenses or regarded by society as "solid citizens" are likely to receive very short sentences—even for very serious crimes. White collar criminals, suburbanites, and businessmen are likely to receive shorter sentences for most offenses simply because, in the rehabilitative mode, they do not "need" as much rehabilitation as the non-white-collar (usually nonwhite) offender. There is nothing pernicious in this; it is inherent in the rehabilitative model that judges and parole board members are likely to see persons similar to themselves as less in need of rehabilitation than people who are different from themselves.[10]

PRISON POPULATION, DISCONTENT, GOOD TIME, AND DISCIPLINE

Critics who argue that determinate sentencing will increase prison population assume essentially three things: (1) a reduction or abolition

---

[7] Of course, this may result in more offenses being committed by those on work release and thus create a furor to terminate the program entirely. But since most offenders will be returned to the community in any event, equality, as well as common sense, supports this proposal.

[8] 63 N.J. 287 (1973).

[9] Ironically, there is good evidence that the parole boards involved in New Jersey have seriously undercut the *Chambers* decision in precisely the manner suggested. New Jersey has three parole boards—one for young male offenders, one for women offenders, and one for adult male offenders. The first two have established matrixes of a type similar to that established by the U.S. Parole Commission. But the women's parole board typically gives longer dates before parole release than does the young male offender board for the same offense. This may be somewhat misleading, since the populations are not totally equivalent (under a utilitarian theory); if adult male parole figures were added to young male parole figures, the results might be altered. But the concern is nevertheless a real one.

[10] At the same time, it is possible that in extreme cases the opposite may be true: A white collar offender may receive a much longer sentence (or parole date) than a non-white-collar person committing the same crime, on the theory that the white-collar criminal "had everything" and therefore did not "need" to commit the crime. Thus, we allow the status of offenders (wealth, age, position, sex, race) to determine our response to their crime. Not only is this suspect in terms of constitutionality and fairness, but it also assumes that we know what rehabilitation means.

of good time credits; (2) an increase in time served by most, if not all, prisoners; and (3) a reduction in the power, or the abolition, of the parole board. We will discuss the first two issues here; the third will be discussed in Chapter 8.

Good Time and Prison Discipline in a Desert Prison

A major contention raised by opponents of a determinate sentence scheme is that the concept virtually requires the abolition of good time. This, it is argued, will have two effects: (1) prison discipline will suffer; and (2) sentences will become longer, and the prison population will increase.

The argument is frequently made that good time revocation, as a potential sanction for serious prison rule violations, is essential to prison discipline. As Messinger and Johnson describe the function:[11]

> Historically, "good time" provisions were the first way in which discretion to shorten prison terms was allocated to the correctional bureaucracy; they were seen as an extension of the executive's pardoning power. It is understandable that such provisions reappear with a move to determinacy since, in the judgement of prison officials, they provide the only reliable incentive, with determined sentences, to conformance. . . . If we have prisons, presumably we must supply those responsible for managing them with some disciplinary tools.

The desert argument against good time is simple—if prison authorities have discretionary control over good time, it will become the coin of favoritism in the prison, and nothing will have been gained in terms of equality of durational punishment: two prisoners convicted of the same crime, sentenced for the same length of imprisonment, will in fact serve different sentences, depending on whether and how much good time they earn (or lose). This undercuts equality of punishment for the offense and, therefore, cannot be allowed.

Moreover, there are other arguments for abolition of good time. First, the punishments available to a prison administrator— segregated housing, loss of privileges, reclassification, and so forth— still compose a heavy armamentarium for those offenses that are truly "prison" offenses and that do not have substantial counterparts in the penal code. Second, to the extent that revocation of good time is allowed to be imposed for offenses that are listed in the penal code, we have resurrected disparity of sentences through administrative fiat.

[11] Messinger and Johnson, *California's Determinate Sentencing Statute: History and Issues*, in DETERMINATE SENTENCING: REFORM OR REGRESSION? 13, 34–35 (1978).

Suppose aggravated assault is punishable, in the code, by a presumptive penalty of three years' imprisonment. Persons who commit aggravated assault in the outside world will receive that penalty. Yet a person who commits the same offense inside the prison will receive, for example loss of good time for ninety days. By allowing two possible systems of punishment for such offenses, we have introduced a disparity of twelve to one (three years to one-quarter year) for the same offense. This not only reintroduces disparity in actual sentencing, but suggests—erroneously—that the crime inside the prison is only one-twelfth as serious as the same crime outside the prison. This not only destroys equality of sentencing, it also treats the victims of the same crime very differently: it says that the prisoner victim of aggravated assault is only one-twelfth as important as the nonprisoner victim of the same crime. To avoid this disparity, good time (and its potential revocation for these offenses) should be abolished, and prison authorities should be required to prosecute, in the free world, all major prison violations.

Some prison officials may object that this is unrealistic—that prosecutions will not occur, either because inmate witnesses are reluctant to speak or are not believed by juries, or because county prosecutors will not prosecute due to lack of funds. These arguments are not sustainable. The American Correctional Association has recently provided, in its accreditation standards for adult correctional institutions, that it is essential that "where an inmate allegedly commits an act covered by statutory law, the case is referred for consideration for criminal prosecution."[12] Furthermore, there is some evidence that lack of witnesses for such major violations—always raised as a potential obstacle to outside prosecution of in prison offenses—is exaggerated.[13] Additionally, the issue of excessive cost to the local jurisdiction prosecuting these cases can be met by providing, as the Model Sentencing and

---

[12] ACA, Manual of Standards for Adult Correctional Institutions § 4320 (1977). A substantial number of national studies are in accord. National Advisory Commission on Criminal Justice Standards and Goals, § 2.11; American Bar Association, Standards Relating to the Legal Status of Prisoners, § 3.3 (Tentative Draft) (1977). Conference of Commissioners on Uniform State Laws, Model Sentencing and Corrections Act, § 4-511 (1978) (MSCA).

[13] Sylvester, Nelson, and Reed, in a recent study of prison homicides, found that of 126 prison homicides occurring in this nation in 1973, 87 (70 percent) were referred to the judicial system and that, of these, 60 percent were convicted (at the time of writing, 14 were still pending, or status was unknown). Furthermore, they found that there were, in almost every case, sufficient witnesses willing to testify to allow prosecution to go forward. A conviction rate of 60 percent is quite substantial even in the free world; there is nothing to suggest, therefore, that in serious crimes inside the prison, the concerns of prison administrators are in fact well founded. S. Sylvester, J. Nelson, and N. Reed, Prison Homicides (1977). See also United States v. Free, 574 F. 2d 1221 (5th Cir. 1978) (prisoner witness in homicide prosecution).

Corrections Act does, that the state will either establish a special office of prison prosecutors or reimburse the county for expenses incurred in such prosecutions.[14]

Finally, the empirical data on good time does not clearly support the critics. Although it does appear that good time revocation was a frequent sanction in the 1950s and 1960s,[15] its use appears to have declined measurably during the 1970s.[16] To the extent that the decline will continue, the argument for retention of good time is immeasurably weakened. Furthermore, some correctional administrators now appear to consider good time more a nuisance than an aid in prison discipline.

It may be suggested, however, that a system that does not allow revocation of major amounts of good time, but nevertheless provides some flexibility in prison punishment, is desirable and, perhaps, consistent with a desert structure. Moreover, since most states now have good time provisions, it is unlikely that this will change rapidly. Indeed, to the extent that the system persists in having "false time," good time will be essential to allow sentence reduction. Thus, Illinois, Indiana, and Ohio each provide for day-for-day good time,[17] while many others provide for high ratios, in a clear effort to reduce the actual time served. If that kind of a scheme is adopted, in contradiction to the suggestions made here, should good time be retained and, if so, with what safeguards?

The obvious answer is "vesting"—protecting the prisoner against revocation of large amounts of good time by providing, in the legislation, that good time earned within a particular period of time "vests" and cannot be revoked. Several states provide for such vesting, albeit at different time periods. Clearly, vesting is an important protection for the prisoner. Moreover, to the extent that vesting occurs frequently, thus forbidding revocation of large amounts of good time, the mechanism increasingly resembles an equality model: every prisoner will earn good time at the same rate, and proportionality among sentences

---

[14] MSCA, §4-512.

[15] See, e.g., Note, *The Problems of Modern Penology: Prison Life and Prisoners' Rights*, 53 IOWA L. REV. 671 (1967); Kraft, *Prison Disciplinary Practices and Procedures: Is Due Process Provided?* 47 N.D. L. REV. 9, 37 (1970); Note, *Prisoners' Gain Time: Incentive, Deterrent or Ritual Response?* 21 U. FLA. L. REV. 103 (1969).

But see Jacob, *Prison Discipline and Inmate Rights*, 5 HARV. CIV. LIB.-CIV. RTS. L. REV. 227, 234 (1970).

[16] Heinz et al., *supra*, note 5 at 6, found that only 2.4 percent of all males had part of their good time revoked in Illinois, but that 21 percent of all female prisoners studied lost good time. Compare this to the New Jersey dichotomous parole practice, noted p. 100, *supra*. It is at least arguable that this decline followed on the heels of *Wolff v. McDonnell*, 418 U.S. 539 (1974), where the Supreme Court held that minimum due process applied in the prison disciplinary setting when good time was involved.

[17] See Chapter 10.

will be sustained. Thus, false time, combined with frequently vesting good time, essentially becomes true time sentencing.

In summary, the notion that prison discipline will collapse if good time revocation is not allowed to sanction major rule violations does not seem supportable: there is evidence that (1) revocation is increasingly used only infrequently; and (2) there are feasible alternatives, which will be just as deterrent of prison violence and more equitable to both the prisoner and his victim than good time revocation. Finally, the notion of good time, and its revocation, is inconsistent with an equality model of sentencing. In short, we need a "flat time" model, once the sentence itself has been set using the presumptive sentence approach as well as aggravating and mitigating circumstances.

Other aspects of prison discipline and dissatisfaction should be mentioned. Opponents of determinate sentencing argue that there will be less reason for prisoners to abide by prison regulations if good time is removed and, consequently, more tension and dissonance in the prison. But any person familiar with the prison riots of the mid-1950s or early 1970s understands that one of the prime grievances felt by prisoners in both those decades was the uncertainty and perceived unfairness of the parole decision and, even more basic, of initial sentencing. Disparity among prison sentences forms one of the main topics of conversation among prisoners. They are often even more aware than attorneys or courts of the significant differences between judges in the same jurisdiction or between judges or courts in different jurisdictions. Thus, whatever the particular sentencing philosophy we carry, if we are at all concerned about the tinderbox effect that disparate sentencing brings to the prison setting, we must seek ways to reduce the discrepancies and then find means of explaining clearly why differences continue to obtain even in the presence of presumptive sentencing. If prisoners believe that they have been treated fairly and equitably, or if they understand the bases for differences in sentence and therefore length of imprisonment, they are more likely to respect the law and its rational qualities and are less likely to be embittered about the differences in their sentences. Thus, explanations of sentences, as well as removal from corrections officials of the power to alter those sentences through manipulation of good time, may well help the prison environment rather than damage it.

Prison Population

If today's lengthy sentences are retained in a purely flat time model, the prison population will clearly increase dramatically, since all our sentences today are nothing but fictions. Today, a seven year sentence, reduced by parole eligibility and good time, probably means an actual term of incarceration of about two years; even a life sentence generally means parole eligibility in twelve years and release in about fifteen. If a seven year sentence actually comes to mean seven years in the prison and life means life, prison populations will unquestionably mushroom in a matter of a few years. There are at least four possible alternatives to increased prison population in a "flat time" world.

The first, most obvious, and best solution would be simply to reduce drastically the sentences now handed out to reflect *true time served*. Several objections, however, are raised to bringing truth to the system. First, it is argued, the public would demand more time to be served, and therefore, the reduction of sentences would be short-lived indeed. This argument is difficult to deal with, because it assumes what public reaction would be. No one, of course, knows what public reaction (assuming we could determine who "the public" is) would in fact be. Legislatures, fearing that public reaction will be adverse, often raise the specter without having really checked the facts; public reaction then becomes what it is alleged to be.[18] It is just as plausible to argue that the public would not be disquieted about shorter sentences if they were informed that every offender would receive that amount of punishment by a presumptive sentencing measure and that the shorter sentences were equal to actual time served now, so that there was in fact no (or little) reduction of actual confinement.

A second, more sophisticated argument against telling the truth is that "the public" (there they are again) does not understand the brutality of prison life and that only exaggerated figures of sentences can convey the actual amount of punishment. In essence, the position is that the public cannot comprehend what deprivation of liberty, even for an hour, means, and therefore to say that the punishment is twenty years in prison probably conveys approximately the amount of suffering that a prisoner who serves three years actually experiences. But the notion, again, is dubious. I believe the public can and does comprehend the impact of imprisonment; moreover, if this is not the case one could argue that there is a duty to inform the public of the actual condition of prison life, thereby perhaps enhancing the possibility for prison reform. Continued prevarication will not achieve that aim. Finally, it is not clear that alleged public irritation about the system's "softness" would be greater than what it now (supposedly) feels when it sees that the system lies—when it sees a prisoner sentenced to twenty years leave the institution after three. How one measures such irrita-

---

[18] This is not to deny that when sporadic incidents by persons on community release programs commit offenses, there is not, in fact, a public outcry. But that outcry is often led, and nurtured, if not engendered, by public decisionmakers. A change in attitude on their part might well soften the furor that does arise.

tion, such displeasure, I do not know. But the burden is upon the opponents of truth to demonstrate beyond cavil both that their hypothesis is true (that public outrage would in fact increase) and that public education, if needed, is unattainable. Short of overwhelming evidence of this phenomenon, the proponents of candor must prevail on this point.

If false time were retained, however, an agency, like the parole board, but with virtually no discretion, could be established to simply set a release date in harmony with a set schedule.[19] The United States Parole Commission, the Oregon Parole Board, and the Corrections Commission of Minnesota now do something very much like this, and there has been no significant uproar.

A third possible solution to this perceived problem would be a return to the practice prevalent in this country in the early 1800s under the determinate sentencing schemes then in effect—the governor's pardon. Between one-third and one-half of all prisoners were pardoned by the governors of Pennsylvania, New York, and Massachusetts during the early years of penitentiary existence.

These last two solutions are not desirable. They perpetuate untruth and, more importantly, would only continue the tension now felt by prisoners as to whether they, in fact, will be released at the time normally set.

Another solution, however, could deal equitably with all persons: to allow the sentencing commission, in its rulemaking procedures, to reassess which offenses, as a generic matter, "deserve" imprisonment.[20] What crimes deserve imprisonment, or any other specific level of punishment, depends, in part, upon what the society is willing to pay to achieve that punishment. Assuming for the moment that a given state was not willing to build eight new prisons, at astronomical sums, to house the increased prison population hypothesized by the opponents of equal sentencing, the commission would be in an ideal situation to simply determine that some crimes, while serious, are simply not serious enough to warrant imprisonment at all, or at least to warrant the length of imprisonment established by the previous rules.[21] Thus, for example, if 10 percent of the prison population were serving a presumptive sentence of two years for jaywalking, the commission could reduce prison population by 10 percent over a two year

[19] See Chapter 8.

[20] Of course, as with all other actions of the sentencing commission, the legislature would have final authority before such a scheme became effective.

[21] The MCSA, *supra* note 12, is eclectic on this. It appears to require such changes to be made by the commission (p. 14), but also says that individual sentencing judges will consider such new mores as well (p. 99).

period by establishing probation as the presumptive sentence for jaywalking or by 5 percent by establishing a presumptive sentence of one year. This change in the guidelines would be justified because it would reflect the seriousness with which society actually considered jaywalking, and additionally, it would reach, in an equitable and fair manner, all jaywalkers.

A further response is required, however. It is frequently argued that prison overcrowding could be eliminated, or at least drastically reduced, by the simple expedient of not incarcerating nondangerous offenders. Proponents of this approach often point to figures, such as those recently published in New Jersey,[22] that indicate that 35 percent or more of prisoners incarcerated have been convicted of nondangerous felonies, such as gambling offenses, drug violations, and so forth. This analysis is faulty on two grounds.

First, not all would agree that all drug offenders or property offenders do not deserve to be incarcerated. Surely not all would agree that some white collar criminals, particularly those involved with governmental corruption, deserve probation. If by nondangerous, this school of thought means nonviolent, then certainly not all nondangerous persons should be assured of nonincarceration for their offenses, which may reflect a very high degree of moral blameworthiness. And if by dangerous, this school of thought includes the governmental corruptor or the large pusher of heroin, one can only say they have joined hands with Humpty-Dumpty, who asserted that a word means only what he wants it to mean.

The second weakness in the argument—that if nondangerous offenders were not imprisoned at all, prison population would decrease, or at least not increase—is, perhaps, more mundane, yet critical. Given the widespread use of plea bargaining, the mere fact that 35 percent of the prison population has been convicted of a nondangerous crime does not mean that that large a percentage has, in fact, committed a nondangerous crime. A conviction for larceny, after all, may mean either that the person committed a crime that in fact involved no danger to the person or that the larceny conviction was the result of a plea bargain from armed robbery. So even if we removed from prison all those whom we would all agree—from whatever viewpoint—did not deserve to be imprisoned, or at least to be imprisoned for so long, it is not clear that we would in fact significantly reduce the prison population, particularly if we added, as a deserts system intends to do, all those who deserve imprisonment, but who under the current discretionary system receive a nonincarcerative sentence.

[22] NEW JERSEY CORRECTIONAL MASTER PLAN 68 (1977).

This, however, assumes that sentences would remain the same and that some device would have to be implemented (or retained) to avoid the overcrowding. What would happen, however, if the legislature were to adopt, either directly or through a sentencing commission, the notion that sentences should be reduced to current actual time served, as several legislatures have done?[23]

Obviously, predicting future prison populations under various sentencing proposals is a hazardous business. Recently, however, a highly sophisticated project attempted to do just that, using several different models of sentencing reform compared to the base run projection of what would occur if sentencing in the systems selected (Massachusetts, federal system, Iowa, South Carolina, California) were simply left alone without change. This study, using a complex dynamic flow model that assumed that certain adaptive changes would be made in some procedures of other agencies, concluded that determinate sentencing would reduce prison population by 1982, assuming that the determinate sentences imposed reflected actual time now served.[24]

Because it is so detailed, it may be of some use to explore that study a bit further. The intriguing point, for our purposes, is that the study posited five separate reforms that could occur in sentencing: (1) a "law and order" reform, in which sentences are generally higher across the board, and incarceration imposed on more offenders; (2) two variants of "mandatory minimum" reforms, in which there would be mandatory minimums for (a) violent offenders and (b) repeat offenders (violent and nonviolent); (3) "reduced" sentences, where the legislature would decide expressly to avoid excessive prison costs, particularly of new construction; and (4) determinate, where the determinate sentence would be based on time currently served in that jurisdiction. The projections for 1982, assuming that 1976 was the base (100) year, are shown in Table 7–1.

Thus, in the federal system, South Carolina, Iowa, and California, determinate sentencing would achieve the lowest population of all reforms except the reduced population form. And in Massachusetts, the effects of any of the reforms are so similar that there is no realistic difference between them. Furthermore, the study projects that determinate sentencing would reduce populations below those to be ex-

---

[23] Pennsylvania, Illinois, and Minnesota have established such commissions, and several other states have considered this step. See Chapter 10. Problems with ascertaining actual time served have already been noted. See Chapter 3, note 19.

[24] ABT ASSOCIATES, PRISON POPULATION AND POLICY CHOICES (2 vols., 1977). See Chapter 3 note 19, *supra,* for an analysis of how "actual time served" should be calculated. The ABT study did not use this approach and thus skewed the results toward longer time served than might otherwise be the case.

Table 7–1. 1982 Prison Population Projections

System	Base Run *(no change)*	Law/ Order	Mandatory Minimum		Reduced	Determinate
			Violent	*Repeat*		
Federal	103	114	N.A.	120	87	103
Massachusetts	101	94	96	93	95	96
Iowa	97	108	92	110	73	89
South Carolina	111	146	120	129	85	115
California[a]	103	126	104	113	83	86

Source: ABT Associates, Prison Population and Policy Choices (2 vols; 1977), vol. I, ch. 6. The data are not so collated. Moreover, there appears to be a conflict between the determinate data in Volume I and that in Volume II, Tables 4.11 and 4.12, but that discrepancy can be erased by assuming, as I think is a reasonable assumption, that Table 4.11 is the simple flow model and 4.12 the dynamic flow model and not vice versa, as they are labeled.

[a] The projections were run before the new California law became effective and are based on California's old indeterminate sentencing scheme.

pected if nothing changes in those systems, except in South Carolina, where the difference is 4 percent.

These findings may not be immune from criticism, particularly from a methodological viewpoint. But they certainly suggest that a sophisticated understanding of the criminal justice system and the adjustments it will make to any sentencing model need not necessarily lead to the conclusion that determinate sentencing will in fact increase prison population over that which would otherwise occur if no change were made at all. Compared with other, possibly more stringent, reforms, moreover, the determinate sentencing model is greatly preferable if our object is not to greatly increase prison population which is the concern we have been considering. Thus, the population problem is either ephemeral or manageable.

SUMMARY

With a properly drawn set of presumptive sentences, prison populations need not burgeon. There is nothing inherent in the presumptive sentence-equality model that precludes considering prison capacity in establishing a proportionate scale of punishments founded in part—but not wholly—on terms actually served under present sentencing schemes.

Prisons in a commensurate desert society should not reduce their efforts at rehabilitation; there is nothing in the desert model that requires it, and there is much within the model supportive of such programs. On the other hand, the notion of good time is philosophically antithetical to a desert model and is not in fact necessary to the maintenance of control inside the prison. Major prison offenses—those likely to now carry good time revocation as a penalty—should be criminally prosecuted, thus treating in prison offenses equally with free world offenses. This is both feasible and sound correctional practice. Moreover, it would show equal concern with prisoner victims as with free world victims and would deter—to the extent that any sanctions deter—serious prison offenses at least as much as the threat of revoked good time now does.

Chapter 8

Abolish Parole?

THE ROLE OF THE PAROLE BOARD

If a good time appears to be both unnecessary and incompatible with a sentencing model based on equality and proportionality, it would seem that *a fortiori,* parole must similarly
be abolished under that model. Parole release has been, if anything,
more discretionary and less principled than sentencing and could be
more destructive of equality than a good time system. Moreover, no
meaningful attempt to structure that discretion had been made prior to
five years ago.[1] Today, in the vast majority of jurisdictions, that is still

---

[1] In the early 1970s, the United States Parole Board (now Commission) did undertake
to substantially structure its own discretion. After a massive and sophisticated study of
its practices, conducted by Dean Don Gottfredson and a staff of researchers, the board
adopted a "matrix" system that determined the "expected" release date of an offender
using only the offense he had committed and a "salient factor score," based on the
offender's past record and certain characteristics that the board considered relevant (and
which seem to have been relevant to some degree) to recidivism. See generally D.
GOTTFREDSON, L. WILKINS, and P. HOFFMAN, GUIDELINES FOR PAROLE AND SENTENCING
(1978). The matrix has been both approved, on the basis that it does in fact predict
recidivism, see generally, UNITED STATES PAROLE COMMISSION RESEARCH UNIT, SE-
LECTED REPRINTS RELATING TO FEDERAL PAROLE DECISION MAKING (1977), and criticized,
on the basis that it is both inaccurate and unfair to minorities. See Coffee, *The Repressed
Issues of Sentencing: Accountability, Predictability and Equality in the Era of the Sentencing Commission,* 66 GEO. L.J. 975 (1978). The matrix itself is included in Chapter 10.
The Oregon parole system has adopted a similar scheme, as has Washington (see
Chapter 10). The matrix-guideline system has weathered well in litigation generally.
Recently, however, the Third Circuit held that the use of the matrix involved serious
constitutional and statutory questions and remanded for further fact finding on the
precise method in which the matrix was used. Geraghty v. United States, 579 F.2d 238
(3rd Cir. 1978). This is not the place to debate the desirability or validity of a matrix, as

true. To retain parole in any form would prima facie seem to be anathema to a commensurate deserts model.

Nevertheless, there are good reasons for carefully considering this issue before simply proceeding apace with abolition of the parole board. Perhaps surprisingly, von Hirsch and Hanrahan have recently argued for the retention—at least for some time—of the parole board.[2] In fact, they urge that the board be given the de jure power to fix all durations of confinement, and would restrict initial desert sentencing (set by the sentencing commission or the legislature) to the in-out decision. They argue that (1) the parole board can better perform the function it now performs—duration setting—while we wait to see whether judges can, in fact, operate under a restricted discretion system; and (2) the board is in the best position to equalize sentences. Because this is the major desert defense of parole retention, even in a substantially modified form, much of this chapter will deal with these arguments.

The Argument for Gradual Abolition—The Parole Board as Safety Net

The von Hirsch/Hanrahan position is that it is not clear that judges will, in fact, be able to sentence consistently with a system set by the legislature or a sentencing commission. They fear that trial judges will be so attuned to false time that they will find the adaption to true time too difficult to manage. Therefore, the argument proceeds, we should move cautiously, leaving the prison duration decision to a parole board operating under properly structured desert criteria and establishing for judges a desert system for the probation-incarceration decision. We should then assess their performance on this system. If the experiment works (i.e., if the judges do not violate the ranges or criteria too frequently), then we can be relatively assured that they will also sentence equitably in determining duration under a restricted discretion system, and the sentencing commission may then establish such a system for the judges and phase out the parole board.[3]

---

such, and certainly not the details of the federal matrix. It does demonstrate, however, that a parole board could structure its discretionary release decision powers. There is some question whether any of these matrixes are sufficiently rigid, however, since the hearing examiner or the board can always go outside the matrix, after stating reasons, and since the board is able to alter the release date on the basis of institutional conduct, a very dubious predicate for predicting recidivism. Furthermore, the federal board determines the "crime committed" not by the crime of conviction, but rather by the "facts" of the case, thereby seriously undermining the plea bargain. See Edwards v. United States, 574 F.2d 937 (8th Cir. 1978); Manos v. United States Bd. of Parole, 399 F. Supp. 1103 (M.D.Pa. 1975). The Oregon board's draft rules previously allowed this, but its current rules have rejected that power.

[2] A. von Hirsch and K. Hanrahan, The Question of Parole: Retention, Reform, or Abolition (1979).

[3] Caleb Foote, certainly no friend of the parole process, has made the same argument.

The argument is strongest in the context in which it was initially made—the federal correctional system. The United States Parole Commission has promulgated a matrix system of release dates[4] and is now giving the prisoner an "early fix"—informing the prisoner early in his incarceration of when he is to be released (all other things being equal) under its guidelines. This, for all practical purposes, is the true sentence. To obliterate that commission and its experience with guidelines before we know how judges will act under a sentencing guidelines system may throw out the tot with the tub.

It is certainly true that the Parole Commission has moved far in the last five years toward apparent equalization of disparate sentences and that the early fix ameliorates much of the animosity that prisoners have felt toward the parole system. Moreover, the task of educating 500 federal trial judges, spread throughout the nation, about the new system is Herculean in scope and argues for cautious reform. Nevertheless, I believe that von Hirsch and Hanrahan are wrong on this phase of the argument.

First, experimentation with judges under an in-out guidelines system will prove nothing about their ability to work well with a durations guideline system. The failure of trial judges to abide by the guidelines, as von Hirsch and Hanrahan fear, could stem from only two sources: (1) misunderstanding of the guidelines; (2) active hostility and manipulation of the guidelines. As to the first, it may well be that some lead time will be necessary to both inform and persuade judges as to the desirability of the guidelines, but that task will be necessary in any event at some point. As to the second, it is certainly consistent to believe that judges who would be hostile to the duration guidelines would deliberately operate well under the in-out guidelines so as to obtain the power—duration setting—that von Hirsch and Hanrahan fear judges will ultimately abuse.

Second, state sentencing judges in Newark, New Jersey, and Denver, Colorado, and elsewhere have been working with variations of sentencing guideline systems. A number of other jurisdictions are in the process of drafting them. While the evaluation of these programs is not yet complete, and while there is some evidence that in at least one of these jurisdictions the guidelines are being substantially ignored, the evidence is certainly not conclusive that judges are incapable of working with such guideline systems now.

Third, I believe the general evidence is that judges are sophisticated enough to know that they are not sentencing to real time and that they

---

Foote, *Deceptive Determinate Sentencing*, in DETERMINATE SENTENCING: REFORM OR REGRESSION? 133 (1978).

[4] See U.S. PAROLE COMMISSION RESEARCH UNIT, *supra* note 1. The matrix can be found in Chapter 10.

often seek to determine how to hide a real sentence under the false time system now in place.

In short, insofar as the argument depends on the proposition that judges cannot adjust to true time, I find it wanting.[5]

Von Hirsch and Hanrahan have one more arrow in the quiver, however. They argue that the abolition of false time would not be publicly acceptable. The concern here is that present sentencing practices tell the public that an offender had been sentenced to confinement to fifteen years, which placates the public. All persons in the system, however, know that the sentence is really approximately three and one-half years (i.e., fifteen divided by three, less good time), which is initial parole eligibility in most states. If (heaven forbid!) the sentencing commission were to tell the public the truth and require the imposition of only a three and one-half year sentence where the crime had received a fifteen-year sentence previously, the public would not understand, and the resulting pressure to increase sentences—now calculated in true time—would be irresistible. Thus, the reduction of sentences and the introduction of true time should be gradual:[6]

> One might, for example, begin with a 6-year sentence, parolable after one-third; then have a 4-year sentence, parolable after one-half; and so forth until one ends with a nonparolable 2-year sentence of actual imprisonment. This would mean there would not, at any one time, be a very large apparent reduction in sentence, as would occur with a sudden shift

---

[5] The final argument in favor of such a plan (not made by von Hirsch and Hanrahan) is that there is a need for some administrative agency to be able to act flexibly when the sentencing commission changes guidelines (e.g., when A was sentenced to eight years for marijuana possession, it was considered much more serious than now when the sentencing commission has reduced the presumptive sentence to one year or to probation); the assumption, probably correct, is that neither the sentencing commission nor the appellate courts are in a position to achieve this end.

That argument, however, assumes that changes in society's perceptions of the seriousness of the crime should be retroactive. In deserts terms, however, this is not necessarily clear. Since the offender (supposedly) was aware of the seriousness with which society viewed the crime at the time of the act, there is no inherent reason why he, although willing to commit the offense anyway, should reap the benefit of a new perception even if it is a better perception. This may seem somewhat harsh, but surely the burden is on the proponents of justify the contrary position. Mercy, of course, might be such an argument, but why mercy should be restricted to this area is unclear. Finally, if retroactivity, as a general principle, is desirable, there would be no reason why it could not be legislated expressly or delegated to either the sentencing commission or the department of corrections, since the application of the new guidelines should not require substantial discretion. That is to say that if all marijuana possessions are to receive the retroactive benefit of a new commission guideline, the process should be fairly automatic. If it is not, then the supporters of the plan assume a need for more discretion than the model would allow.

[6] VON HIRSCH and HANRAHAN, ABOLISH PAROLE? 36 (Executive Summary, LEAA, 1978).

from dual to single time. And it would give the public more opportunity to get used to a new way of reckoning sentence time.

This argument is difficult to accept, if for no other reason than that it again raises the spectacle of the public's reaction to changes in the criminal justice system. Perhaps the public does really want its pound of flesh; but it seems just as plausible that the cry of the public is simply a shorthand method of saying that many elected officials are afraid that the public will react adversely and therefore argue that the public will so act. Furthermore, the argument assumes that the public does not understand our current charade. I find no evidence to support that; indeed, I would suggest that the average member of the community now understands that a fifteen-year sentence means three and one-half and that he or she is frustrated by the duplicity with which the system operates. I do not claim to know that this is true, but I do suggest that unless the opponents of candor in criminal justice can demonstrate it not to be so, the presumption should be in favor of truth.

Furthermore, even if judges are subject to public pressure, I believe that the argument fails to recognize that parole boards are, or at least appear to be, as responsive to such pressures as judges; it is scarcely news that boards often change their paroling practices in response to perceived public pressures.[7] Reliance on the parole board being able to stick by its guidelines under such pressure, but an unwillingness to concede that judges may be just as able to stick by theirs[8] is what I find weak. I remain unpersuaded that continuation of the sentencing shell game is desirable.[9]

This is not to deny the true political dangers to which Hanrahan and von Hirsch point. But at some point, as even they admit, we must

---

[7] N. MORRIS, THE FUTURE OF IMPRISONMENT 48 (1974).

[8] This assumes that the judges will consider the guidelines set by the commission sufficiently "theirs," which is another reason for having judges on the commission. The argument that parole boards are better able to enforce their guidelines on recalcitrant hearing examiners does ring true; but I am not so persuaded by this that I am willing to assume nefarious trial judges.

Perhaps more importantly, the ability of the board to force conformity may in fact be a disadvantage, for it could suppress legitimate disagreement about the substantive content of the guidelines. Trial judges, not being so directly jeopardized, may more readily dispute the guidelines, thus leading to further discussion of their desirability. Some independence on the part of the persons actually applying the guidelines will be beneficial, rather than detrimental, assuming the independence is not simply used arbitrarily.

[9] There is also the point that the present system leads to public disenchantment when a person sentenced to what is purportedly a fifteen year sentence in fact leaves prison after three and one-half years. This, of course, is a utilitarian argument, but since the entire argument is framed in pursuit of utilitarian persuasion of legislatures, it seems not unfair to respond in kind.

confront the prospect of actually reducing sentences to time served and abolishing the parole board. The gradualistic approach which they endorse seems to me to bear more dangers than the peremptory one: (1) the parole board will become increasingly more entrenched and able to prepare for the final fight over its abolition; (2) inertia will remain on the side of the board and make abolition eventually more difficult; (3) the confrontation over "true time" sentencing will eventually have to be fought in any event.

I do not propose that these problems will be easily solvable. But for the same reason that I believe it is unfair and inaccurate to ascribe to the desert philosophers the current trend in harsh sentencing, I believe it unwise to support perpetuation of the false time system in the hope that, twenty years from now, we may be able to turn to true time. In the end, I would propose to von Hirsch and Hanrahan the opposite stance—let us abolish parole and institute true time sentencing. If the public pressure (or political fear of public pressure) results in increasingly higher sentences from the Commission, then (as happened in the early 1900s) we can institute some form of regularized agency which can once again lie to the public. But let us see whether that is necessary; let us not assume that it is.

The Board as Sentence Equalizer

The second argument for retention is that if all postsentencing discretion is removed, there will be no effective check upon those judges who fail to follow the standards. Theoretically, appellate review of sentences is available to provide this check, but appellate review, even where available in this country,[10] has proved unable to do so now,[11] and there is little reason to believe that this will suddenly change. Moreover, even if judicial appellate review were the solution, it is a time-consuming process, and at least initially, there will be a need for speedy review of sentences to structure the judicial decision. Furthermore, the standard for reversing or modifying a sentence is likely to be too weak ("clearly unreasonable"; "unwarranted") to serve as a meaningful check on deviations from the guidelines. Appellate review, therefore, is probably an insufficient method of achieving such conformity in the period immediately following enactment of the new sentencing system.

In effect, the parole board under the von Hirsch/Hanrahan scheme would become an administrative appellate review tribunal for sentenc-

---

[10] Approximately twenty-three states now have appellate review of sentences, at least on the books.

[11] See Chapter 3.

ing deviations while judicial appellate review was being put in place. Some argue that this is already one major function of the board— discrete equalization behind the walls of the prison, secure from public clamor of disparate sentences. But the weight of evidence does not clearly support such an assertion.[12] Indeed, Dean Morris has suggested that boards, subject to public pressure, may have actually increased sentence lengths.[13] Where disparate minimum sentences have been imposed, the board would have to disregard the low disparate sentences and still could not affect the high disparate minimum.[14]

Moreover, as Dean Morris has said with regard to this problem, "Don't underestimate the capacity of all of us to not be moved by the suffering of others."[15] The evidence, in short, is certainly not clear that boards in fact do equalize sentences; the argument appears to be mostly a rationalization to retain the board, rather than one drawn from statistical analysis of actual parole board data.[16]

California has provided a possible solution—its Community Release Board, established at the same time that its presumptive sentencing scheme became effective, reviews every sentence from every judge in the jurisdiction; if the sentence is out of line with other sentences imposed throughout the state, it remands the sentence for reconsideration in light of this information. The board is given sufficient staff, computers, and information with which to perform this massive task.

For all practical purposes, the Community Release Board is the parole board, since it performs the same function that parole boards

---

[12] Sacks, *Promises, Performance and Principles: An Empirical Study of Parole Decisionmaking in Connecticut*, 9 CONN. L. REV. 347 (1977). Two other recent studies of parole board operations did not directly deal with the issue of whether the board attempted to equalize sentences. Nevertheless, since neither study (one of the Illinois board, the other of an unnamed midwestern state) appeared to find any evidence that the board did consider such a function, at least a negative implication might be drawn that those boards, at least, did not so act. See Heinz, Heinz, Senderowitz, and Vance, *Sentencing by Parole Board: An Evaluation*, 67 J. CRIM. L. & CRIM. 1 (1967); Scott, *The Use of Discretion in Determining the Severity of Punishment for Incarcerated Offenders*, 65 J. CRIM. L. & CRIM. 214 (1974).

[13] Morris, *supra* note 7 at 48.

[14] Sacks, *supra* note 12, posed the following situation: five offenders are sentenced. *A* receives a minimum sentence of two years; *B, C,* and *D* a minimum of three years; and *E* a minimum of four years for the same crime and under the same basic circumstances. The board cannot achieve fully equity unless it holds everyone until *E* may be released; but it may achieve partial equity by holding *A* for an additional year beyond his minimum. Still, as Sacks suggests, there is little factual data to demonstrate that current parole boards do this, either consciously or as a matter of mere happenstance.

[15] Comments, DETERMINATE SENTENCING: REFORM OR REGRESSION? 108 (LEAA 1978).

[16] The argument is somewhat more accurate if the board has devised a relatively rigid scheme such as that used by the U.S. Parole Commission; but even that evidence is not compelling, particularly since the commission uses many factors almost surely not consistent with the desert approach.

are now alleged latently to perform—equalization of sentences. I agree that in those jurisdictions where the board is now so functioning, the board could remain to perform this function, rather than create a new board or a new bureaucratic agency to perform this task. That may, however, be true only in Oregon, California, and the federal system.

It may be objected that courts will not accept review or change of their sentence by an administrative, as opposed to a judicial, body. But parole boards today actually do precisely that, usually without any judicial review of that decision at all.[17] In fact, several federal courts, faced with challenges to the United States Parole Commission guidelines on the grounds that the guidelines are, in fact, administrative manipulations of judicial sentencing, have spurned the challenge.[18] With proper discussion prior to implementation of this system, there should be relatively little active hostility on the part of trial judges to such a system. Moreover, the board could accomplish this review relatively early in the prisoner's incarceration, thus achieving the early fix that von Hirsch, Morris, and others urge.

THE ROLE OF PAROLE SUPERVISION

Abolition of the parole board does not necessarily mean abolition of parole supervision. In principle, there are two functions now performed by parole: (1) providing early release from prison; and (2) supervision of the releasee and, if necessary, revocation of the grant of conditional liberty. It is clearly possible to conceive of the second without the discretionary administrative release mechanism.

Parole supervision today, however, is not clearly effectual. In *The Question of Parole*, von Hirsch and Hanrahan have compellingly gathered the data that demonstrates that, in terms of recidivism, parole is either ineffective or at best, that there are little data that supports its effectiveness.[19] While there are some studies that indicate that parole may slightly affect the recidivism rate,[20] von Hirsch and

---

[17] This is not contrary to the earlier argument, which was that there is little, if any, evidence that parole boards, in reviewing these sentences, actually equalize them.

[18] But see Geraghty v. United States, 579 F.2d 238 (3d Cir. 1978). And see Hayburn's Case 2 U.S. 409 (1792).

[19] Citing Robison, *The California Prison, Parole and Probation System: It's Time To Stop Counting, Technical Supplement No. 2, A Special Report to the Assembly* (April 1969); I. WALLER, MEN RELEASED FROM PRISON (1974); *Bay Area Discharge Study: Preliminary Summary of Findings* (1977); Hudson, *An Experimental Study of the Differential Effects of Parole Supervision for a Group of Adolescent Boys and Girls—Summary Report* (March 1973).

[20] Gottfredson, Some Positive Changes in the Parole Process (presented at the American Society of Criminology meeting, November 1, 1975); Lerner, *The Effectiveness of a Definite Sentence Parole Program*, 15 CRIMINOLOGY 211 (1977).

Hanrahan properly charge that these data are simply insufficient grounds upon which to base a continued parole supervision function. On the basis of this information, they argue for the abolition of parole supervision.

Moreover, the conditions of liberty that confront a parolee in many jurisdictions[21] are repugnant to any notion of fairness. Requirements that the parolee obtain the permission of his parole officer before he marry, obtain a driver's license, leave the state, and so forth are both demoralizing to the parolee and appear ineffective in terms of either rehabilitation or surveillance.

Similarly, the case loads that confront most parole officers today often render meaningless any attempt to do much more than simply control the parolee. Recent studies indicate that parole officers generally cannot spend more than seven to ten minutes per month with a given parolee—obviously too short a time in which to accompany any kind of task.

Furthermore, the conditions that now attach to parole are means rather than ends, and generally negative means, at that. The parolee is not required, for example, to work on community service projects for X hours per day/week/month, nor is he required to place himself under the supervision of a parole officer for large periods of time during a given period. He is simply left at will; the officer's basic task becomes an ad hoc, post hoc, evaluation of the parolee's conduct.

These weaknesses argue strongly in favor of abolishing parole conditions and, hence, parole supervision, at least as we know it today. But there is one fly in the ointment—the same arguments, virtually without exception, could be used against probation supervision and, indeed, against any nonincarcerative sentencing alternative presently in operation. If these arguments are sufficient to justify abolition of parole supervision, they are similarly sufficient to justify—indeed require—abolition of probation supervision. That would mean, in essence, that there would be no valid alternatives to incarceration as a sentencing sanction. For those who wish to reduce the use of prison as a punishment, this is untenable.

This, of course, does not necessarily argue that parole supervision should be retained, as modified; it merely suggests that a new form of parole supervision, compatible with a deserts model, is possible. It would surely be possible to retain probation, reconstituted as a meaningful sanction, without retaining its postconfinement analog, parole;

[21] Some jurisdictions have recently rewritten their conditions to remove many of these arcane conditions; but most retain them. AMERICAN BAR ASSOCIATION RESOURCE CENTER ON CORRECTIONAL LAW AND LEGAL SERVICES, SURVEY OF PAROLE CONDITIONS (1974).

but a decision to retain punitive parole supervision could be sustained on the basis that shorter prison sentences, followed by truly punitive parole, would likely be more acceptable to the sentencing commission and, ultimately, the legislature. If so, then incarceration time, even for those sentenced to imprisonment, could be reduced, without necessarily reducing the total sanction imposed on the offender and without skewing the requirement of proportionality of sanction.

A serious question then develops, however: if the person on conditional liberty in fact ignores the conditions, what should be done with him? The present system has a ready answer—failure to abide by the conditions of parole demonstrates that the prisoner has not yet been fully rehabilitated. Thus, return to the prison for more treatment is necessary.

This could not be true in a commensurate deserts model. If, of course, the parolee commits a new crime, then deserts requires new punishment for that offense. But if the violation is one of a technical condition—an act that would not require or allow incarceration if committed by a member of free society—incarceration would be both disproportionate to that offense and, additionally, would render sentences for other offenses (for which incarceration is in fact required) equally disproportionate.[22] Yet, if the punishment of parole is to have any effect, there must be some punishment for its violation.

The argument is not utilitarian: it does not posit that punishment must be meted out to the first parole violator in order to deter later parole violations. Instead, it is that a person who chooses to ignore a valid command—even a noncriminal command—of the state must be sanctioned; that is his fair punishment. It is a thorny question. While one can easily envision a scale of escalating punishment, increasingly restrictive of the parolee's freedom, which could meet most situations, the crux will come when the "most serious" nonincarcerative alternative has been tried and been ignored. Is prison then justified, as punishment for recalcitrance? The probable answer is yes—if even brief (ten day) incarceration is permissible for relatively minor criminal offenses (shoplifting, speeding, etc.), then it is permissible for violation of a very serious condition of conditional liberty.[23] Therefore, the point

---

[22] Von Hirsch and Hanrahan develop this thesis brilliantly, *supra* note 2.

[23] Von Hirsch and Hanrahan disagree. See *id.*, ch. 7–8.

My colleague, Jon Hyman, has suggested what I find a compelling analog—prison escape. Assuming that an escape is a walkaway in which there is no harm to others created, there is no apparent reason why it should be punished—there has been no risk created or harm committed from the mere fact of the departure. Nevertheless, since the individual has sought to avoid the punishment that society has a right to impose and that he deserves, there is something morally culpable in that act alone that justifies punishment. The same problem, of course, may arise in other public crimes; but the

is generally valid: if probation or parole can be made sufficiently onerous, without reaching the level of arbitrary oppression that current parole conditions (if actually enforced) could not reach, a middle ground can be found.

SUMMARY

Parole today serves two functions: (1) release, and (2) supervision of the released offender on the streets. The first is, I believe, unnecessary in a properly structured sentencing system that pursues equality of punishment, and the board's functions in this regard should ultimately be abolished. As an interim measure, however, the board could be retained to serve as the first step of appellate review of sentences subject to later judicial oversight. The second function—street supervision—might be retained, assuming that the conditions of liberty were proportionate to the amount of discomfort that the offender deserved in this phase of his punishment. Some ingenuity will be required to establish such a list of conditions, particularly with regard to remedies in case of violation. But the board could continue to impose—and monitor—such conditions, with some function as an administrative determination of whether the parolee has complied with the conditions.[24]

---

notion seems to explain why a person refusing, after great attempts have been made, to abide by the punishment imposed may be further punished. (This is, of course, different from the issue of habitual offenders, since they have already suffered the full punishment initially imposed.)

[24] Von Hirsch and Hanrahan argue at length in their new book (*supra* note 2) that lack of full due process at parole revocation militates against its retention, since it means that a parolee could be reimprisoned (1) on the basis of less evidence than is required at trial; or (2) for a noncriminal offense. These weaknesses are concededly great, but there are two difficulties with their conclusion that the weaknesses cannot be overcome: (1) the same weaknesses apply to probation revocation, which again would argue that probation (and other nonincarcerative sanctions) would have to be abolished; (2) it would be possible to introduce most due process requirements into revocation proceedings, even to the point of abolishing the board's function and giving all such functions to a court, which is already true in probation revocation proceedings today. They recognize this last point, and agree that if parole supervision is retained, sanctions should be imposed by the judiciary, under a "beyond a reasonable doubt" standard of proof. On the latter point, however, the argument suffers from overkill: there are many serious sanctions today that do not require proof beyond a reasonable doubt and that are imposed for noncriminal offenses. Contempt of court, for example, may result in incarceration, even if noncriminal in nature. This may be both question begging and insufficient; but unless they are willing to argue that all grievous losses require all due process protections (and, as to one—jury trial—this is not even required in all criminal matters), the argument must fail, at least as the law stands today.

Chapter 9

Prosecutorial Discretion and Sentencing Reform

HYDRAULIC DISCRETION

A particularly depressing criticism against any proposal for sentencing reform is that it is irrelevant, since it tinkers with only one part of an entire system, blindly ignoring the effect that such reform will have on the other parts. Specifically, the argument is that to opt for affecting judicial sentencing rather than parole decisions is to opt for sentencing by plea bargain.[1] This criticism is aimed not only at desert sentencing; as *Doing Justice* observed, "The problem of how to limit plea-bargaining discretion . . . inheres in any theory that advocates that sentencing be governed by a consistent set of standards."[2] Nevertheless, the presence of plea bargaining is especially anathema to the desert model of sentencing, since the model seeks consistent sentencing not only because equality is basically a desirable goal, but because all persons who commit the same offense should receive both the sanction and social stigma of having committed that offense. If plea bargaining allows some offenders to incur reduced stigma, the goal of equality of desert will have been seriously undermined.

Of the various critics who have made the argument, none has more

[1] Heinz, et al., *Sentencing by Parole Board: An Evaluation* 67 J. Crim. L. & Crim. 19 (1976). Accord, Clear, Hewitt, and Regoli, *Discretion and the Determinate Sentence: Its Distribution, Control, and Effect of Time Served,* 24 CRIME & DELINQ. 428, 443 (1978); Golding, *Criminal Sentencing: Some Philosophical Considerations,* in J. CEDERBLOM and W. BLIZEK, JUSTICE AND PUNISHMENT 89, 100 (1977).

[2] A. VON HIRSCH, DOING JUSTICE 106 (1976).

clearly summarized the position than Professor Alschuler, who declares:[3]

> Eliminating or restricting the discretionary powers of parole boards and trial judges is likely to increase the powers of prosecutors, and these powers are likely to be exercised without effective limits through the practice of plea bargaining. The substitution of fixed or presumptive sentences for the discretion of judges and parole boards tends to concentrate sentencing power in the hands of officials who are likely to allow their decisions to be governed by factors irrelevant to the proper goals of sentencing—officials moreover, who typically lack the information, objectivity and experience of trial judges. . . .
>
> If the reformers hope to do more than reallocate today's lawless sentencing power in a way that will give prosecutors an even heavier club, they must exhibit greater courage. They must view the criminal justice system as a system, recognize that the idea of equal justice is currently threatened more by the practices of prosecutors than by those of trial judges, and bite the bullet on the question of plea bargaining.

Professor Alschuler argues, and I agree, that such enhanced prosecutorial discretion would be unfortunate; however ungainly judicial disparity may have been, or may be, judges do not (usually) sentence in order to gain higher political office or to win reelection. Nor are they advocates so blind to the cause of justice that they ignore even the most simple demands of fairness.[4] Enhanced prosecutorial discretion, then,

---

[3] Alschuler, *Sentencing Reform and Prosecutorial Power: A Critique of Recent Proposals for "Fixed" and "Presumptive" Sentencing*, 126 U. PA. L. REV. 550, 577 (1978). Accord, Tonry, Sentencing Guidelines and Sentencing Commissions—An Assessment of the Sentencing Reform Proposition in the Criminal Code Reform Act of 1977 (unpublished), p. 140.

[4] In a recent discussion with two federal prosecutors, I asked them to consider whether the United States Parole Commission's practice, discussed *infra*, of looking at the crime the offender actually committed, even if he had pled and been convicted of a lower one, did not arguably vitiate the plea bargain and, if so, whether the U.S. Attorney might not be under a duty—ethical or otherwise—to at least bring to the attention of defendant and his counsel the parole commission's practice. The response greatly depressed me—both argued that it was up to defense counsel to know this, and if he did not, the defendant could always seek relief on the basis of incompetent counsel. Defense counsel should know this, the argument went, even though the regulations were published in the Federal Register, one of the least likely spots for an attorney unaccustomed to federal criminal practice to look and although both agreed that the defendant was being deluded by the plea. The argument that prosecutors should have the obligation to inform defense counsel of the parole commission's practice is easy to make; it is far less easy, however, to suggest why this particular piece of information should be made available when both case law and practice allow the prosecutor to hide other pieces of information which are similarly devastating to the original plea. See J. BOND, PLEA BARGAINING AND GUILTY PLEAS (2nd ed., 1978).

One possible distinction would be that at least much of the information that the

is undesirable, for at least the same reason that enhanced judicial discretion would be undesirable.

It is far from certain, however, either that prosecutorial discretion will be rampant or that plea bargaining will increase if sentencing reform is undertaken. In the first place, the legal realists who argue that reform is undesirable because it will lead to unchecked prosecutorial discretion fail to consider the myriad factors that feature the system as we now know it or as it might become under a new approach. For example, in the nineteenth century, it was the governor's office, with the extensive use of the pardon power, that effectively exercised ultimate sentencing discretion, not the prosecutor.[5] Furthermore, if one assumes that the system will, as a whole, seek to evade the impact of a new system, there is no reason not to assume that the other parts of the system will similarly seek to evade it. Thus, for example, Professor Alschuler quotes a prosecutor who declares—boasts may be the better word—"I have yet to see the policy that an assistant district attorney couldn't get around when he wanted to."[6] Assuming that this is true, the error lies in believing that such ingenuity resides only in the prosecutor's office; one could equally say that any judge who wished to evade the determinate sentencing scheme or undercut any prosecutor who sought to evade it could do so—if he wanted to. Judges could, for example, simply refuse to accept guilty pleas engineered by what they believed to be too potent a weapon by the prosecution. Or, in those cases where prosecutors had overcharged and no plea had been obtained, judges, as fact finders, could simply refuse to find the facts required for the higher charge.

The point is that if one assumes with the neolegal-realist school that one part of the system is going to ignore the new legislation and the spirit that attends it, there is no reason to believe that other parts of the system will simply quietly acquiesce in that undoing. One must assume either that all parts will act equally nefariously or that, within reason, none will.

---

prosecutor need not disclose is related to the specific case and, therefore, is initially unknown to either advocate, whereas the board's practice is known to the prosecutor before the case begins. Moreover, the information present in criminal statutes (such as parole ineligibility for some offenses) is at least more arguably available than information buried in the Federal Register. Still, the distinction is not strongly compelling; the conclusion I would reach is that the prosecutor should bear the burden of informing the defense counsel, and hence the defendant, of all such matters of law and practice to which defense counsel will not have equal access in fact. This may conflict with the game theory of prosecution, but appears, ultimately, much fairer.

[5] This is not to urge such a result; it simply indicates that the cataclysm envisioned by the critics is not the only possible scenario and that this potential use of power might indirectly at least check the prosecutorial power.

[6] Alschuler, *supra* note 3 at 73.

Furthermore, Professor Alschuler's point fails to consider other pressures on the prosecutor, outside the judicial system itself, to act consistently with the spirit of the new laws. First, of course, there will be the pressure not to charge so as to increase significantly the existing prison population. Second, public pressure to lengthen sentences, or at least to seek substantial sentences, may in fact increase, but it is at least as likely that as the cost of increased prison populations becomes clear, this pressure may decrease. No one can tell with certainty at this point.

Nor is it clear that plea bargaining will increase as the critics have suggested. The Twentieth Century Fund, in its report endorsing presumptive sentencing did acknowledge that there might be an increase in charge bargaining.[7] But von Hirsch suggested that under a presumptive sentence scheme, the defendant will be less willing to bargain, since the threat of an uncharacteristically severe punishment if he goes to trial will be removed.[8] And the Council of State Governments, after studying four states' proposals for determinate sentencing, concluded that the effect on plea bargaining was unclear.[9]

Moreover, one could argue that the prosecutor will be less willing to charge bargain down under a presumptive sentence system. Today, the prosecutor may view bargaining as a "no lose" proposition. He obtains the relief of not having to go to trial. But he knows, or should, that the mitigation that he has ostensibly given in terms of reduced charges may well be reinstated by the sentencing judge (although this is highly unlikely) or by the parole board. Thus, Dawson relates that in Kansas, the pardon attorney was more likely to refuse commutation to a prisoner who had plea bargained, telling him, "You have already had your clemency."[10] Indeed, this is now the explicit policy of the United States Parole Commission, which openly acknowledges that, in determining the "seriousness of the offense" for the *y* axis of its matrix system, it looks not at the offense to which the offender pleaded guilty, but to the "real" offense. Thus, for example, a defendant convicted of armed robbery, with a salient factor score of, for example, 9, will not be released on parole until he has served at least forty months. The defendant convicted of robbery, with the same salient factor score, will be released after twenty-six months, an apparent difference of fourteen months. But if the latter defendant's file, including the presentence

---

[7] TWENTIETH CENTURY FUND, FAIR AND CERTAIN PUNISHMENT 26 (1976).

[8] VON HIRSCH, *supra* note 2 at 105.

[9] COUNCIL OF STATE GOVERNMENTS, DEFINITE SENTENCING: AN EXAMINATION OF PROPOSALS IN FOUR STATES 34–53 (1976).

[10] R. DAWSON, SENTENCING 221 (1969).

report and the examination under Rule 11, demonstrates that he "actually" committed armed robbery, the board will treat him as it treats the first defendant;[11] thus the benefit of the bargain has been lost.[12]

Under a presumptive sentence system, however, the parole board would be unable to perform this sleight of hand, and prosecutors might not be so willing to reduce charges, since the reduction would in fact carry a factual impact on the duration of sentence. The prosecutor who was concerned about his public record would not wish his armed robbers actually returning to the community in the time that robbers normally do; the politically ambitious prosecutor (of which, rumor has it, there are at least a few in this country) might be wary of plea bargaining.[13]

I do not know that any of these hypotheses will occur; it may well be that the critics are correct and that prosecutorial discretion will increase and plea bargaining escalate.[14] But neither I nor the opponents of presumptive sentencing can know, since we have had little time to become experienced with these systems. It is, at best, premature to condemn the reforms on the notion that they cannot work.

Regardless of whether the critics are correct, however, their argument that "since" plea bargaining will increase, sentencing reform should be foregone, is clearly overkill. As Dean Norval Morris has said: "I disagree with Alschuler's argument that sentencing reform should

---

[11] This practice and the cases upholding it (thus far) are cited in Chapter 8.

[12] It could be argued, of course, that the defendant has still reduced the maximum amount of incarceration possible and thus retains the benefit of the bargain. But when parole is granted to virtually everyone, and usually very soon after first eligibility, this benefit is, as a matter of fact, very small indeed.

[13] Theoretically, of course, defense attorneys, under the present system, should similarly be unwilling to bargain, since the bargain is often illusory. But this does not happen for several reasons. First, defense attorneys are not as aware of parole board practices as they ought to be. Second, many attorneys consider that their job ends upon conviction, or at least upon sentence, and have not sought to learn about parole boards. Third, few state parole boards have any guidelines and continue to operate under the vague mandate that release should occur "when the defendant is ready to return to society." Many defense attorneys basically agree with that philosophy and are not willing to second guess parole boards. Fourth, the board's "readjustment" of the plea bargain occurs invisibly, inside the prison, and often under the vague rubric outlined above or some equally unilluminating phrase, so that the defense attorney cannot be sure that the board is "really" undermining the plea bargain. (I.e., if the board says that it is delaying release because the prisoner lacks a good parole plan, or has been insubordinate to prison officials, the defense attorney cannot go behind that to determine whether the decision to delay was actually based on the board's evaluation of the real crime.) The publication of the U.S. Parole Commission's admission as to what it does is in this regard not only strikingly illuminating; it is unique.

[14] Since plea bargaining now accounts for between 70–90 percent of all convictions, however, this escalation may be small in any event.

wait on the achievement of better control of charge and plea bargaining, but I certainly agree . . . that such bargaining may well frustrate reforms in legislative and judicial sentencing."[15] Indeed, one point that is almost always ignored is that in a system where judicial, parole board, and good time discretionary decisions are eliminated or heavily restricted, control of prosecutorial discretion is not only interesting—it becomes important. So long as there are three bodies, each with substantial discretion to ignore the impact of the other two and each able to either enforce or fail to enforce the other's discretionary decisions, control of only one part of the system—particularly the preliminary parts—would be irrelevant. Parole reform in an indeterminate, fully discretionary model would be relatively meaningless if judges could set distressingly high minima or maxima or if prosecutors could seek and obtain convictions on a very high seriousness level. Similarly, control on plea bargaining discretion would be relatively fruitless if judges or parole boards could then undo the discretionary decision. In short, it is only by severely reducing the discretion in two (or more) parts of the system either simultaneously or seriatim that reform in the other parts of the system truly becomes meaningful.

So even if the presumptive sentence model is justly accused of concentrating the discretion all in the hands of the prosecutor (which I doubt for reasons already indicated), that is not necessarily an indictment. Having narrowed the locus of discretion to the extent that it is exercised or exercisable, true reform of the entire system may become more plausible. We should turn, then, to the possible methods of reforming prosecutorial discretion. The discussion is not exhaustive; it is intended merely to show that such control is feasible if good faith attempts are made by all involved.

ABOLISH PLEA BARGAINING?

It appears, or at least it has been argued, that plea bargaining has been part of the criminal justice system for at least the last century.[16] Whatever the case, it is undeniably true that during the last fifteen years, we have become increasingly aware of its presence and of its

---

[15] Morris, *Conceptual Overview and Commentary on the Movement Toward Determinacy*, in DETERMINATE SENTENCING: REFORM OR REGRESSION? 1, 6 (LEAA 1978).

[16] See M. HEUMANN, PLEA BARGAINING 27–33 (1977); Miller, *The Compromise of Criminal Cases*, 1 So. CAL. L. REV. 3 (1927). It has also been argued, far less convincingly, that other methods of compromise or of avoiding the jurisdiction of the criminal courts can also be seen as "plea bargaining," thus suggesting that plea bargaining can be traced to benefit of clergy and other methods of the middle ages. See Note, The Plea Bargain in Historical Perspective, 23 BUFF. L. REV. 499 (1974).

powerful impact on the criminal justice system.[17] Within that period, two major works—one a tract by the American Friends Service Committee[18] and the other a national report by a federally funded study supported by the Department of Justice[19]—have called for the complete abolition of plea bargaining.

Needless to say, these calls have met widespread incredulity and scoffing. Some, arguing that the courts would be crushed under a caseload pressure of enormous proportions, say the proposal is unrealistic.[20] Others argue that even those who say that they want to abolish the process still want to retain discretion in the "extraordinary" case and that, therefore, the pressure to expand the definition of "extraordinary" would eventually lead back to the present system.[21]

The question has increased in intensity recently with the publication of a debate between several leading scholars on comparative criminal procedure concerning the presence (or absence) of plea bargaining in the continental systems, particularly in Germany.[22] Each of these scholars agree that, in Germany, the prosecutor is under a statutory duty to prosecute fully and completely every alleged offense, with the exception of those by which he may proceed by "penal order," which is basically a nolo contendere type procedure. This notion of full prosecution for all offenders—called the *Legalitatsprinzip* (legality principle)—is seen as restricting, or even forbidding, the use of prosecutorial discretion. Moreover, German law allows any citizen dis-

---

[17] The literature is enormous. For at least a sample, see the bibliography in HEUMANN, *supra* note 16; or the two bibliographies published by LEAA, PROSECUTORIAL DISCRETION: THE DECISION TO CHARGE (1975) and PLEA BARGAINING, A SELECTED BIBLIOGRAPHY (1976).

[18] STRUGGLE FOR JUSTICE (1971).

[19] NATIONAL ADVISORY COMMISSION ON CRIMINAL JUSTICE STANDARDS AND GOALS, COURTS, §3.1 (1973) (Abolition desirable by 1978).

[20] These critics, however, do not deal with the mounting evidence that plea bargaining is not a result of high prosecutor or defense case loads. See HEUMANN, *supra* note 16; Frankelstein, *A Statistical Analysis of Guilty Plea Practices in the Federal Courts,* 89 HARV. L. REV. 293 (1975). Both these works compared heavy case load jurisdictions with light jurisdictions and found roughly the same amount of bargaining. Moreover, Heumann found that most defendants want to plead guilty and get it over with and that the bargaining is simply a bonus to their initial desires in any event.

[21] HEUMANN, *supra* note 16 at ch. 7.

[22] K. DAVIS, DISCRETIONARY JUSTICE IN EUROPE AND AMERICA (1976); Goldstein and Marcus, *The Myth of Judicial Supervision in Three "Inquisitorial" Systems: France, Italy and Germany,* 87 YALE L.J. 240 (1977); Jescheck, *The Discretionary Powers of the Prosecuting Attorney in West Germany,* 18 AMER. J. COMP. L. 508 (1970); Langbein and Weinreb, *Continental Criminal Procedure: "Myth" and Reality,* 87 YALE L.J. 1549 (1978) (responded to by Goldstein and Marcus, *Comment on Continental Criminal Procedure,* 87 YALE L.J. 1570 (1978)); Pugh, *Ruminations re Reform of American Criminal Justice (Especially Our Guilty Plea System): Reflections Derived From a Study of the French System,* 36 LA. L. REV. 947 (1976); Vouin, *The Role of the Prosecutor in French Criminal Trials,* 18 AMER. J. COMP. L. 493 (1970).

pleased by the refusal of a prosecutor to pursue a case to take the prosecutor to court; additionally, the prosecutor is subject to criminal liability if he cannot justify the refusal on the basis of lack of sufficient evidence to proceed or some other similar justification.[23] As one of the writers put it.[24] "The decisive idea is . . . that it is one of the primary tasks of the state to guarantee fairness and justice without considerations of expediency, matters which have very little to do with retribution." Similar, though not identical, restrictions on prosecutorial discretion were allegedly found in both the French and the Italian systems.

Professors Goldstein and Marcus, however, were unpersuaded that these conclusions were accurate and conducted their own study, from which they concluded that in all three countries the prosecutor had, and exercised, substantial discretion in whether, and if so how much, to prosecute. In particular, they pointed to a process in the French system that allowed the prosecutor to "correctionalize" (reduce) the charge before the case came to trial. They then observed that the defendant, while barred from admitting his guilt, often failed to contest vigorously the state's evidence. From this they concluded that a deal was struck by which the prosecutor would correctionalize in exchange for a failure of defense from the defendant; they characterized this as plea bargaining. Similar processes were alleged to be present in Germany and Italy.

Professors Weinreb and Langbein dissented, both generally and specifically, arguing that, in fact, the principle of legality was observed in virtually all instances and that the existence of prosecutorial discretion not to prosecute did not necessarily indicate the existence of plea bargaining.[25]

Which of these views is correct—or more correct—is not critical to our discussion here, for both sides of the argument are agreed that in

---

[23] Herrmann, *Rule of Compulsory Prosecution and the Scope of Prosecutorial Discretion in Germany*, 41 U. CHI. L. REV. 468 (1974). In at least one jurisdiction in this country, failure to prosecute may lead to criminal prosecution or removal, even without a demonstration of corruption. State v. Winne, 12 N.J. 152, 96 A.2d 63 (1953). See Ferguson, *Formulation of Enforcement Policy: An Anatomy of the Prosecutor's Discretion Prior to Accusation*, 11 RUTGERS L. REV. 507 (1957).

[24] Jescheck, *supra* note 22 at 511.

[25] This important point is often ignored by writers who fail to differentiate the discretion not to prosecute—which may (and should) be based on considerations of the likelihood of conviction—and the discretion in plea bargaining, which is generally based on perceived social, not legal, goals such as saving court time. See J. Hyman, Prosecutorial Discretion in a Desert Society (unpublished), for a more discriminating analysis. The former decision is certainly not necessarily incompatible with a desert theory, which only posits that if there is evidence that a crime has been committed, the sanctions imposed should be equal, not dependent on the negotiating abilities of the parties.

these jurisdictions, there is a consensus that trials are desirable and that informal arrangements are not to dominate the legal process. Neither the Goldstein-Marcus writings nor those of any other scholar thus far suggest that the rampant dealing that occurs in this country characterizes proceedings on the Continent. Indeed, one remains convinced, after reading these critiques, that the essential difference is one of attitude—that prosecutors in those countries are less advocates and more impartial assessors and often use their power simply to dismiss charges, rather than continue to press in the hopes of gaining some defense concession. Perhaps it is more attitude than formal structure that needs to be reexamined if we are to even begin to abolish plea bargaining in this country. It would certainly not be novel to suggest that the adversary system sometimes defeats real justice and that a further incorporation of inquisitorial approaches to criminal justice might, in fact, achieve fairer and more equitable results. But even if one stops short of that position, the charge to our prosecutors to reassess the value of efficiency would be of immense value.

CONTROLLING PLEA BARGAINING

Even if abolition is not feasible or desirable, there is no question but that controlling prosecutorial discretion, and in particular the plea bargaining process, has consumed much discussion in the last decade. At least three modes of controlling these activities have been suggested, in addition to those already referred to in the German system.

Guidelines

Two methods for providing plea bargaining guidelines for prosecutors have been suggested. One is that the prosecutor's office itself establish guidelines in the same way that guidelines will be established for the sentencing decision. Some offices now have, or profess to have, such guidelines,[26] and with the advent of presumptive sentencing ranges established by a commission, and increasing number of prosecutor's offices may feel that plea bargaining guidelines are necessary and desirable. These guidelines are subject to review, formal or informal, by the nonaccommodating judge, the chief prosecutor, or in some instances, the attorney general. Problems of disparity from county to county might ultimately have to be resolved by some statewide mechanism, which could be evolved over a period of time.

A second possible guideline solution, proposed by Professor Zal-

---

[26] Cf. C. Vance, The Prosecutor's Discretion: A Statement of Policy of the District Attorney of Harris County (1974); Kuh, *Plea Bargaining: Guidelines for the Manhattan District Attorney's Office*, 11 Crim. L. Bull. 48 (1975).

man[27] and endorsed with some hesitation by Professor Alschuler, is that the sentencing commission guidelines could themselves incorporate a presumptive sentence for the crime if there is a trial and a presumptive sentence if the defendant pleads guilty without trial (discount rate). As Professor Alschuler says, this "open articulation of the principles that makes our system of plea bargaining effective should indeed cause us to blush." Nevertheless, recent United States Supreme Court decisions[28] make it unlikely that such an expressed and open articulation of the price one pays for the constitutional right of jury trial would be held unconstitutional.

If the sentencing commission's schedules in fact recognize a reduction in the presumptive sentence to those who plead guilty, plea bargaining might be reduced. A defendant who knows that by merely pleading guilty (as opposed to bargaining for the plea) to the crime charged, he may receive a sentence reduction of one year, may have little incentive to negotiate with the prosecutor for a pled down charge and a different presumptive sentence.[29] The difficulty with such a system, of course, is that it does not, in fact, reduce plea bargaining. It only reduces prosecutorial plea bargaining, replacing the prosecutor with the sentencing commission. But the commission, at least, does not suffer the weakness of partiality, and its guidelines would essentially support pleas as a method of efficiency. To the extent that the actual process of negotiation is seen by both sides as desirable and productive, they will resist any such attempt to replace face-to-face bargaining with standardized discounts for guilty pleas.

Administrative Review

In one sense, every prosecutor is reviewed by her or his superior, who will also evaluate the plea bargains made. This could be strengthened by a requirement that the prosecutor articulate in writing the reasons for accepting the plea. This review, however, is meaningless to the defendant (who has already been sentenced) and nearly so to the rest of the criminal justice system, since such a review is able neither to retroactively affect a specific sentence nor to inform the public, including defendants and their counsel, of the office's plea-bargaining policies. If administrative review is selected as the control

---

[27] Zalman, *supra* p. 63, n. 9. See also Hoffman & De Gostin, *An Argument for Self-Imposed Explicit Judicial Sentencing Standards*, 3 J. Crim. Just. (1975).

[28] See, e.g., Bordenkircher v. Hayes, 434 U.S. 357 (1978); United States v. Jackson, 390 U.S. 570 (1968). But see, Brady v. United States, 397 U.S. 742 (1970).

[29] To be effective, the sentencing commission would have to distinguish between pleas to crimes charged in the indictment—which would result in reductions—and pleas to lesser induced offenses, which would not, since only this would effectively reduce prosecutorial plea bargaining.

mechanism, therefore, it must be more public than the internal office review now practical. Indeed, several suggestions have been made that the prosecutor's office apply the state's administrative procedure act to its operation, including the establishment of guidelines, as well as continued in-house review.[30]

Judicial Participation in or Review of the Plea Bargain Process

Many recent proposals for change in the plea bargain process have involved making the process public and, in fact, making the judge an active participant in the process.[31] Although this raises problems of judicial independence and possible coercion on the defendant, it at least poses the possiblity of introducing an impartial third party to the bargaining session.

An intriguing, and more radical, variation of that suggestion was made several years ago in a Yale Law Journal note.[32] That note urged that plea bargaining become, in effect, a "minitrial"; after hearing the facts (with some limitations on evidence) and arguments, the judge (whose sole function would be to sit at these pretrial discussions) would indicate to the defendant two possible sentences—one if he pled guilty now and one that would be imposed if he decided instead to go to trial and were found guilty. The trial judge (who would not know of this finding) would be bound by the latter decision in the event of trial. Thus, the defendant would know, prior to trial, the precise discount rate for pleading guilty.[33]

These suggestions may seem fanciful. But they at least indicate that serious and imaginative proposals are being made to deal with the problem of prosecutorial discretion and plea bargaining. It is likely that they will be more carefully scrutinized and perhaps adopted once the plea-bargaining process means, in fact, as much to the defendant as it means to the prosecution.

Attitudinizing

The monstrous gerundial with which this section begins nevertheless reflects an important part of analysis of ways in which plea bar-

---

[30] Bubany and Skillern, *Taming the Dragon: An Administrative Law for Prosecutorial Decision Making*, 13 AMER. CRIM. L. REV. 473 (1976); Neumann, *The New Era of Administrative Regularization: Controlling Prosecutor and Discretion through the Administrative Procedure Act*, 3 UNIV. OF DAYTON L. REV. 23 (1978).

[31] Gallagher, *Judicial Participation in Plea Bargaining: A Search for New Standards*, 9 HARV. CIV. LIB.–CIV. RTS. L. REV. (1974).

[32] Note, *Restructuring the Plea Bargain*, 82 YALE L.J. 286 (1972). Cf. L. WEINREB, DENIAL OF JUSTICE (1977).

[33] This is similar to the Zalman-Hoffman position, except that here the "sentence" would be more "individualized."

gaining may be altered. Those who argue that enactment of a more equalized, consistent sentencing scheme, whether based on a principle of commensurate deserts or not, will not achieve their goals ignore the potential impact of the enactment itself. Prosecutors, judges, and others now in the system cannot fail to note the antipathy toward unregulated plea bargaining that an enactment calling for more even-handed determinations of punishment would evoke. The prosecutor quoted earlier by Professor Alschuler argued that a prosecutor could avoid any limitation on discretion if he wanted to do so. But any actor in the system must feel some allegiance, however small, to the prevailing policy of the system, whatever his own personal views. To the extent that prosecutors recognize that they are engaging in practices that cannot be squared with articulated legislative philosophy, they may retreat from bargaining.

Realities and practicalities usually govern people's actions, and it would be naive to argue that simply because the system had adopted a presumptive sentence model based on desert principles, plea bargaining will end. Just as naive, however, is the notion that whatever the articulated philosophy, life will continue as always, without even a notice of the change in philosophy. If ideology is not the sole determinant of people's actions, it is also too important to ignore; the impact upon plea bargaining of the fact that the legislature has endorsed a notion inimical to plea bargaining may be substantial.[34]

SUMMARY

Commensurate deserts and plea bargaining are essentially incompatible; the utilitarian drive for the efficiency that is the articulated justification for plea bargaining is antithetical to the moral impetus behind the movement for consistency in punishment. If plea bargaining were to continue in its present degree, this conflict alone could wreck the new experiments on the shoals of utilitarianism.

But plea bargaining may not increase under a presumptive sentence model; indeed, it may decrease of its own accord. First, prosecutors may themselves feel more constrained in reducing the sanction, and stigma, imposed upon an offender, particularly if the model prescribes the sanction that feels right for that crime. Second, there may be outside pressures—judicial refusal to accept bargains, executive pardons, and so forth—that may convince the prosecutor to rein his discretion.

---

[34] Goldstein and Marcus, *The Myth of Judicial Supervision, supra* note 22 at 283: "In the end these Continental systems rely more on their ideology and on the assumption that officials adhere to the ideology. . . ."

Finally, if the realists are correct and prosecutorial discretion is increased and is used, there will undoubtedly be a further call for restricting such discretion through either guidelines, administrative review, or some other mechanism. While these methods will not achieve as much as a basic change in attitude, nor as quickly, it is likely that, in the long run, consistency in sentencing will become a reasonably accomplished fact. It took, after all, nearly seventy-five years for the rehabilitative, medical, indeterminate notion of sentencing to take hold, and even today it is often ignored. No one can expect that the move to less arbitrary sentencing will be achieved overnight. But that is no reason not to start.

Chapter 10

Reform: Illusion or Reality?

STANDARDS OF EVALUATION

Thus far, we have explored the theory of deserts sentencing, noting the spots at which debate still continues and suggesting resolutions of at least some of these issues. But as noted in the introduction, a great deal of sentencing change, some of it in the name of just deserts, has occurred in the last few years, and much more is imminent. It seems prudent, therefore, to examine the legislation that has already been promulgated to determine whether in fact consistency and equality in sentencing has become a reality.

To evaluate these proposals, we should first restate the basic principles a desert-equality model would require:

1. The sanction imposed should be based primarily, if not exclusively, on the crime and therefore should be roughly the same for all persons who commit that crime; this sentence can be called the presumptive sentence.
2. This sanction should be proportionate to the crime.
3. Variations from the typical or presumptive sentence should be based primarily, if not exclusively, on factors concerned with the manner in which the crime was perpetrated; the offender's characteristics should be irrelevant or, at best, only peripherally considered in setting the sentence.
4. Even where variation is allowed, it should not be allowed, except in extraordinarily unique circumstances, across types of sentence (i.e., probation should generally not be available for crimes for which the presumptive sentence is imprisonment, and vice versa).
5. The amount of variation from the presumptive sentence allowed should be very small. This is required not only to reduce possible

disparities, but also on the theory that the core of the sentence must be based on the crime.

6. Maximum possible sentences—actual time served—should be small, since in most instances the need for punishment can be achieved without enormously lengthy incarcerations. Five years actual time served would seem to be the maximum feasible sentence for all but the most heinous offenses.

7. The sentence structure should be such that there is little or no overlap among crimes or classes of crimes. That is, the lowest sentence for, for example, the most serious class should ideally be higher than the highest sentence for the next most serious class, even after aggravating and mitigating circumstances are considered; to provide otherwise would allow crimes of different severity to be punished equally or, even worse, allow a more serious crime to be treated with less severity than a less serious crime. If that ideal is not possible, overlap should be avoided in the higher crime classes and tolerated in the lower seriousness crimes.

8. Postsentence methods for reducing an imposed sanction must be minimal, or the potential for great disparity again appears. Thus, good time should be abolished or, if retained, should be a very small percentage of the total duration, protected by vesting provisions so that the actual amount of possible variation from the deserved sentence will be small.

9. Mechanisms must be established to prevent preconviction disparity; plea bargaining must be limited through guidelines established by the prosecutors themselves or some other agency.

We have also discussed other aspects of implementation of the model—(1) that it would be more desirable (though not essential) to have the sentencing standards established by an independent agency; (2) that the role of appellate review, by whatever agency, should be broad for nonpresumptive sentences and very narrow for presumptive sentences; and (3) that parole surveillance could be retained as a punishment, but that parole release should become so automatic that parole boards could be abolished.

Obviously, it would be both foolish and unrealistic to expect any sentencing reform in the real world to reflect fully each of those points. There are, after all, serious debates about some of these points (first offenders, overlap, etc.) that could reasonably be decided either way. Further, the political process is subject to pressures that reject the entire notion of commensurate deserts and limits on judicial discretion. Even a legislature responsive to the notions of deserts will find it impossible not to yield on some points, in the hope that the resistance to the reform as a whole will be lessened. Thus, for example, legislatures might require presentence reports to placate probation officers or judges or both, even though under a system that looks at the crime and not the criminal that document could and should be brutishly succinct.

Nevertheless, if we are to assess the reforms thus far carried out in the name of commensurate deserts, we should use these major points as a lodestar, recognizing that wholesale adoption of any legislative plan is not likely. The next pages, then, summarize, with some comments, the legislation, parole regulations, or court rules that have been adopted or proposed in the various states in an alleged attempt to follow the deserts model.[1] The sketches are short and do not fully exhaust these provisions. Only the highlights are mentioned. Thereafter, data from one of these jurisdictions (California) will be presented and weighed against the model. The final section of this chapter will seek to deal with the question of whether, in light of the findings in the two preceding sections, one should simply give up the ghost of the chances for reform.

THE PRESENT STATUS OF SENTENCING REFORM

Alaska
Legislation. Alaska's newly enacted legislation adopts a definite term of imprisonment, as follows:

	First Offense		Second Offense	Third and More
	Maxi-mum	Mini-mum		
Class A[3]	22.5	3[2]	Presump-tive 10 yrs	Presump-tive 15 yrs
Class B	7	0	Presump-tive 5 yrs	Presump-tive 10 yrs
Class C	3	0	Presump-tive 2 yrs	Presump-tive 4 yrs

For first offenders in all three classes (except Class A offenders "using" a "firearm"), the judge may set any minimum deemed proper. For

[1] In the summer of 1978, I wrote to the clerk of each state supreme court, the clerk of each legislative body in every state, and the parole board in every state, asking the status of changes along these lines. The survey that follows is based upon that data as well as on information that I have acquired through other sources. It attempts to be, but almost surely is not, complete, at least through June 1978. Activity after that date is unlikely to have been noted.

[2] Three year minimum if defendant "used" a "firearm"; otherwise no minimum.

[3] Does not include murder.

repeat offenders, variation from the presumptive sentence is allowed only when the judge finds specifically stated factors in mitigation or aggravation (there are thirteen aggravating and twelve mitigating factors stated), with a maximum increase or decrease of 50 percent (e.g., a second offender, Class A, has a range of 5–15, with a presumptive of 10; a third offender, Class C, has a range of 2–6, with a presumptive of 4).

If a judge finds "by clear and convincing evidence" that "manifest injustice" would result if another mitigating or aggravating factor, not listed, were not considered, he may consider it. In such an instance, he is to send the record to a newly established sentencing panel, consisting of three judges, who determine whether, in fact, "manifest injustice" would result. If so, the panel sentences; if not, they remand for sentencing in accord with normal procedures.

First offenders are eligible for parole at one-third of the sentence imposed; recidivists apparently are not to be paroled. Similarly, first offenders (except murderers and Class A firearm users) are eligible for probation; second offenders are not.

Good time is granted at the rate of one day for every three. Alaska already has appellate review of sentencing, and there is nothing in this bill that appears to affect that process.[4]

Parole.   The Alaska Parole Board is developing parole guidelines with a grant from the National Institute of Corrections. The guidelines are expected to be completed some time in 1979.

Arizona

Arizona's new legislation, enacted in 1977 and effective October 1, 1978,[5] follows the notion of presumptive sentences, according to the class of felony, as follows:[6]

Class	First Offense		Second Offense		Third Offense	
	Presumptive	Range	Presumptive	Range	Presumptive	Range
2	7	5 1/4–14	10 1/2	7–21	15 3/4	14–28
3	5	3 3/4–10	7 1/2	5–15	10 1/4	10–20
4	4	2–5	4 1/2	4–8	7 1/2	8–12
5	2	1–2 1/2	2 1/4	2–4	3 3/4	4–6
6	1 1/2	3/4–1 3/8	2 1/4	1 1/2–3	3 3/4	3–4 1/2

[4] See Erwin, *Five Years of Sentence Review in Alaska*, 5 U.C.L.A.—ALASKA L. REV. 1 (1975).

[5] There have been many amendments. This summary is based on the legislation prior to the amendments.

[6] There is an ambiguity in the language of the provisions here, but this appears to be the proper interpretation.

The range of variation, which is scaled according to class of offense, from the presumptive sentence is based on the presence or absence of aggravating and mitigating circumstances. The circumstances specified in the statute are relatively narrow and well defined, thereby emulating what would be a reasonably predictable sentencing pattern. Moreover, they tend to be more desert oriented than most such attempts. The judge must place the evidence for his conclusion "in the record." However, in both the aggravating and mitigating provisions, the legislature allows the judge to also consider "any other factors which the court may deem appropriate to the ends of justice." While the specification of factors may be used as an indication of the types of factors that should be considered, there is no guarantee that the courts will so interpret that section; if not, then the trouble taken in listing the factors is futile.

Arizona also provides longer sentences for persons who have "used or exhibited" a "deadly weapon or dangerous instrumentality" or if "serious physical injury" was inflicted, the maximum again depending upon the crime for which the defendant now stands convicted and the number of previous convictions. Again, these sentence determinations seem to be totally within the discretion of the trial judge.

Recidivists are not eligible for probation. Parole eligibility for recidivists is also restricted, depending on the class of crime of current convictions and number of past convictions.

Arizona already has appellate review of sentences, and that is apparently unchanged; a new provision, however, allows the state to appeal if the presumptive sentence is not imposed. The standard for appeals by defendant is whether the sentence is "greater than under the circumstances . . . ought to be inflicted"; no standard appears to be articulated for review when the state appeals.

Parole is retained, with eligibility at one-half the sentence imposed. Good time is repealed.[7]

Arkansas
The legislature has established a committee to study determinate sentencing.

California
Legislation. In 1976, after several years of intense legislative struggle, California adopted what was the first presumptive sentence legislation. California's approach is, even today, the closest to the notion of consistent sentencing and restriction of judicial discretion. It is also

---

[7] The whole code is reviewed in Gerber, *Arizona's New Criminal Code: An Overview and Critique*, 3 ARIZ. ST. L.J. 483 (1977).

enormously complex, and the summary below only scans the surface of that complexity.

Essentially, California establishes four classes of crimes, although they are not so labeled in the legislation. They are as follows, with ranges:

	Presumptive Sentence	Range of Sentence
Class A	6	5–7
Class B	5	4–6
Class C	3	2–3
Class D	2	16 months–3 years

The judge may sentence within the range on the basis of aggravating and mitigating factors. These factors are not detailed in the legislation, but the California Judicial Council has provided a list of seventeen aggravating and fourteen mitigating factors (see *infra*).

The legislation also provides for enhancements to the sentence that take the sentence outside the range. These enhancements, and the duration of the addition to sentence, are specifically spelled out in the statute and are described in more detail in Chapter 6.

Administrative review of all sentences is provided by the Community Release Board, which is to determine whether a sentence is within the range of sentences normally given for that offense and offender characteristics. If the board determines that there is disparity, it is to remand the sentence to the sentencing judge, along with its reasons for finding the sentence out of conformity. If the sentencing judge adheres to the original sentence, there is no clear appellate review process.

There is parole supervision for one year, with specified procedures and penalties for nonobservance of the parole conditions.

Since the passage of the initial act, there has been a constant stream of amendatory language; much of this was passed in 1977, before the effective date of the bill, and is known as A.B. 476. In 1978, the legislature passed S.B. 709, which increased the possible sentences for over forty crimes.

California has dealt intricately with the problem of consecutive sentences. The judge is to select one crime as the primary crime and then treat all others as subsidiary. For the subsidiary crimes, a consecutive sentence may (not must) be imposed; if one is imposed, only one duration is allowed—one-third the middle sentence for that crime. Thus, if an offender has committed crime A, with a four year presumptive, and crime B, with a three year presumptive, assuming no aggravation or mitigation, enhancements, and the like, the sentence could be either five years (four years for A, one year for B), or four and one-third (three years for B, one and one-third for A). Nothing requires the judge to select one offense against another as the primary offense.

Good time is three months for every eight served plus an additional month for every eight of participation in prison programs. Good time vests, and the amount subject to loss is limited per incident.

The legislation mandates that the system be studied to determine the effects of the new scheme on criminal justice generally. Thus, within five years at a maximum, we should have some clear ideas as to the precise effect of the California experiment.

Judicial.   As indicated, the Judicial Council, pursuant to the statute, has promulgated a list of factors that may be considered by the sentencing judge in determining whether to vary from the presumptive sentence yet remain within the one year range. These factors, as discussed more fully in Chapter 6, are so vague and wide that they effectively give to the sentencing judge full discretion within a two year range; several reflect the "Catch-22 syndrome" described in Chapter 6.

Because California was the first state that attempted meaningful sentence reform, and because it is a key state in corrections, and because the move from a nearly totally indeterminate system to a relatively determinate use was so striking, it has already been the subject of significant comment.[8]

Colorado
Legislation.   In 1977, Colorado enacted legislation, effective April 1979, that can fairly be described as determinate. It provides, for first offenders, presumptive terms of life, seven and one-half years, four and one-half years, two years, and one and one-half years respectively for class 1, 2, 3, 4, and 5 offenses. Recidivists are increased one class for each past offense. Thus, a two time loser who has committed a class 4 felony is treated as a class 2 felon, with a presumptive term of seven and one-half years. All sentences carry a one year parole term.

---

[8] Cassou and Taugher, *Determinate Sentencing in California: The New Numbers Game*, 9 PACIFIC L.J. 1 (1978); McGee, *California's New Determinate Sentence Law* 42 FED. PROB. 3 (March 1978); Messinger and Johnson, *California's Determinate Sentencing Statute: History and Issues*, in DETERMINATE SENTENCING: REFORM OR REGRESSION? 13 (1978); Oppenheimer, *Computing A Determinate Sentence . . . New Math Hits the Courts*, 51 CAL. ST. B.J. 604 (1976); Uelmen, *Proof of Aggravation Under the California Uniform Determinate Sentencing Act: The Constitutional Issues*, 10 LOYOLA (L.A.) L. REV. 725 (1977); Comment, *Senate Bill 42—The End of the Indeterminate Sentence*, 17 SANTA CLARA LAW. 133 (1977). California will also be the focus of a major LEAA grant to study the effects of determinate sentencing.

A court may increase or decrease the presumptive sentence by 20 percent on the basis of (unspecified) aggravating or mitigating circumstances.

All offenders except those sentenced for life are eligible for probation. Good time of ten days per month vests monthly. Extra meritorious good time of not more than one month for six served is also available.

There does not appear to be appellate review.

Judicial.   Denver, Colorado, was one of the sites of the Kress study[9] on sentencing guidelines and has had them in effect for several years.

Parole.   The board is seeking funding to establish parole guidelines.

Connecticut

In 1978, Connecticut considered, but rejected, a bill that would have instituted a complex form of presumptive sentencing. The presumptive sentence would be found by a matrix, on one axis of which was the offense, ranked by class of seriousness, and on the other axis the offender's past criminal record. As noted in Chapter 5, not only the number of past convictions, but the crimes involved, would be considered in determining the proper box of the matrix from which the presumptive sentence would be chosen. The judge could then aggravate or mitigate by 15 percent and, for compelling reasons, in writing, could go above or below the range. Some of the mitigating circumstances and most of the aggravating circumstances were arguably desert oriented. In addition, assault on the elderly, or second and third degree assault generally, could be increased by one class in the judge's discretion.

Probation was available except for murder, kidnapping, and other Class A offenses.

Connecticut already had appellate review, although it has been recently examined and found severely wanting.[10] There is nothing in the act that would have changed that.

Although the legislation itself set the initial presumptive sentences, a seven person sentencing commission, appointed respectively by the

[9] Kress, *Who Should Sentence: The Judge, the Legislature, or. . . . ?* 17 JUDGES JOURNAL 12 (1978).

[10] See Samuelson, *Sentence Review and Sentence Disparity: A Case Study of the Connecticut Sentence Review Division*, 10 CONN. L. REV. 5 (1977).

superior court judge, the governor, and the leaders of the legislature, was established to study the impact of the new sentencing scheme and to promulgate sentencing guidelines for the efficient implementation of the legislation.

Good time was retained, at the rate of six days a month (20 percent); no vesting was provided. Parole release was made nondiscretionary, but parole supervision, for a period of at least one year, was retained.

Delaware

Delaware is currently considering presumptive sentencing legislation. The legislation would establish the following schedule:

	Presumptive	Mitigating	Aggravating
Class B	20	15	25
Class C	15	12	18
Class D	10	8	12
Class E	7	6	8

Prior felonies would be considered as an aggravating factor, along with others, as well as a list of mitigating factors. Probation would be available for all offenders except Class A, which are dealt with in separate provisions of the existing code and which would not be altered (Class A offenses are capital).

A Criminal Sentence Review Board, much like California's Community Release Board, would be established both to review every prison sentence and to collect sentencing data and recommend changes to the legislature. The board would consist of three judges, one from the supreme court, one from the equity division, and one from superior (trial) court. Each member would serve a year, and the assignment would then rotate to another judge.

Day for day good time is provided and vests every thirty days; no more than thirty days, therefore, can be revoked for any prison infraction. For all but Class A offenders, parole is abolished.

Florida

In 1978, the Florida legislature enacted a presumptive sentencing scheme, with relatively wide ranges. This, however, was vetoed by the governor. Currently, the Florida Supreme Court has appointed a committee to investigate determinate and presumptive sentencing and to report no later than January 1, 1979.

The legislation would have provided for the following schedule (excluding life and capital punishment sanctions):

Class	Presumptive	Aggravating	Mitigating
1st Degree	10	15	5
2d Degree	5	10	3
3rd Degree	2	7	0

Additionally, a three year term would be imposed for each past conviction of a "violent felony" (defined in the act). The criteria for aggravation and mitigation were to be set by the supreme court. One year
enhancements for other felonies were also allowed, except that in extraordinary cases, recidivists and those convicted of capital offenses
were not eligible for probation. The supreme court was to establish
procedures, "if any," for appellate review.

Good time, on a sliding scale, from three months per year for the
first year to nine months per year for over five years, was retained and
apparently not vested. Discretionary parole release was retained. The
board has been mandated by other legislation to establish parole
guidelines that were to be ready by December 1, 1978.

Idaho

A legislative proposal for studying determinate sentencing was on
the ballot in Idaho in November 1978.

Illinois

Illinois' newly enacted legislation, like that of Indiana and Maine,
discussed later in this chapter, is a good example of sentencing reform
that calls itself "just deserts," but that is in fact a determinate sentencing scheme run wild. The schedule for offenses is:

Class	Minimum	Maximum	Enhanced Sentences
X	6	30	30–60
1	4	15	15–30
2	3	7	7–14
3	2	5	5–10
4	1	3	3–6

Nothing in the statute provides guidelines for the discretionary des-
ignation of a determinate sentence—for example, for a Class 1 offense
between four and fifteen—although both the supreme court and the
simultaneously established sentencing commission are to provide such
guidance later. The sentencing commission, composed of twelve persons, three appointed by the governor, three by each house, and three
circuit (trial) judges, has not yet begun its work according to my
information, and it is not clear what power it has in any event.

The code abolishes parole, but retains good time on a day for day basis, thus reducing the lengthy sentences imposed. Since there is frequent vesting of such good time, the actual sentences will be almost one-half that which the judge imposed—a retention of false time.

Probation is available to most offenders, except murderers, Class X offenders, and Class 1 and 2 repeaters. The statute provides, in fact, a presumption in favor of probation for those eligible; an exhaustive list of aggravating and mitigating factors, based on the Model Penal Code, is intended to guide this discretionary decision.

There is appellate review, and there is a "rebuttable presumption" that the sentence imposed is "proper." The court may increase or decrease a sentence.

Indiana

Indiana, perhaps more than any other state with the possible exception of Maine, demonstrates the difficulties referred to in the introduction of this book. In 1976, the legislature enacted new penal legislation, which became effective October 1, 1977. In its large features, the scheme is determinate and presumptive sentencing. The ranges of sentencing, however, are so wide that the legislature has neither abolished nor restricted disparity or discretion in sentencing. The sentences allowed are as follows:

	Presumptive	Maximum	Minimum
Murder	40	60	30
Class A	30	50	20
Class B	10	20	6
Class C	5	8	2
Class D	2	4	May be reduced to a misdemeanor

The judge is to determine where within this enormous range the sentence will fall by looking to listed aggravating and mitigating circumstances, the vast majority of which are rehabilitational. Unfortunately, as noted in Chapter 6, these factors are exceptionally vague, and additionally, there is the escape clause that the judge may consider any nonlisted factor he considers relevant.

Furthermore, most of the offenses actually span two or three felony classes, since serious bodily injury, use of the threat of deadly force, and several other factors will allow the judge to increase the class of felony.[11]

---

[11] See Clear, Hewitt, and Regoli, *Discretion and the Determinate Sentence: Its Distribution, Control, and Effect on Time Served*, 24 CRIME AND DELINQ. 428, 433 (1978).

Indiana also provides for habitual offender sentences, by adding an additional fixed term of thirty years to the base sentence. A habitual offender is defined as a person who has been convicted of two prior unrelated convictions of any felony.

As in Illinois, the legislature has sought to soften the blow of these lengthy sentences by provision of concomitantly high good time. Three classes of offenders are created: Class I receives one for one good time, Class II one for two good time, and Class III no good time. Thus, a Class I offender (based on institutional behavior) will actually serve only half his time. Since there is no vesting provision, however, the possibility of revocation of vast amounts of good time remains. Every person released before the expiration of the term (which is almost certain to be every prisoner) is placed on parole for the remainder of the sentence, but if parole is not revoked within one year, discharge is mandated. If the prisoner is returned on parole revocation, however, the parole board then functions as a normal parole board, making discretionary decisions as to release. (E.g., if a prisoner serving a ten year sentence is put on parole after five years (earning 50 percent good time), and is then revoked, he is returned to the prison for the remaining five years; his release then depends on the parole board, whose decisions are, apparently, to be as unregulated as they currently are.)

The legislature further made all second felonies ineligible for probation, as well as some first offenders. Clear, Hewitt and Regoli, however, suggest that there is already evidence that prosecutors are bringing charges of "attempt," which do not fall within the exclusion, rather than charges for the consummated offense.

The Indiana legislation has already been subjected to academic criticism. "When determinate sentences are combined with incapacitative and deterrent goals, the results may be harsh sentences that are never regularly enforced and hidden discretionary powers that are regularly abused." [12] Professor von Hirsch also comments: [13] "If Indiana's punishments are commensurate only to the extent that the formal penalty scheme is disregarded, this scarcely speaks for the justice of the formal scheme."

Iowa

In 1978, a bill to establish a sentencing commission composed of five members appointed by the Iowa Supreme Court died in committee and is unlikely to be resuscitated. The commission would have established

[12] See Clear, Hewitt, and Regoli, *supra* note 11 at 445.

[13] Von Hirsch, The New Indiana Sentencing Code, Is It Determinate Sentencing? (presented at a colloquium on the Code, September 1978), at 197.

determinate, presumptive guidelines only for duration, not for the in-out decision. Periods of confinement "shall reflect the average of the periods of confinement actually served by persons convicted in Iowa of committing similar crimes. . . ." The commission was also to have established aggravating and mitigating circumstances. The parole board would have been abolished.

Maine

Maine was the first state to actually take legislative action toward sweeping sentence reform in the mid-1970s. On May 1, 1976, its act abolishing parole and abandoning the indeterminate sentence became effective. Virtually nothing else about the Maine scheme, however, is similar to the just deserts notion. Although judges must select a specific, determinate sentence, the ranges for these sentences are notably broad:

Class	Maximum Term
Murder	Life, or any term with a minimum of twenty-five years
A	20
B	10
C	5
D	1

There is no presumptive sentence, no required minimum, and no list of aggravating and mitigating factors; nor is there appellate review. The discretion of the judge is unlimited and unchecked.

Once sentenced, moreover, the prisoner may obtain reduction of the sentence at any time on motion of the department of corrections to the sentencing judge—merely a new mechanism for parole or at least early relief. Further, good time is earned at the rate of six days per month, with an additional two days per month deducted on the basis of special work assignments.

Massachusetts

The report of a specially established committee to study uniform sentencing procedure is due in December 1978.

Michigan

Michigan is currently considering a kaleidoscope of bills affecting sentencing reforms, many of which would establish pieces of a determinate sentencing scheme. All of these bills are presently in committee. Because their references sometimes vary and sometimes conflict, there is no easy way to summarize their potential effect.

It appears that the bills all agree that the schedule for first offenders should be as follows:

	Presumptive	Minimum	Maximum
Class A	7	3	21
Class B	5	2	15
Class C	3	1	9
Class D	2	0	6
Class E	None	0	3

The bills differ on the sentences for repeat offenders. Leaving aside specific crimes where the sentence for first offenses is unique (mandatory minimum or life), the differences would appear to be:

	Second Offense	Third	Fourth
S.B. 648	Up to 31½	Up to 42	Up to life; Class E—15 yrs.
S.B. 4218	Min of 1 year	Min of 2 years	Min of 20; Class E—4 yrs.
S.B. 1462	Up to 45(A)	Up to 60(A)	Life; Class E—15 years
	30(B)	40(B)	
	15(C)	20(C)	
	7½(D)	10(D)	
	3(E)	4(E)	

There is also a host of complex rules for relatively singular cases, which need not be repeated here.

The various proposals list aggravating and mitigating factors that allow deviation from the presumptive sentence. Some bills would appear to let the sentencer go outside the range, but that seems unlikely in the majority of the bills being considered. Probation appears to be available except in murder or treason or other specifically named offenses.

Appellate review, in the court of appeals, is available for excessive sentences; the court may not increase the sentence. A sentence deviating from the presumptive sentence, but within the maximum and minimum range, will be overturned only for an abuse of discretion.

Good time, apparently nonvesting, is provided at five days per month.

Minnesota

In 1978, Minnesota enacted one of the nation's two statutes providing for a sentencing commission (Illinois being the other). The act provides for a nine member commission; three of the members are designated by title (chief justice, commissioner of corrections, chairman of the Minnesota Corrections Board); four (representing, respectively, public defender, county attorneys, and the public) are appointed by the governor; and two are district court judges appointed by the chief justice. Thus, both the composition of the commission and method of selection are intended to assure diversity and participation by all aspects of the criminal justice system. The commission is an independent body, which tends to assure that it will not unduly reflect the concerns of any one part or constituency, but seek to equitably balance all interests.

The commission is given authority to promulgate guidelines for both the in-out decision and the duration decision, a significant and desirable change from the initial legislative proposals. It is statutorily mandated to establish presumptive sentences; the sentences must reflect both the seriousness of the crime and the offender's characteristics. Again by statute, the range is narrow—the actual sentence allowable by the guidelines may vary from the presumptive sentence by no more than 15 percent. A second offender, for whatever offense, is to receive a minimum of three years.

To avoid the possibility of severe overcrowding (see Chapter 7), the commission is enjoined to "take into substantial consideration" current sentencing and release practices, but is not bound by them. Good time—one day for every two—remains; there is vesting of earned good time, but an infraction can result in the loss of future good time for an appropriate period.

Finally, the commission is expressly empowered to act as a data collector and disperser of information once its guidelines go into effect.

The guidelines become effective four months after they are submitted to the legislature, unless the legislature affirmatively "provides otherwise." This provision is not clear and might allow the legislature to interfere with some parts of the guidelines but not others, a highly undesirable result; instead, the provision should be interpreted to mean that the legislature can only "provide otherwise" as to whether the guidelines take effect at all or whether the commission must try again.

Minnesota's act is unquestionably the best conceived of all sentencing reform legislation thus far passed. By establishing a commission, the legislature has removed the policy decisions one step from public tumult, but has retained ultimate power over the effectiveness of the final result. Furthermore, the composition of the commission is precisely what is necessary—diversity of viewpoints and diversity of selection processes attempt to ensure both negotiation and compromise in the development of rules that directly and importantly affect every part of the criminal justice system. In short, the sentencing commission provisions of the act are quite good indeed and should, with only minor modification, serve as a model to the nation; many of the provisions of the model act proposed in Appendix A are taken verbatim from the Minnesota legislation.

The act further provides for appellate review of sentencing. Here, the language is somewhat more ambiguous. The guidelines established by the commission are said to be "advisory" to the district courts; the appellate review provisions seem to underscore this by providing that the supreme court (which serves as the appellate tribunal) may change any sentence that is "inconsistent with statutory requirements, unreasonable, inappropriate, excessive, unjustifiably disparate, or not warranted by the findings of fact issued by the district court." In short, whether the sentence is inside or outside the guidelines, the supreme court may equally change the sentence. This part of the act is highly debatable; the act would better provide that the guidelines have presumptive weight and that sentences which fall outside the allowable range are presumptively invalid. In practice, however, it is likely that the supreme court would take this position.

Release is automatic at the end of sentence, less good time earned, and there is a period of community supervision equal to the remaining time left to serve on the sentence.

Nebraska

Although there was a legislative report in 1977 recommending determinate sentencing, no legislation to that effect has been introduced in 1978.

New Jersey

Legislation.   In 1978, New Jersey enacted criminal code legislation to become effective September 1, 1979. The legislation did not affect parole at all, so that discretionary parole release is still unfettered.[14] The newly enacted code provides for four classes of felonies, each of which has a presumptive sentence. Variations from the presumptive sentence are allowed upon judicial findings, in writing, of aggravating or mitigating factors. This list includes the typical amalgam of deterrent, rehabilitative, retributive, and incapacitative factors discussed in Chapter 6. The court may also lower the crime by one degree if there are sufficient mitigating factors present.

[14] The governor is expected to introduce in early 1979 a parole reform act that would establish a presumptive parole release date of one-third of the sentence, less good time. This would substantially lessen the otherwise long sentences passed under the legislation described in the text. It is widely assumed that the reform bill will pass.

First offenders of third or fourth degree crimes "should" receive a nonincarcerative sentence; some first and second degree crimes carry a "presumption" of incarceration, but probation is available for all crimes.

The legislation establishes "extended term" sentences for four types of persons: (1) "persistent" offenders (third felony of any kind); (2) a person engaged in any "continuing criminal activity in concert with two or more persons . . . (who) has knowingly devoted himself to criminal activity as a major source of livelihood"; (3) a "dangerous, mentally abnormal person whose commitment for an extended term is necessary for protection of the public"; and (4) a person who committed the crime for hire.

There is no indication in the legislation of a right to appellate review nor of the standard to be applied if there is appellate review. For the past five years or so, however, New Jersey has had appellate review of sentences, but the standard applied ("manifest injustice") and the few reported case law decisions leave little hope that appellate review will be a means of establishing a "common law of sentencing."

The legislation does not establish a sentencing commission, but erects a "Criminal Justice Commission," which is primarily an advisory group to the legislature. The commission has power only to collect data and to report to the legislature.

Judiciary. As indicated in the text, Essex County, New Jersey (Newark), was one of the test sites for sentencing guidelines under the LEAA study headed by Professor Jack Kress. Those guidelines have been challenged as unconstitutional under the state constitution, but have thus far been upheld.[15] The extent to which the judges in Essex County are using the guidelines, however, and the depth of that reliance is not now clear; it appears that they are being used, if at all, only as informational and not directional.

Prior to the passage of the new code, the state administrative office of the courts conducted a massive project to discover the extent of disparity in sentencing in New Jersey. That report was made public on October 23, 1978, and establishes sentencing guidelines for the entire state. The guidelines are offense-specific and are said to be only informational. They have multiple factors that the judge should consider. The complexity of the guidelines and the fact that they reflect past sentencing practices throughout the state makes it likely that it will be some time before they have real effect. Moreover, when the new code becomes effective, the guidelines will be of questionable importance.

[15] State v. Whitehead (No. 2856-76, Essex County Superior Court, May 10, 1978).

New York

In 1977, pursuant to legislative mandate, the New York Parole Division promulgated a matrix system for determining parole release. The axes of the systems, as with other systems, were prior record and present offense. The division was also legislatively instructed, however, that in making individual decisions, institutional adjustment, parole plans, and the risk to the community were to be considered. Therefore, the division provides that the hearing examiner may go outside the matrix guidelines on the basis of aggravating or mitigating circumstances; unfortunately, these are not articulated.

As with other parole guideline systems (Oregon; federal), the issue of disparity on the in-out decision cannot be touched. Good time calculations become essentially irrelevant for purposes of parole release and have meaning only for mandatory release. The guidelines provide actual time served prior to first release as follows:

Prior Criminal History

Class	Good	Fair	Poor	Very Poor
7	12–15 mos.	13–16 mos.	14–17 mos.	15–18 mos.
6	13–18	15–20	18–22	20–24
5	14–20	18–23	22–26	25–29
4	21–24	23–28	27–32	31–36
3	23–28	26–31	29–34	32–40
2	23–38	23–43	38–48	43–53
1	40–70	60–80	70–90	80–120

In short, a level 5 offense has the range, in terms of acual time served, of between 14–29 months; a level 2 offense, between 23–53 months. The board may revise or modify the guidelines in whole or in part.

North Carolina

North Carolina has currently pending a bill on commensurate desert sentencing. The schedule provided in the bill is:

Class	No Priors	Prior Convictions
B	20	25 if prior is class C, D, or E; 30 if class B or two priors of C, D, or E.
C	10	12 if prior is class D or E. 14 if one prior of B or C or two or more class D priors.
D	5	6 if one prior of class E; 7 if one prior of B, C, or D or two or more class E priors.
E	2	3 if one prior of class E; 4 if one prior of class B, C, or D or two or more class E priors.

The judge may raise or lower the presumptive sentence on the basis of aggravating or mitigating factors, some of which are listed in the statute. Probation is available for all offenders. Day for day good time is provided. There is a ninety-day parole period after release.

Ohio

Ohio's determinate sentencing bill would provide the following schedule of punishments:

	First Offense			Second Offense or Higher		
	Presumptive	Minimum	Maximum	Presumptive	Minimum	Maximum
First Degree	8	6	10	15	12	18
Second Degree	5	3	7	9	7	11
Third Degree	3	2	4	6	4	8
Fourth Degree	2	1	3	6	4	8

Variations from the presumptive sentence would be based upon aggravating or mitigating circumstances, which are listed, but are not exclusive. Probation appears to be available to all offenders.

Appellate review in the court of appeals is established, but there does not appear to be an express statutory standard of review.

Day for day good time, vesting every thirty days, is provided, meaning that no more than thirty days can be revoked for any single prison infraction.

Parole does not appear to be expressly retained, but the bill retains "shock parole," initially a concept by which an offender, sentenced for a long period of incarceration, would be released by the judge after six months, just before jurisdiction to alter the sentence expired. The notion was to "shock" the prisoner with the experience of prison. That idea is now codified and allows shock parole under a number of conditions once six months has passed. It is not clear whether "shock" parole must now be effected at six months, or whether, any time after six months, the court may institute it. If the latter, the provision is essentially one for parole as we know it: discretionary release, at any time during the sentence, based primarily upon the risk that the offender presents.

Oregon

In early 1977, the Oregon parole board accepted in principle the notion of just deserts and commensurate sentencing and began to put such principles into action. The board, following the general lead of the U.S. Parole Commission, adopted a matrix approach to determining actual dates of parole release (subject to good institutional behavior). In mid-1977, the legislature essentially ratified this approach, leaving to the board the development of precise guidelines and criteria. The legislature did, however, establish an Advisory Commission on Prison Terms and Parole Standards to work on these guidelines; the Advisory Commission was composed of the five members of the board of parole, five district court judges appointed by the Chief Justice, and to break ties, the governor's counsel.

By March 1978, the Commission had promulgated draft rules, to take effect later that year unless public reaction suggested otherwise. Although the summary below will not always attempt to distinguish between the new rules and the old ones, some changes will be so noted.

The guidelines, then, provide as follows: A matrix, with axes for the severity of the offense and the criminal history of the offender, is generally applied in determining the prisoner's parole release date. Each box in the matrix has a relatively narrow range (six to eight months) for release. Thus, for example, a class 4 offense, committed by an offender with a good criminal history score, will result in a parole release date some sixteen to twenty-two months after sentence. A class 6 offense, committed by a very poor risk offender, will receive a sentence between eighty-six and one hundred and forty-four months.

Obviously, the spans within a given box of the matrix may be narrow (as in the class 4 example) or very broad (as with the class 6 example). In these latter situations the discretion of the parole board is enormous and merely reintroduces the possibility of disparity of durational times. The board has total discretion within those ranges—any time set within the minimum and maximum is allowed. In addition to this, the board may go outside the already flexible matrix when it finds the presence of any mitigating or aggravating factor. These are specified in a long list (Appendix E to the board's rules), which can be extended by the board. The increases (or decreases) of time allowed by the aggravating and mitigating circumstances do not themselves appear to be great; for example, in our "class 4, good history" case, the board is restricted to a six month increase or decrease outside the guidelines. The six month variation also applied to many other offenders—for example, class 3 with a "fair" history. But when added to the already potentially wide range inside the matrix, the total picture resembles the typical discretionary system today in place. Thus, in the "class 4, good history," the original range is sixteen to twenty-two months; with the "aggravating and mitigating" range added, the final range for that one category of offense and offender is ten to twenty-eight months; the maximum is almost three times the minimum, and the additional time is one and one-half years allowable on the basis of one aggravating factor versus one mitigating factor. In the "class 6, very poor" case, the original range is eighty-six to one

hundred and forty-four months; the variation for aggravation or mitigation is twenty-four months. The result is a range of sixty-two to one
hundred and sixty-eight months—a nine year variation. When it is
remembered that this is not the sentence, but actual time served, the
breadth of the ranges is staggering.

The commission has attempted to set some limits—the mere presence of an aggravating or mitigating factor, for example, does not allow
the board simply to go off the charts entirely. Moreover, such factors
must be shown to be present by the preponderance of the evidence, a
substantial safeguard if adhered to honestly.

Unfortunately, this is not the only difficulty with the new parole
guidelines. Additionally, the board may refuse to set parole release
dates for the following persons: (1) a person who has committed a
particularly violent offense; (2) a third time offender convicted of a
class A or B felony; or (3) "where the record includes a psychiatric or
psychological diagnosis of severe emotional disturbance." Furthermore, "Dangerous Offenders," defined under O.R.S. 161.725 and
161.735, need not receive eligibility dates.

Thus, recidivists or "dangerous offenders," either under statutory
definition or parole board application of its own "violent offense"
catagory, will not necessarily receive the benefit of the certainty that is
the hallmark of the desert model, which the guidelines purport to
adopt. In excluding these categories entirely from the guidelines, the
new rules unhappily restore much of the discretion that was the initial
target of the restrictive rules that the board initially adopted.

On the positive side, many of the sentences for "moderate" offenses
appear to be shorter than in other states. See p. 166, *infra.*

Pennsylvania

In November, 1978 Pennsylvania enacted legislation that would
create an eleven member sentencing commission, with appointments
made by the supreme court, both houses of the legislature, and the
governor.[16] The latter, who has three appointments, must appoint a
defense attorney, a prosecutor, and a law professor or criminologist.
After establishing tentative guidelines, the commission must hold
public meetings to allow testimony by the public and by specifically
named groups. The guidelines, which are to work within the
framework of current sentencing law, become effective unless rejected
in their entirety by the legislature. The commission is also to remain in
power to collect data on sentencing and to make further guideline
changes. One provision would declare that in sentencing generally,

---

[16] The analysis here is based on the May 23, 1978, version of the bill.

even before the promulgation of the commission's guidelines, the sentence imposed should call for the (minimum amount of) confinement consistent with gravity of the offense, protection of the public, and the rehabilitative needs of the defendant. The bill removes the words "minimum amount" preceding confinement, which may suggest an incapacitative theme.

The bill would also establish appellate review of sentences and carefully delineate different standards of review for sentences inside and outside the guidelines.

United States

Legislation. In February 1978, the Senate passed S. 1437, the massive federal criminal code reform act. Part of that act was a carefully constructed new sentencing system; while the act had weaknesses in detail, it accepted in scope the notion of presumptive sentencing and restriction of sentencing discretion. A sentencing commission, established in the judicial branch, was to perform the functions suggested in Chapter 4—establishment of sentencing ranges, review of their operation and data gathering, proposals for change, and the like. The purposes by which the commission was to be guided were unfortunately broad and included virtually all utilitarian and desert purposes together. The sentencing provisions of the act were also mixed, and substantial judicial discretion was subject to the commission's ranges. Appellate review was provided, but there was no clear standard of review. Probation was generally available, except in specified crimes or in other specific instances.

The act was hardly "perfect" from the viewpoint of a model of consistency, but it strove mightily in that direction. It is carefully analyzed by Coffee[17] and by Tonry.[18] Nevertheless, the act broke new ground for the federal system and augured to be a bellweather for other systems as well.

Unfortunately, the act died in the House of Representatives Judiciary Committee, which published a totally different code, including a totally different sentencing scheme. Since neither S. 1437, nor its House replacement, H.B. 6869, was passed, it is likely that the new Congress will be required once more to consider these two massively different attempts to codify the federal criminal code.

---

[17] Coffee, *The Repressed Issues of Sentencing: Accountability, Predictability, and Equality in the Era of the Sentencing Commission*, 66 GEO. L.J. 975 (1978).

[18] Tonry, Sentencing Guidelines and Sentencing Commissions—An Assessment of the Sentencing Reform Proposition in the Criminal Code Reform Act of 1977 (unpublished).

Parole. As indicated in other parts of this book, the United States Parole Commission was the inaugurator of attempts to bring consistency to sentencing, at least in terms of those actually sentenced to confinement. Beginning in 1972, the commission undertook a series of steps geared toward equalizing, at least to some degree, the actual times served for persons who had committed the same crime.[19] The history of these steps, and analyses of them, can be found in the work of Gottfredson, Wilkins, and Hoffman.[20]

The form which the "guidelines" took is that of a matrix, one axis of which is the offender's crime, and the other the offender's "salient factor score", a configuration of factors apparently connected with recidivism potential. The most recent matrix, and the most recent salient factor score form, are shown in Table 10–1.

Virginia

A bill similar to the Model Sentencing and Corrections Act died in the Virginia Assembly in 1978, but may be resuscitated in 1979. The bill would have provided statutory maximum sentences, but then established a sentencing commission to promulgate guidelines that could have much lower actual presumptive sentences, maxima and minima. The aggravating and mitigating factors are similar to those of the MSCA.

Appellate review in the Supreme Court of Virginia would have been available, if there was a misapplication of the guidelines or if the sentence was unduly disproportionate to sentences imposed on similar offenders for similar offenses.

Day-to-day good time was provided, but ninety days could be withheld by a disciplinary board, and up to two years could be withheld by the director personally. Parole would cease after a transition period.

Washington

Legislation. Washington currently has pending a carefully thought out and articulate sentencing reform act. It establishes a sixteen person "criminal sanctions board" to promulgate "sentencing standards and guidelines." Seven of the members are members of the parole board; the other nine are the chief justice, the attorney gen-

[19] One difficulty with the board's practice is that it allows the board to deal with the offender on the basis of what he actually did, rather than the offense of which he was convicted, thus undercutting the plea bargain that the defendant may have made.

[20] GUIDELINES FOR PAROLE AND SENTENCING (1978). See also UNITED STATES PAROLE COMMISSION RESEARCH UNIT, SELECTED REPRINTS RELATING TO FEDERAL PAROLE DECISIONMAKING (1977).

Table 10–1. United States Parole Commission Guidelines for Decisionmaking. [Customary total time to be served before release (including jail time)]

Offense Characteristics—Severity of Offense Behavior (examples)	Offender Characteristics—Parole Prognosis (salient factor score)			
	Very good (11 to 9)	Good (8 to 6)	Fair (5 to 4)	Poor (3 to 0)
Adult				
Low: Escape open institution or program (e.g., CTC, work release)—absent less than 7 d; Marihuana or soft drugs, simple possession (small quantity for own use); Property offenses (theft or simple possession of stolen property) less than $1,000	6–10	8–12	10–14	12–18
Low moderate: Alcohol law violations; Counterfeit currency (passing/possession less than $1,000); Immigration law violations; Income tax evasion (less than $10,000); Property offenses (forgery/fraud/theft from mail/embezzlement/interstate transportation of stolen or forged securities/receiving stolen property with intent to resell) less than $1,000; Selective Service Act Violations	8–12	12–16	16–20	20–28
Moderate: Bribery of a public official (offering or accepting); Counterfeit currency (passing possession $1,000 to $19,999); Drugs: Marihuana, possession with intent to distribute/sale (small scale (e.g., less than 50 lb)); "Soft drugs", possession with intent to distribute/sale (less than $500); Escape (secure program or institution, or absent 7 d or more—no fear or threat used); Firearms Act, possession/purchase/sale (single weapon: not sawed-off shotgun or machine gun); Income tax evasion ($10,000 to $50,000); Mailing threatening communication(s); Misprison of felony; Property offenses (theft/forgery/fraud/embezzlement/interstate transportation of stolen or forged securities/receiving stolen property) $1,000 to $19,999; Smuggling/transporting of alien(s); Theft of motor vehicle (not multiple theft or for resale)	12–16	16–20	20–24	24–32

High:
  Counterfeit currency (passing/possession $20,000 to $100,000)
  Counterfeiting (manufacturing)
  Drugs:
    Marihuana, possession with intent to distribute/sale (medium scale (e.g., 50 to 1,999 lb))
    "Soft drugs", possession with intent to distribute/sale ($500 to $5,000)
  Explosives, possession/transportation
  Firearms Act, possession/purchase/sale (sawed-off shotgun(s), machine gun(s), or multiple weapons)
  Mann Act (no force—commercial purposes)
  Theft of motor vehicle for resale
  Property offenses (theft/forgery/fraud/embezzlement/interstate transportation of stolen or forged securities/receiving stolen property) $20,000 to $100,000

15–20	20–26	26–34	34–40

Very high:
  Robbery (weapon or threat)
  Breaking and entering (bank or post office-entry or attempted entry to vault)
  Drugs:
    Marihuana, possession with intent to distribute/sale (large scale (e.g., 2,000 lb or more))
    "Soft drugs", possession with intent to distribute/sale (over $5,000)
    "Hard drugs", possession with intent to distribute/sale (not exceeding $100,000)
  Extortion
  Mann Act (force)
  Property offenses (theft/forgery/fraud/embezzlement/interstate transportation of stolen or forged securities/receiving stolen property) over $100,000 but not exceeding $500,000
  Sexual act (force)

26–36	36–48	48–60	60–72

Greatest I: Aggravated felony (e.g., robbery: Weapon fired—no serious injury); explosive detonation (involving potential risk of physical injury to person(s)—no serious injury occurred); robbery (multiple instances (2–3)). Hard drugs (possession with intent to distribute/sale—large scale (e.g., over $100,000)); sexual act—force (e.g., forcible rape)

Greatest II: Aggravated felony—serious injury (e.g., injury involving substantial risk of death, or protracted disability, or disfigurement); aircraft hijacking; espionage; kidnapping; homicide (intentional or committed during other crime)

40 to 55	55 to 70	70 to 85	85 to 110

Greater than above—however, specific ranges are not given due to the limited number of cases and the extreme variation possible within the category.

161

Table 10–1. continued

SALIENT FACTOR SCORE

Case name .... Register. No. .... □ □

Item A .... □

No prior convictions (adult or juvenile) = 3.
1 prior conviction = 2.
2 or 3 prior convictions = 1.
4 or more prior convictions = 0.

Item B .... □

No prior incarcerations (adult or juvenile) = 2.
1 or 2 prior incarcerations = 1.
3 or more prior incarcerations = 0.

Item C .... □

Age at first commitment (adult or juvenile):
26 or older = 2.
18 to 25 = 1.
17 or younger = 0.

Item D .... □

Commitment offense did not involve auto theft or check(s) (forgery/larceny) = 1.
Commitment offense involved auto theft or check(s) = 0.

Item E .... □

Never had parole revoked or been committed for a new offense while on parole, and not a probation violator this time = 1.
Has had parole revoked or been committed for a new offense while on parole, or is a probation violator this time = 0.

Item F .... □

No history of heroin or opiate dependence = 1.
Otherwise = 0.

Item G .... □

Verified employment (or full-time school attendance) for a total of at least 6 mo during the last 2 yr in the community = 1.
Otherwise = 0.

Total score .... □

162

eral, the director of the department of social services, and six persons appointed by the governor (three of whom must be a sitting judge, a prosecutor, and a criminal defense attorney). The board's rules, once promulgated, take effect unless the legislature remands them for consideration. Once the standards are adopted, the nine non–parole board members drop off.

The statute sets out the parameters of the guidelines and differentiates sentences for each class of offense and for recidivists within that class. The additional sentence for prior offenses depends primarily upon the class of prior offense and the number of priors. There are explicit definitions of "violent offenses" and "persistently violent offenders" that increase the sentences or make an offender ineligible for probation.

The proposed act also establishes appellate review of sentences by regional "sentence review panels" of three superior court judges and the standards for review—if the sentence is "clearly excessive (or lenient)." No review of a sentence within the board's guidelines is allowed; any sentence not within the guidelines will carry with it an effective presumption of invalidity, which must be overcome on appeal.

Probation is available only to persons not convicted of a "violent offense" or to a first offender of a nonviolent offense. Specific conditions of probation are listed. Good time appears to be abolished.

The penalties outlined in the act are quite low, generally—Class B felonies carry a presumptive sentence of one year, if the offender has no priors, and a maximum of three years if the crime was not violent and if the offender has two or less priors and none of them is violent. A persistently violent offender convicted of a Class B offense may receive a sentence between eight and ten years, but only if the crime of conviction was a violent one; otherwise the maximum is five years. Similar restrictions are placed on other sentences, although the court may impose an "exceptional" sentence outside these ranges if "excessive danger" to the public would occur. The board is instructed, in establishing the sentences, to consider the conditions of prisons and jails, but not the bedspace available.

Finally, the act takes the first few tentative steps toward regulating plea bargaining, the first such attempt in the country.

Parole. While the legislature is contemplating this act, the parole board has already promulgated rules and regulations that are the most complex of any such regulations in the country. They establish fourteen classes of crimes, ranging from very specific (forcible rape) to generic terms (theft, drug offenses). Each crime carries a base term, the minimum of time to be served before considering action for parole.

Each crime additionally carries a series of aggravating factors, some very detailed indeed, that increase the base term by a highly specific amount of time. Thus, the base time for murder is forty-two months. There are nine aggravating factors, ranging from "victim forced to another location" (increase of twelve months) to "victim was vulnerable" (thirty-six months) to "weapon only by offender" (eighteen months).

The aggravating factors are sometimes excruciatingly detailed (see Chapter 6 for Washington's provisions on the vulnerable victim of rape, by age). Also, the amount of increased time that a single factor will bring varies with the offense. Thus, "physical force by offender" increases the murder sentence by eighteen months, manslaughter by forty-two months, and a sexual molestation sentence by nine months. (The sentences in the first two cases therefore become sixty months for murder (forty-two base plus eighteen increase), but sixty-nine for manslaughter (twenty-seven base plus forty-two for physical force).

Variations are allowed on the basis of aggravating or mitigating factors not otherwise declared. The variation allowed depends on the guideline term. Similarly, prior crimes increase the base term, but again by a specific number of months depending both on the prior offense and the present offense. Thus, a prior crime of robbery adds twenty-four months if the present crime is murder, twelve months for assault, and six months for a drug offense. A prior conviction of assault adds twenty-four months for assault, manslaughter, or murder; twelve for sex or robbery; and six for property or drugs.

It seems clear that the Washington legislation and the parole board guidelines are symbolic—both attempt to vary sentences on the basis of both new crime and prior record, with specifics in each. Similarly, the aggravating and mitigating factors notion is sliced exceptionally thin by the parole board, and the legislation carries the same flavor.

Wisconsin

In 1978, the Wisconsin Assembly passed joint resolution 79, mandating the legislative council to study possible revisions of the sentencing system, including possible determinate sentences and parole abolition. That study is now being conducted. The legislature has already considered one such bill (A.B. 828), but it was not reported out of committee.

* * *

This analysis, however sketchy, of the enacted, pending, and rejected legislation and administrative and judicial action demonstrates the ambiguity of the data. It is rarely a question of whether the glass is half full or half empty. In some very meaningful ways, the states have attempted to reorient their sentencing schemes around a model of restricted judicial discretion. On the other hand, in a number of these jurisdictions, that attempt seems, at least initially, to have gone awry. The wide ranges of sentences, for example in Indiana, Maine and Illinois; the availability of probation as an alternative to imprisonment for many crimes; and the numerous variations of treatment for recidivists or "dangerous" offenders are clear indications that the thrust of the desert/equality model of sentencing, which focuses on the crime and eschews prediction, has not been fully implemented.

Moreover, the enormous differences among the states leaves little hope that there will be anything like equality among the jurisdictions. Interstate comparisons are exceptionally difficult, given the differences of definitions of crimes, as well as the provisions for good time, probation, and other possible variations from sentences that may occur. Nevertheless, even a dip in the pond may be illuminating. The charts in Table 10–2, intended to indicate likely release dates in five states for four typical crimes, are based upon the following assumptions: (1) the likely sentence is the presumptive sentence or, where there is no presumptive sentence, the midpoint in the allowable range(s); and (2) the prisoner earns the maximum amount of good time possible. They demonstrate the wide range of sanctions possible for the same offense by an offender with the same prior records. No aggravating or mitigating circumstances are considered.[21]

The distressing disparity shown here leaves little hope that either inter- or intrajurisdictional equity will result. But perhaps that is too quick a conclusion. Perhaps the actual record of the use of these provisions, within one jurisdiction, will be better than one might anticipate: perhaps the trial courts will not vary the sentences as much as they could or as much as the loose wording of the statutes clearly permits. Perhaps the spirit of the new law will govern its letter.

Here, however, the few facts we have are no more encouraging. Since most sentencing change has occurred so recently, there is really no information on whether judges, parole boards, prosecutors, and so forth have misused the process (leaving aside, of course, the extent to which the legislature has, either knowingly or not, failed to achieve anything like a deserts process). But there are data from one location—California. Before we cast too heavy a shroud over the possible abuses to which the present legislation could lead, we should at least examine the sketchy data from California. California, after all,

---

[21] Even this comparison is suspect. Maine retains a form of "parole release," so that its numbers are high. Illinois' figures are based upon current statutory maxima, but the Sentencing Commission may lower these.

Table 10–2. Average Actual Time Served Under Selected Determinate Models—Four Offenses.

State	Likely Sentence (in years)	Good Time (in years)	Release (in years)
Forcible Rape—First Offense			
Maine	10	2	8
California	4	1 1/3	2 2/3
Indiana	10	5	5
Illinois	18	9	9
Oregon	—	—	5
Narcotics Dealing—First Offense			
Maine	5	1	4
California	4	1 1/3	2 2/3
Indiana	30	15	15
Illinois	10	5	5
Oregon	—	—	1 1/2
Simple Burglary—2 Priors			
Maine	2 1/2	1/2	2
California	5	1 2/3	3 1/3
Indiana	20	10	10
Illinois	18	9	9
Oregon	—	—	4
Simple Burglary—First Offense			
Maine	2 1/2	1/2	2
California	2	2/3	1 1/3
Indiana	5	1	4
Illinois	5	2 1/2	2 1/2
Oregon	—	—	1 1/2

has legislation which is the closest, at least on paper, to the presumptive sentencing model; there is a narrow range, with a middle normal sentence; while increases are possible, there must be findings of facts, with relatively specified parameters. Parole is abolished, and good time is virtually automatic. If, thus far, there is any jurisdiction that has hopes of achieving something like equality of sentences, California would appear to be it. Let us look, then, at the data we now have.[22]

THE CALIFORNIA DATA

California Penal Code Section 1170.4 instructs the judicial council to collect and disseminate data on sentencing under the new penal code,

---

[22] LEAA has recently announced a large grant for the purpose of studying the California system; that study, which will be ready in about two years, will obviously be based upon more data than we now have. These conclusions, then, are highly tentative.

which has been described in the previous section. Carrying out this mandate, the council has published a quarterly periodical entitled *Sentencing Practices Quarterly.*[23] The *Quarterly* is almost exclusively statistical; there is no attempt in narrative form to describe sentencing practices nor to go behind the figures to determine, for example, the effect that prosecutorial charging decisions have upon sentencing.[24] Instead, the *Quarterly* reflects only the end result of the sentencing process. Thus, the information is somewhat incomplete and certainly cannot be held conclusive. Nonetheless, the information that the data do provide may be useful in determining the effect of a just deserts sentencing model. This analysis is based on the *Quarterly* published in September, 1978.

Tables 10–3 and 10–4 provide some disturbing data for the advocate of equality in sentencing. As was true in prereform days, it appears that the vast bulk of offenders, and clearly the majority of all offenders except for homicides and robberies, are receiving no prison sentence at all. Thus, only 27 percent of assaults, 31 percent of sexual offenses, and 9 percent of family offenses resulted in prison sentences. In property crimes, not a single offense resulted in more than a 40 percent imprisonment rate, and in many instances, the rate was well below one-third. In such a situation, the availability of probation appears to have undermined the notion that persons who commit similar crimes should be punished similarly.

In fact, the facial appearance may be misleading. Although the records indicate a high percentage of "nonincarceration," other information from that same report declares that of persons placed on probation, between 70–85 percent were required, as a condition of probation, to spend some time in jail. Indeed, the overall incarceration rate, both jail and prison, was somewhere near seventy-five percent.[25] This figure, however, is still misleading, for it does not acknowledge that the amount of time spent in jail or on probation is surely much less than the average time spent in prison, if the sentence is one of imprisonment.[26]

A supporter of controlled sentencing might then analyze the California data to suggest that, in effect, notwithstanding the legisla-

---

[23] Available from Administrative Office of the Courts, Judicial Council of California, 601 McAllister St., San Francisco, CA 94102.

[24] This is one of the tasks to be undertaken in the LEAA study.

[25] CALIFORNIA JUDICIAL COUNCIL, SENTENCING PRACTICES QUARTERLY 7 (Sept. 1978).

[26] The use of jail as a condition of probation was widespread in California prior to the adoption of the new law; its continuance suggests that nothing much has really changed. Furthermore, there are serious questions as to whether, as a penological matter, probation conditioned on the service of some jail time is either sensible or effective. Those questions, of course, are not relevant here, but they should be noted to suggest that the courts either think the practice is sound (from what viewpoint?) or do not care.

Table 10–3. Superior Court Dispositions of Persons Convicted of Felonies and Alternate Felony/Misdemeanors (By most serious crime if multiple convictions)—State Total—Quarter Ending 12/31/77.

Code and Section	Crime or Category	Total Number of Cases	State Prison Sentences			
			Total		Determinate Number	Indeterminate Number
			Number	Percent of all Dispositions		
	CRIMES AGAINST PERSONS					
	HOMICIDES					
PC187*	Murder, first degree	[Not tabulated due to special sentencing rules]				
PC187**	Murder, second degree	87	75	(86)	14	61
PC192(1)	Voluntary Manslaughter	83	51	(61)	17	34
PC192(3)\(a)	Vehicular manslaughter—gross negligence	53	8	(15)	4	4
[A]	Other homicides and attempts	72	38	(53)	0	38
	TOTAL HOMICIDES	295	172	(58)	35	137
	ROBBERIES					
PC211	Robbery [includes first and second degree crimes committed before 7/1/77]	898	550	(61)	217	333
[B]	Other robberies and attempts	59	17	(29)	8	9
	TOTAL ROBBERIES	957	567	(59)	225	342
	ASSAULTIVE BEHAVIOR					
PC242	Battery on a peace officer	106	14	(13)	8	6
PC245(a)	Assault wih a deadly weapon	549	162	(30)	59	103
[C]	Other assaultive behavior on a peace officer	61	19	(31)	11	8
[D]	Other assaultive behavior	97	27	(28)	15	12
	TOTAL ASSAULTIVE BEHAVIOR	813	222	(27)	93	129

Code	Category					
	SEXUAL OFFENSES					
C261(2)+(3)	Forcible rape	109	70	(64)	20	50
PC288	Lewd acts on child	125	20	(16)	3	17
[E]	Other prohibited intercourse and attempts	69	13	(19)	5	8
[F]	Other sexual offenses	85	19	(22)	3	16
	TOTAL SEXUAL OFFENSES	388	122	(31)	31	91
	KIDNAPPING					
[G]	Kidnapping, false imprisonment and attempts	52	15	(29)	4	11
	FAMILY OFFENSES					
[H]	Family offenses	44	4	(9)	0	4
	TOTAL CRIMES AGAINST PERSONS	2549	1102	(43)	388	714
	CRIMES AGAINST PROPERTY					
	ARSON					
[I]	Arsons, burnings and attempts	64	12	(19)	3	9
	BURGLARIES					
PC459*	Burglary, first degree	299	111	(37)	44	67
PC459**	Burglary, second degree	1764	537	(30)	216	321
PC459/664	Attempted burglary	70	16	(23)	9	7
	TOTAL BURGLARIES	2133	664	(31)	269	395
	THEFT					
PC487(1)	Grand theft—amount over $200	346	73	(21)	12	61
PC487(2)	Grand theft—person	235	59	(25)	14	45
PC487(3)	Grand theft—auto	122	39	(32)	9	30
VC10851	Vehicle theft	288	67	(23)	30	37
PC666	Petty theft with a prior	58	19	(33)	9	10
[J]	Other thefts and attempts	49	9	(18)	5	4
	TOTAL THEFTS	1098	266	(24)	79	187

Table 10-3. continued

Code and Section	Crime or Category	Total Number of Cases	State Prison Sentences		Deter-minate Number	In-deter-minate Number
			Total			
			Num-ber	Percent of all Dis-positions		
	FRAUDS, FORGERIES AND EMBEZZLEMENTS					
PC470	Forgery	288	96	(33)	25	71
PC476a	Issuing check with insufficient funds	144	40	(28)	9	31
W11483(2)	Welfare fraud	122	3	(2)	0	3
[K]	Credit card offenses	65	12	(18)	5	7
[L]	Other frauds, forgeries, and embezzlements	89	22	(25)	9	13
	TOTAL FRAUDS, FORGERIES, AND EMBEZZLEMENTS	708	173	(24)	(48)	(125)
	OTHER CRIMES AGAINST PROPERTY					
PC496	Receiving stolen property	517	112	(22)	29	83
[M]	Other crimes against property	43	2	(5)	0	2
	TOTAL OTHER CRIMES AGAINST PROPERTY	560	114	(21)	29	85
	TOTAL CRIMES AGAINST PROPERTY	4563	1229	(27)	428	801
	DRUG LAW VIOLATIONS					
HS11350	Possession of narcotics, opiates, morphine, heroin, etc.	383	100	(26)	17	83
HS11351	Possession for sale of same	196	84	(43)	18	66
HS11352	Sale of same	344	99	(29)	17	82
HS11357	Possession of concentrated cannabis	68	1	(1)	1	0
HS11359	Possession for sale of marijuana	100	7	(7)	3	4
HS11360	Sale of marijuana	135	9	(7)	0	9

Code	Offense					
HS11377	Possession of nonnarcotic dangerous drugs, LSD, etc.	133	15	(11)	4	11
HS11378	Possession for sale of same	62	9	(15)	1	8
HS11379	Sale of same	111	10	(9)	1	9
[N]	Other controlled substance violations	57	7	(12)	1	6
[O]	Other drug law violations	81	17	(21)	1	16
	TOTAL DRUG LAW VIOLATIONS	1670	358	(21)	64	294
	PENAL INSTITUTION OFFENSES					
PC4532	Escape from jail	98	22	(22)	10	12
[P]	Contraband offenses	68	15	(22)	10	5
[Q]	Other penal institution offenses	58	43	(74)	24	19
	TOTAL PENAL INSTITUTION OFFENSES	224	80	(36)	44	36
	OTHER OFFENSES					
PC12021	Felon with a firearm	103	44	(43)	20	24
[R]	Other weapon and explosive offenses	63	8	(13)	2	6
VC23101	Felony drunk driving	120	12	(10)	5	7
PC32	Accessory	67	9	(13)	0	9
PC182	Conspiracy	52	12	(23)	2	10
[S]	Other offenses	122	8	(7)	2	6
	TOTAL OTHER OFFENSES	527	93	(18)	31	62
	TOTAL—ALL OFFENSES	9533	2862	(30)	955	1907

Table 10-3. continued

Code and Section	Crime or Category	Total Number of Cases	Probation — Total: Number	Probation — Total: Percent of all Dispositions	Probation — Percent of Probation Dispositions: With Jail as Condition	Probation — Percent of Probation Dispositions: Without Jail as Condition
	CRIMES AGAINST PERSONS					
	HOMICIDES					
PC187*	Murder, first degree		[Not tabulated due to special sentencing rules]			
PC187**	Murder, second degree	87	0	(—)	—	—
PC192(1)	Voluntary Manslaughter	83	30	(36)	(8)	(13)
PC192(3)(a)	Vehicular manslaughter—gross negligence	53	39	(74)	(92)	(8)
[A]	Other homicides and attempts	72	31	(43)	(87)	(13)
	TOTAL HOMICIDES	205	100	(34)	(89)	(11)
	ROBBERIES					
PC211	Robbery [includes first and second degree crimes committed before 7/1/77]	898	214	(24)	(89)	(11)
[B]	Other robberies and attempts	59	27	(46)	(85)	(15)
	TOTAL ROBBERIES	957	241	(25)	(89)	(11)
	ASSAULTIVE BEHAVIOR					
PC242	Battery on a peace officer	106	72	(68)	(64)	(36)
PC245(a)	Assault with a deadly weapon	549	321	(58)	(81)	(19)
[C]	Other assaultive behavior on a peace officer	61	28	(46)	(57)	(43)
[D]	Other assaultive behavior	97	56	(58)	(80)	(20)
	TOTAL ASSAULTIVE BEHAVIOR	813	477	(59)	(77)	(23)

Code		Col 1	Col 2	(%)	(%)	(%)
	SEXUAL OFFENSES					
PC261(2)+(3)	Forcible rape	109	18	(17)	(67)	(33)
PC288	Lewd acts on child	125	69	(55)	(62)	(38)
[E]	Other prohibited intercourse and attempts	69	48	(70)	(77)	(23)
[F]	Other sexual offenses	85	55	(65)	(62)	(38)
	TOTAL SEXUAL OFFENSES	388	190	(49)	(66)	(34)
	KIDNAPPING					
[G]	Kidnapping, false imprisonment and attempts	52	31	(60)	(87)	(13)
	FAMILY OFFENSES					
[H]	Family offenses	44	35	(80)	(66)	(34)
	TOTAL CRIMES AGAINST PERSONS	2549	1074	(42)	(79)	(21)
	CRIMES AGAINST PROPERTY					
	ARSON					
[I]	Arsons, burning and attempts	64	43	(67)	(60)	(40)
	BURGLARIES					
PC459*	Burglary, first degree	209	151	(51)	(87)	(13)
PC459**	Burglary, second degree	1764	967	(55)	(81)	(19)
PC459/664	Attempted burglary	70	47	(67)	(77)	(23)
	TOTAL BURGLARIES	2133	1165	(55)	(81)	(19)
	THEFT					
PC487(1)	Grand theft—amount over $200	346	223	(64)	(66)	(34)
PC487(2)	Grand theft—person	235	147	(63)	(89)	(11)
PC487(3)	Grand theft—auto	122	66	(54)	(83)	(17)
VC10851	Vehicle theft	288	164	(57)	(86)	(14)
PC666	Petty theft with a prior	58	32	(55)	(84)	(16)
[J]	Other thefts and attempts	49	32	(65)	(81)	(19)
	TOTAL THEFTS	1098	664	(60)	(79)	(21)

Table 10-3. continued

Code and Section	Crime or Category	Total Number of Cases	Probation		Percent of Probation Dispositions	
			Total		**With Jail as Condition**	**Without Jail as Condition**
			Number	Percent of all Dispositions		
	FRAUDS, FORGERIES AND EMBEZZLEMENTS					
PC470	Forgery	288	160	(56)	(78)	(22)
PC476a	Issuing check with insufficient funds	144	91	(63)	(67)	(33)
W11483(2)	Welfare fraud	122	113	(93)	(58)	(42)
[K]	Credit card offenses	65	42	(65)	(79)	(21)
[L]	Other frauds, forgeries, and embezzlements	89	55	(62)	(65)	(35)
	TOTAL FRAUDS, FORGERIES, AND EMBEZZLEMENTS	708	461	(65)	(69)	(31)
	OTHER CRIMES AGAINST PROPERTY					
PC496	Receiving stolen property	517	317	(61)	(80)	(20)
[M]	Other crimes against proptery	43	40	(93)	(52)	(48)
	TOTAL OTHER CRIMES AGAINST PROPERTY	560	357	(64)	(77)	(23)
	TOTAL CRIMES AGAINST PROPERTY	4563	2690	(59)	(78)	(22)
	DRUG LAW VIOLATIONS					
HS11350	Possession of narcotics, opiates, morphine, heroin, etc.	383	248	(65)	(75)	(25)
HS11351	Possession for sale of same	196	94	(48)	(88)	(12)
HS11352	Sale of same	344	205	(66)	(80)	(20)
HS11357	Possession of concentrated cannabis	68	50	(74)	(62)	(38)

Code	Offense					
HS11359	Possession for sale of marijuana	100	90	(90)	(78)	(22)
HS11360	Sale of marijuana	135	125	(93)	(69)	(31)
HS11377	Possession of nonnarcotic dangerous drugs, LSD, etc.	133	104	(78)	(63)	(37)
HS1378	Possession for sale of same	62	49	(79)	(78)	(22)
HS11379	Sale of same	111	98	(88)	(79)	(21)
[N]	Other controlled substance violations	57	45	(79)	(64)	(36)
[O]	Other drug law violations	81	56	(69)	(62)	(38)
	TOTAL DRUG LAW VIOLATIONS	1670	1164	(70)	(74)	(26)
	PENAL INSTITUTION OFFENSES					
PC4532	Escape from jail	98	38	(39)	(89)	(11)
[P]	Contraband offenses	68	44	(65)	(86)	(14)
[Q]	Other penal institution offenses	58	12	(21)	(92)	(8)
	TOTAL PENAL INSTITUTION OFFENSES	224	94	(42)	(88)	(12)
	OTHER OFFENSES					
PC12021	Felon with a firearm	103	52	(50)	(83)	(17)
[R]	Other weapon and explosive offenses	63	41	(65)	(71)	(29)
VC23101	Felony drunk driving	120	99	(82)	(80)	(20)
PC32	Accessory	67	45	(67)	(71)	(29)
PC182	Conspiracy	52	37	(71)	(70)	(30)
[S]	Other offenses	122	94	(77)	(60)	(40)
	TOTAL OTHER OFFENSES	527	368	(70)	(72)	(28)
	TOTAL—ALL OFFENSES	9533	5390	(57)	(77)	(23)

Table 10-3. continued

Code and Section	Crime or Category	Total Number of Cases	Total — Number	Total — Percent of all Dispositions	Percent of Misdemeanor Sentences — With Jail	Percent of Misdemeanor Sentences — Without Jail	Other Dispositions — Number	Other Dispositions — Percent of all Dispositions
	CRIMES AGAINST PERSONS							
	HOMICIDES							
		[Not tabulated due to special sentencing rules]						
PC187*	Murder, first degree	87	0	(—)	—	—	12	(14)
PC187**	Murder, second degree	83	0	(—)	—	—	2	(2)
PC192(1)	Voluntary Manslaughter	53	4	(8)	(75)	(25)	2	(4)
PC192(3)(a)	Vehicular manslaughter—gross negligence	72	0	(—)	—	(25)	3	(4)
[A]	Other homicides and attempts							
	TOTAL HOMICIDES	295	4	(1)	(75)	(25)	19	(6)
	ROBBERIES							
PC211	Robbery [includes first and second degree crimes committed before 7/1/77]	898	0	(—)	—	—	134	(15)
[B]	Other robberies and attempts	59	0	(—)	—	—	15	(25)
	TOTAL ROBBERIES	957	0	(—)	—	—	149	(16)
	ASSAULTIVE BEHAVIOR							
PC242	Battery on a peace officer	106	12	(11)	(83)	(17)	8	(8)
PC245(a)	Assault with a deadly weapon	549	25	(5)	(64)	(36)	41	(7)
[C]	Other assaultive behavior on a peace officer	61	10	(16)	(70)	(30)	4	(7)
[D]	Other assaultive behavior	97	4	(4)	(75)	(25)	10	(10)
	TOTAL ASSAULTIVE BEHAVIOR	813	51	(6)	(71)	(29)	63	(8)

	SEXUAL OFFENSES							
PC261(2)+(3)	Forcible rape	109	0	(—)	—	—	21	(19)
PC288	Lewd acts on child	125	0	(—)	—	—	36	(29)
[E]	Other prohibited intercourse and attempts	69	3	(4)	(—)	(100)	5	(7)
[F]	Other sexual offenses	85	1	(1)	(100)	(—)	10	(12)
	TOTAL SEXUAL OFFENSES	388	4	(1)	(25)	(75)	72	(19)
	KIDNAPPING							
[G]	Kidnapping, false imprisonment and attempts	52	3	(6)	(33)	(67)	3	(6)
	FAMILY OFFENSES							
[H]	Family offenses	44	2	(5)	(50)	(50)	3	(7)
	TOTAL CRIMES AGAINST PERSONS	2549	64	(3)	(66)	(34)	309	(12)
	CRIMES AGAINST PROPERTY							
	ARSON							
[I]	Arsons, burnings and attempts	64	0	(—)	—	—	9	(14)
	BURGLARIES							
PC459*	Burglary, first degree	299	0	(—)	—	—	37	(12)
PC459**	Burglary, second degree	1764	70	(4)	(81)	(19)	190	(11)
PC459/664	Attempted burglary	70	2	(3)	(100)	(—)	5	(7)
	TOTAL BURGLARIES	2133	72	(3)	(82)	(18)	232	(11)
	THEFT							
PC487(1)	Grand theft—amount over $200	346	22	(6)	(59)	(41)	28	(8)
PC487(2)	Grand theft—person	235	10	(4)	(90)	(10)	19	(8)
PC487(3)	Grand theft—auto	122	8	(7)	(88)	(12)	9	(7)
VC10851	Vehicle theft	288	23	(8)	(78)	(22)	34	(12)
PC666	Petty theft with a prior	58	4	(7)	(100)	(—)	3	(5)
[J]	Other thefts and attempts	49	5	(10)	(100)	(—)	3	(6)
	TOTAL THEFTS	1098	72	(7)	(78)	(22)	96	(9)

Table 10-3. continued

Code and Section	Crime or Category	Total Number of Cases	Misdemeanor Sentences after Conviction of Crime Punishable Alternatively as Felony or Misdemeanor				Other Dispositions	
			Total		Percent of Misdemeanor Sentences			
			Number	Percent of all Dispositions	With Jail	Without Jail	Number	Percent of all Dispositions
	FRAUDS, FORGERIES AND EMBEZZLEMENTS							
PC470	Forgery	283	10	(3)	(90)	(10)	22	(8)
PC476a	Issuing check with insufficient funds	144	6	(4)	(50)	(50)	7	(5)
W11483(2)	Welfare fraud	122	5	(4)	(60)	(40)	1	(1)
[K]	Credit card offenses	65	5	(8)	(80)	(20)	6	(9)
[L]	Other frauds, forgeries, and embezzlements	89	5	(6)	(60)	(40)	7	(8)
	TOTAL FRAUDS, FORGERIES, AND EMBEZZLEMENTS	708	31	(4)	(71)	(29)	43	(6)
	OTHER CRIMES AGAINST PROPERTY							
PC496	Receiving stolen property	517	41	(8)	(78)	(22)	47	(9)
[M]	Other crimes against property	43	0	(—)	—	—	1	(2)
	TOTAL OTHER CRIMES AGAINST PROPERTY	560	41	(7)	(78)	(22)	48	(9)
	TOTAL CRIMES AGAINST PROPERTY	4563	216	(5)	(78)	(22)	428	(9)

DRUG LAW VIOLATIONS

Code	Offense							
HS11350	Possession of narcotics, opiates, morphine, heroin, etc.	383	0	(—)	—	—	35	(9)
HS11351	Possession for sale of same	196	0	(—)	—	—	18	(9)
HS11352	Sale of same	344	16	(5)	(50)	(50)	40	(12)
HS11357	Possession of concentrated cannabis	68	0	(—)	—	—	1	(1)
HS11359	Possession for sale of marijuana	100	0	(—)	—	—	3	(3)
HS11360	Sale of marijuana	135			—	—	1	(1)
HS11377	Possession of nonnarcotic dangerous drugs, LSD, etc.	133	11	(8)	(73)	(27)	3	(2)
HS11378	Possession for sale of same	62	0	(—)	—	—	4	(6)
HS11379	Sale of same	111	0	(—)	—	—	3	(3)
[N]	Other controlled substance violations	57	3	(5)	(100)	(—)	2	(4)
[O]	Other drug law violations	81	3	(4)	(100)	(—)	5	(6)
	TOTAL DRUG LAW VIOLATIONS	1670	33	(2)	(67)	(33)	115	(7)

PENAL INSTITUTION OFFENSES

Code	Offense							
PC4532	Escape from jail	98	29	(30)	(100)	(—)	9	(9)
[P]	Contraband offenses	68	0	(—)	—	—	9	(13)
[Q]	Other penal institution offenses	58	1	(2)	(100)	(—)	2	(3)
	TOTAL PENAL INSTITUTION OFFENSES	224	30	(13)	(100)	(—)	20	(9)

OTHER OFFENSES

Code	Offense							
PC12021	Felon with a firearm	103	7	(7)	(100)	(—)	0	(—)
[R]	Other weapon and explosive offenses	63	4	(6)	(50)	(50)	10	(16)
VC23101	Felony drunk driving	120	4	(3)	(100)	(—)	5	(4)
PC32	Accessory	67	7	(10)	(86)	(14)	6	(9)
PC182	Conspiracy	52	0	(—)	—	—	3	(6)
[S]	Other offenses	122	13	(11)	(38)	(62)	7	(6)
	TOTAL OTHER OFFENSES	527	35	(7)	(69)	(31)	31	(6)
	TOTAL—ALL OFFENSES	9533	378	(4)	(76)	(24)	903	(9)

Table 10-3. continued

[A] PC187*/664:PC187**/664;PC192(2).

[B] PC211/664;PC214/664.

[C] PC240;PC245(b); PC417(b).

[D] PC136(b); PC136(b)/664; PC217; PC220; PC221; PC222; PC244; PC246; VC23110(b).

[E] PC261(1); PC261(2)+(3)/664; PC261.5; PC261.5/664; PC264.1.

[F] PC266; PC266f; PC266h; PC266i; PC285; PC286; PC288/664; PC288a; PC314.

[G] PC207; PC207/664; PC209; PC236.

[H] PC270; PC273a(1); PC273d; PC278; PC278.5.

[I] PC447a; PC448a; PC449a; PC449b; PC449c; PC450a; PC451a; PC452.

[J] PC485; PC487/664; PC667; VC10851/664.

[K] PC484e(4); PC484f; PC484f/664; PC484g.

[L] I1916.3; CC30.20(a); CC3020(a); CC25110; IC556; PC424; PC470a; PC472; PC474; PC475; PC475a; PC476; PC484b; PC502.7(f); PC503; PC504a; PC508; PC529 (3); PC530; PC532; PC548; PC548/664; RT19406; VC4463; W118910.

[M] PC496/664; PC518; PC518/664; PC524; PC593; PC594(b).

[N] HS11355; HS11366; HS11382; HS11382/664; HS11500.5; HS11910; HS11911; HS11912.

[O] BP4390; HS11173; HS11358; HS11361; HS11368; HS11530; HS11530.5; HS11531.

[P] PC4535; PC4573; PC4573.5; PC4573.5/664; PC4573.6; PC4574.

[Q] PC4501; PC4501.5; PC4502; PC4530(a); PC4530(b); PC4530(c); PC4532/664; PC4534; PC4600; WI3002.

[R] HS12305; PC12020; PC12025; PC12090; PC12220; PC12303; PC12303.2; PC12303.3; PC12560.

[S] EL29731; GC1090; PC67; PC68; PC69; PC118; PC137; PC138; PC148.1; PC337a; PC405a; PC597(a); PC647a; PC653f; PC1319.4; VC20001; VC23106; W111054.

Table 10–4. DETERMINATE PRISON SENTENCES IMPOSED (By crime with the greatest principal term if multiple convictions) STATE TOTAL—QUARTERS ENDING 9/30/77 and 12/31/77 Combined[a]

Code and Section	Crime or Category (with penalty range if applicable)	Number of Cases	Penalty Range					
			Lower		Middle		Upper	
			No.	%	No.	%	No.	%
	CRIMES AGAINST PERSONS							
[D-A]	Homicides	35	8	(23)	21	(60)	6	(17)
PC211	Robbery (2, 3, or 4 years)	224	20	(9)	126	(56)	78	(35)
PC245(a)	Assault with a deadly weapon (2, 3, or 4 years)	64	5	(8)	42	(66)	17	(27)
[D-B]	Sex offenses	33	2	(6)	12	(36)	19	(58)
[D-C]	Other crimes against persons	48	2	(4)	27	(56)	19	(40)
	TOTAL CRIMES AGAINST PERSONS	404	37	(9)	228	(56)	139	(34)
	CRIMES AGAINST PROPERTY							
PC459*	Burglary, first degree (2, 3, or 4 years)	46	3	(7)	29	(63)	14	(30)
PC459**	Burglary, second degree (16 months; 2 or 3 years)	252	23	(9)	172	(68)	57	(23)
[D-D]	Theft (16 months; 2 or 3 years)	86	9	(10)	62	(72)	15	(17)
[D-E]	Frauds, forgeries, and embezzlements (16 months; 2 or 3 years)	54	3	(6)	36	(67)	15	(28)
[D-F]	Other crimes against property and attempts	53	3	(6)	38	(72)	12	(23)
	TOTAL CRIMES AGAINST PROPERTY	491	41	(8)	337	(69)	113	(23)
	OTHER CRIMES							
[D-G]	Drug offenses	67	11	(16)	37	(55)	19	(28)
[D-H]	Penal institution offenses	51	20	(39)	22	(43)	9	(18)
[D-I]	Other crimes	41	5	(12)	25	(61)	11	(27)
	TOTAL OTHER CRIMES	159	36	(23)	84	(53)	39	(25)
	TOTAL ALL CRIMES	1054	114	(11)	649	(62)	291	(28)

Table 10-4. continued

Code and Section	Crime or Category (with penalty range if applicable)	Number of Cases	12022 Enhancement[b] (one year)		
			Number Charged and Found	Percent Imposed	Percent Stricken
	CRIMES AGAINST PERSONS				
[D-A]	Homicides	35	6	(67)	(33)
PC211	Robbery (2, 3, or 4 years)	224	55	(84)	(15)
PC245(a)	Assault with a deadly weapon (2, 3, or 4 years)	64	1	(—)	(—)
[D-B]	Sex offenses	33	3	(100)	(—)
[D-C]	Other crimes against persons	48	9	(89)	(—)
	TOTAL CRIMES AGAINST PERSONS	404	74	(82)	(14)
	CRIMES AGAINST PROPERTY				
PC459*	Burglary, first degree (2, 3, or 4 years)	46	2	(50)	(50)
PC459**	Burglary, second degree (16 months; 2 or 3 years)	252	2	(100)	(—)
[D-D]	Theft (16 months; 2 or 3 years)	86	1	(100)	(—)
[D-E]	Frauds, forgeries, and embezzlements (16 months; 2 or 3 years)	54	0	(—)	(—)
[D-F]	Other crimes against property and attempts	53	0	(—)	(—)
	TOTAL CRIMES AGAINST PROPERTY	491	5	(80)	(20)
	OTHER CRIMES				
[D-G]	Drug offenses	67	1	(—)	(100)
[D-H]	Penal institution offenses	51	0	(—)	(—)
[D-I]	Other crimes	41	0	(—)	(—)
	TOTAL OTHER CRIMES	159	1	(—)	(100)
	TOTAL ALL CRIMES	1054	80	(81)	(15)

Code and Section	Crime or Category (with penalty range if applicable)	Number of Cases	12022.5 Enhancement[b] (two years)		
			Number Charged and Found	Percent Imposed	Percent Stricken
	CRIMES AGAINST PERSONS				
[D-A]	Homicides	35	13	(85)	(15)
PC211	Robbery (2, 3, or 4 years)	224	68	(88)	(12)
PC245(a)	Assault with a deadly weapon (2, 3, or 4 years)	64	16	(69)	(31)
[D-B]	Sex offenses	33	0	(—)	(—)
[D-C]	Other crimes against persons	48	6	(83)	(17)
	TOTAL CRIMES AGAINST PERSONS	404	103	(84)	(16)
	CRIMES AGAINST PROPERTY				
PC459*	Burglary, first degree (2, 3, or 4 years)	46	3	(67)	(33)
PC459**	Burglary, second degree (16 months; 2 or 3 years)	252	2	(50)	(50)
[D-D]	Theft (16 months; 2 or 3 years)	86	0	(—)	(—)
[D-E]	Frauds, forgeries, and embezzlements (16 months; 2 or 3 years)	54	0	(—)	(—)
[D-F]	Other crimes against property and attempts	53	1	(100)	(—)
	TOTAL CRIMES AGAINST PROPERTY	491	6	(67)	(33)
	OTHER CRIMES				
[D-G]	Durg offenses	67	0	(—)	(—)
[D-H]	Penal institution offenses	51	0	(—)	(—)
[D-I]	Other crimes	41	0	(—)	(—)
	TOTAL OTHER CRIMES	159	0	(—)	(—)
	TOTAL ALL CRIMES	1054	109	(83)	(17)

Table 10–4. continued

Code and Section	Crime or Category (with penalty range if applicable)	Number of Cases	12022.7 Enhancement[b] (three years)		
			Number Charged and Found	Percent Imposed	Percent Stricken
	CRIMES AGAINST PERSONS				
[D-A]	Homicides	35	0	(—)	(—)
PC211	Robbery (2, 3, or 4 years)	224	7	(100)	(—)
PC245(a)	Assault with a deadly weapon (2, 3, or 4 years)	64	0	(—)	(—)
[D-B]	Sex offenses	33	2	(100)	(—)
[D-C]	Other crimes against persons	48	3	(100)	(—)
	TOTAL CRIMES AGAINST PERSONS	404	12	(100)	(—)
	CRIMES AGAINST PROPERTY				
PC459*	Burglary, first degree (2, 3, or 4 years)	46	5	(100)	(—)
PC459**	Burglary, second degree (16 months; 2or 3 years)	252	0	(—)	(—)
[D-D]	Theft (16 months; 2 or 3 years)	86	0	(—)	(—)
[D-E]	Frauds, forgeries, and embezzlements (16 months; 2 or 3 years)	54	0	(—)	(—)
[D-F]	Other crimes against property and attempts	53	0	(—)	(—)
	TOTAL CRIMES AGAINST PROPERTY	491	5	(100)	(—)
	OTHER CRIMES				
[D-G]	Drug offenses	67	0	(—)	(—)
[D-H]	Penal institution offenses	51	0	(—)	(—)
[D-I]	Other crimes	41	0	(—)	(—)
	TOTAL OTHER CRIMES	159	0	(—)	(—)
	TOTAL ALL CRIMES	1054	17	(100)	(—)

Code and Section	Crime or Category (with penalty range if applicable)	Number of Cases	667.5(a) Enhancement[b] (three years)		
			Number Charged and Found	Percent Imposed	Percent Stricken
	CRIMES AGAINST PERSONS				
[D-A]	Homicides	35	1	(100)	(—)
PC211	Robbery (2, 3, or 4 years)	224	2	(—)	(100)
PC245(a)	Assault with a deadly weapon (2, 3, or 4 years)	64	0	(—)	(—)
[D-B]	Sex offenses	33	1	(100)	(—)
[D-C]	Other crimes against persons	48	1	(100)	(—)
	TOTAL CRIMES AGAINST PERSONS	404	5	(60)	(40)
	CRIMES AGAINST PROPERTY				
PC459*	Burglary, first degree (2, 3, or 4 years)	46	0	(—)	(—)
PC459**	Burglary, second degree (16 months; 2 or 3 years)	252	2	(—)	(100)
[D-D]	Theft (16 months; 2 or 3 years)	86	0	(—)	(—)
[D-E]	Frauds, forgeries, and embezzlements (16 months; 2 or 3 years)	54	0	(—)	(—)
[D-F]	Other crimes against property and attempts	53	0	(—)	(—)
	TOTAL CRIMES AGAINST PROPERTY	491	2	(—)	(100)
	OTHER CRIMES				
[D-G]	Drug offenses	67	0	(—)	(—)
[D-H]	Penal institution offenses	51	0	(—)	(—)
[D-I]	Other crimes	41	0	(—)	(—)
	TOTAL OTHER CRIMES	159	0	(—)	(—)
	TOTAL ALL CRIMES	1054	7	(43)	(57)

Table 10–4. continued

Code and Section	Crime or Category (with penalty range if applicable)	Number of Cases	667.5(b) Enhancement (one year)		
			Number Charged and Found	Percent Imposed	Percent Stricken
	CRIMES AGAINST PERSONS				
|D-A|	Homicides	35	1	(100)	(—)
PC211	Robbery (2, 3, or 4 years)	224	25	(76)	(24)
PC245(a)	Assault with a deadly weapon (2, 3, or 4 years)	64	5	(80)	(20)
|D-B|	Sex offenses	33	3	(67)	(33)
|D-C|	Other crimes against persons	48	4	(25)	(75)
	TOTAL CRIMES AGAINST PERSONS	404	38	(71)	(29)
	CRIMES AGAINST PROPERTY				
PC459*	Burglary, first degree (2, 3, or 4 years)	46	8	(100)	(—)
PC459**	Burglary, second degree (16 months; 2 or 3 years)	252	21	(52)	(48)
|D-D|	Theft (16 months; 2 or 3 years)	86	8	(50)	(50)
|D-E|	Frauds, forgeries, and embezzlements (16 months; 2 or 3 years)	54	10	(40)	(60)
|D-F|	Other crimes against property and attempts	53	14	(100)	(—)
	TOTAL CRIMES AGAINST PROPERTY	491	61	(67)	(33)
	OTHER CRIMES				
|D-G|	Drug offenses	67	8	(100)	(—)
|D-H|	Penal institution offenses	51	0	(—)	(—)
|D-I|	Other crimes	41	2	(100)	(—)
	TOTAL OTHER CRIMES	159	10	(100)	(—)
	TOTAL ALL CRIMES	1054	109	(72)	(28)

Code and Section	Crime or Category (with penalty range if applicable)	Number of Cases	Multiple count cases[a]		
			Number	Percent Consecutive	Percent Concurrent
	CRIMES AGAINST PERSONS				
[D-A]	Homicides	35	2	(50)	(50)
PC211	Robbery (2, 3, or 4 years)	224	65	(32)	(49)
PC245(a)	Assault with a deadly weapon (2, 3, or 4 years)	64	10	(20)	(40)
[D-B]	Sex offenses	33	12	(50)	(17)
[D-C]	Other crimes against persons	48	15	(33)	(27)
	TOTAL CRIMES AGAINST PERSONS	404	104	(34)	(41)
	CRIMES AGAINST PROPERTY				
PC459*	Burglary, first degree (2, 3, or 4 years)	46	14	(71)	(14)
PC459**	Burglary, second degree (16 months; 2 or 3 years)	252	23	(48)	(35)
[D-D]	Theft (16 months; 2 or 3 years)	86	6	(33)	(67)
[D-E]	Frauds, forgeries, and embezzlements (16 months; 2 or 3 years)	54	15	(33)	(47)
[D-F]	Other crimes against property and attempts	53	5	(40)	(—)
	TOTAL CRIMES AGAINST PROPERTY	491	63	(48)	(33)
	OTHER CRIMES				
[D-G]	Drug offenses	67	12	(25)	(50)
[D-H]	Penal institution offenses	51	0	(—)	(—)
[D-I]	Other crimes	41	2	(100)	(—)
	TOTAL OTHER CRIMES	159	14	(36)	(43)
	TOTAL ALL CRIMES	1054	181	(39)	(39)

Table 10–4. *continued*

Code and Section	Crime or Category (with penalty range if applicable)	Number of Cases	Mean Sentence Imposed (Years)[d]	Range of Sentence Imposed (Years)[d]
	CRIMES AGAINST PERSONS			
[D-A]	Homicides	35	(—)	(—)
PC211	Robbery (2, 3, or 4 years)	224	4.27	2.00–10.33
PC245(a)	Assault with a deadly weapon (2, 3, or 4 years)	64	3.71	2.00–8.00
[D-B]	Sex offenses	33	(—)	(—)
[D-C]	Other crimes against persons	48	(—)	(—)
	TOTAL CRIMES AGAINST PERSONS	404		
	CRIMES AGAINST PROPERTY			
PC459*	Burglary, first degree (2, 3, or 4 years)	46	3.98	3.00–11.00
PC459**	Burglary, second degree (16 months; 2 or 3 years)	252	2.33	1.33–5.00
[D-D]	Theft (16 months; 2 or 3 years)	86	2.19	1.35–5.00
[D-E]	Frauds, forgeries, and embezzlements (16 months; 2 or 3 years)	54	2.36	1.33–5.00
[D-F]	Other crimes against property and attempts	53	(—)	(—)
	TOTAL CRIMES AGAINST PROPERTY	491		
	OTHER CRIMES			
[D-G]	Drug offenses	67	(—)	(—)
[D-H]	Penal institution offenses	51	(—)	(—)
[D-I]	Other crimes	41	(—)	(—)
	TOTAL OTHER CRIMES	159		
	TOTAL ALL CRIMES	1054		

[D-A] PC187**; PC192(1); PC192(3)(a)

[D-B] PC261(2)+(3); PC261.5; PC288; PC288/664; PC288a(c); PC288a(d)

[D-C] PC207; PC211/664; PC217; PC220; PC221; PC236; PC240; PC242; PC245(b); PC246; PC273d

[D-D] PC487; PC666; VC10851

[D-E] PC470; PC472; PC474; PC475a; PC476a; PC484f

[D-F] PC447a; PC449c; PC459*/664; PC459**/664; PC484f/664; PC487/664; PC496

[D-G] BP4390; HS11350; HS11351; HS11352; HS11357; HS11359; HS11377; HS11378; HS11379; HS11382

[D-H] PC4501; PC4501.5; PC4502; PC4530(b); PC4532; PC4573.6; PC4574; PC4600

[D-I] PC182; PC1319.4; PC12020; PC12021; VC20001; VC23101.

189

tion, the presumptive sentence in most crimes has in fact become probation, with only the serious offender receiving any time in state prison at all. Although this would contradict the notion that aggravating circumstances should be used only to increase the duration of sentence, and not the type of sanction,[27] if the data show that persons sent to prison were receiving durational sentences only slightly longer than the duration of probation imposed on the average offender (whether or not considering the jail term as well), perhaps the practice would be tolerable.

Unfortunately, the data demonstrate that even this second level hope is not fulfilled. For second degree burglary, for example (the most numerous conviction offense), 70 percent are not incarcerated in state prison, but of those, 55 percent receive probation. Of that 55 percent, 81 percent receive some duration of jail sentence. Thus, 45 percent of all second degree burglaries lead to jail incarceration and another 30 percent to prison incarceration. What, then, is the average prison sentence for this crime? Table 10–4 shows that for this crime the mean sentence, to state prison, is thirty-two months. If we convert that to "actual time likely to be served" (i.e., subtracting the good time earnable under California law), we conclude that persons sentenced to state prison will serve approximately twenty-one months in incarceration.

The conclusions, of course, are exceptionally tentative. Nevertheless, this one example indicates that:

1. The average sentence for second degree burglary is (an assumed six–eight) months in the county jail, followed by probation.
2. Thirty percent of persons committing this crime are sent to state prison for twenty-one months, roughly three and one-half times that of the average sentence, not even counting the physical differences between state prison and county jail.[28]
3. Of those sentenced to state prison, 57 percent were sentenced to at least three years, which, when discounted by good time, is twenty-seven months—four and one-half times that of the normal sentence.
4. Some number of persons, incalculable from the data, received five year sentences, that, when discounted, amount to forty-eight months—six to eight times the normal sentence of incarceration.

If the differences in sentence can be so great under a system that attempts somewhat scrupulously to follow the notion of presumptive

---

[27] See ch. 6, *supra*.

[28] It may, contrarily, be suggested that six months in a county jail is equivalent to two years in a state prison.

sentences, for a crime that is relatively innocuous and for which there ought to be only minor variations in sentence, the possibilities of variations for the major offenses would seem to abound.

The figures are more difficult when dealing with other crimes, however, since we must, in addition to guessing at the probation-jail time, make rough guesses as to other factors. Nevertheless, let us take robbery. Forty-one percent of robbers received probation, but virtually all of those (90 percent) did receive some jail time as a condition of probation. Let us, then, assume that this time was eight months. Table 10–4 shows that another 9 percent of all robbers sentenced to prison received a sentence at the lower penalty range (two years, discounted to eighteen months). Conveniently, this sums to 50 percent. Thus, we can roughly say that the average robber received ten months incarceration. But Table 10–4 tells us that the average sentence imposed on robbers sentenced to the state prison was 4.27 years. With the removal of 9 percent at the bottom, this will indicate that the remaining half of the robbers in the sample received a prison sentence of roughly 4.3 years, which, again discounted by good time, suggests that the mean time then served was thirty-nine months—four times the average robber. Similarly, there were some robbers who received sentences of 10.33 years. Again, we do not know, from Table 10–4, how many fit into this category. But it demonstrates that even for those incarcerated (not including the 16 percent who were given "other disposition"), the time of incarceration, discounted for good time, ranged from (roughly) eight months to ninety-three months—an eleven time multiple.

Thus, the absolute range is disquietingly wide under this theoretically rigid California system. Moreover, even within the range of prison sentences, the numbers of persons sentenced outside the range, and sentences double and triple the normal sentence, is substantial. Within this group, for example, the majority in every crime category (except sex offenses) is being sentenced to the middle term. This, initially, would indicate that the presumptive approach may be taking hold. Closer inspection, however, indicates that this is not so. While the middle term may be applied in most crimes, there is also, in most instances, some factor that is used to enhance the sentence as well. Thus, we have the data found on page 192.

Further, in terms of enhancements, the percentages indicate that the vast majority of charged enhancements are imposed: 75 percent of one year enhancements; 83 percent of two year enhancements; and 83 percent of three year enhancements. The data do not reveal, however, the extent to which prosecutors are failing to charge deserved enhancements, and it is thus not possible to derive from this information

Crime	Number of Cases	Number Using Enhancements or Multiples	Percent in Which Middle Term Changed
Robbery	224	223	100
Assault	64	32	50
Sex Offenses	33	21	67
Other Persons Offenses	48	38	75
Burglary (1st)	46	30	66
Burglary (2nd)	252	28	20
Theft	86	15	17
Fraud	54	25	47
Other Property Offenses	53	20	43

the critical data about evenhandedness of charging that would be necessary to totally evaluate the California system.

IS REFORM POSSIBLE?

This analysis demonstrates that the movement toward changing the sentencing structure in this country is well under way. A number of state legislatures have affirmatively grasped the nettle and adopted, in theory at least, the proposition that sentences should become more equal, more consistent, and more fully based on the crime rather than the criminal. Perhaps nothing more than this could be expected in the first attempts of legislatures to deal with the enormously difficult problems of seeking equality in sentencing.

That there are some systems that seem not to have actually understood the approach, or to have only half understood, or even to have used it as an excuse for simply increasing sentences, should not surprise, howevermuch it may disappoint. Moreover, the California data, while not hopeful, should not be taken as a sign that the system cannot work. The attempt by any bureaucracy to manipulate any new approach is to be expected. Ready acceptance of a new theory cannot be anticipated. When the notion of parole was first enunciated, for example, many courts sought to undermine the system by imposing sentences with minimum sentences just below the maximum sentence.[29] Similar resistance to the notion of standardized sentences is predicta-

[29] Indeed, this still occurs. See People v. Tanner, 387 Mich. 683, 199 N.W. 2d 202 (1972).

ble. Instead, one can hope that, over a long period of time, the atmosphere in the criminal justice system will change as more and more proponents of the desert system come into positions of power—success by accretion, rather than by fiat, is the typical pattern.

There is strong reason to be hopeful, moreover, because many states that have adopted some semblance of commensurate deserts sentencing have not rushed headlong into the process, but established quasi-legislative agencies, such as the sentencing commission or the parole board, to more carefully study the results in other jurisdictions before they implement the theory in their own states. These commissions will be instructed by the weaknesses and failings of the first fledgling attempts to carry the notion to fruition.

Pragmatically, moreover, those states that have, either consciously or unconsciously, pursued the path of increasing punishments without the restriction of parsimony and proportionality will discover quickly that untenable increases in the number of prisons will be required in order to effectuate these unrealistically high sentences. Most jurisdictions, I believe, will then eschew that path, because of the intolerably high financial costs, and seek to reduce the number of prisoners in some other way. This may—although not necessarily will—result in either reductions of sentences for those convicted of minor crimes or the substitution of probation for imprisonment as the typical sanction for some types of crime. By this means, indirect as it is, it is likely that we will establish a presumptive sentence of probation for some offenses and a presumptive sentence of incarceration for other offenses, with rare transferences across the types of sentences.

In short, the rather unhappy picture sketched by the review of present proposals or actions taken with regard to sentencing reform is not necessarily indicative of the future path that reform will take. Attempts to mold the old system into the new framework were clearly anticipatable; the issue now is whether that will continue to be the course in future proposals.

There is much to be hopeful about. Legislatures have recognized the need for reevaluation of their sentencing systems; many have taken a gradual approach to the changes required, thereby giving themselves the opportunity to more fully assess the immediate impact of such change. The continued debate about these measures, moreover, will more fully crystalize the strengths and weaknesses in a presumptive sentence model and afford new opportunities to devise schemes to correct the weaknesses while accepting the basic premises of that system.

It is always possible to oppose suggestions for change on the grounds that they will simply afford the opportunity for increased harshness and arbitrariness. But "law and order" has never been known to sit idly by waiting for the door of reform to open; instead, those who seek equality and rationality in sentencing must voice both their own disagreements with the theory of commensurate deserts and their views on other attempted reforms. Fear of regression should not be the rationale for not trying to improve the system.

✳

Appendix A
Sentencing Reform Act of 1979

1. Declaration of Principles and Purposes
It is the purpose of this Act to:

(1) eliminate unjustified disparity and promote uniformity in sentencing for persons convicted of crimes of similar seriousness;

(2) provide for the promulgation of standards for criminal sentences which will assure that a criminal offender is punished by the imposition of a sentence he deserves commensurate with the seriousness of the offense as aggravated or mitigated by the circumstances of his particular offense;

(3) make the criminal justice system accountable to the public and reaffirm societal norms by reflecting community condemnation of the criminal act;

(4) allow each convicted offender sentenced to imprisonment to know at the time at which such sentence is imposed the actual duration of his confinement;

(5) maintain appropriate incentives for good institutional behavior;

(6) provide for the promulgation of standards for the charging of criminal violations and reduction of criminal charges for persons charged with criminal violations;

(7) provide for the gradual reintegration into the community of criminal offenders serving terms of continuous confinement in penal institutions;

(8) achieve conditions in penal institution in which the security of each inmate is ensured, the inmate's physical and mental health is preserved, and voluntary programs of improvement are available.

2. Sentencing Guidelines Commission:
Established Membership

(a) There is hereby established the Sentencing Guidelines Commission (Commission), comprised of eleven members, as follows:

(1) The Chief Justice of the Supreme Court;

(2) Two district court judges appointed by the Supreme Court;

(3) One public defender appointed by the Governor upon recommendation of the state public defender;

(4) One County attorney appointed by the Governor upon recommendation of the board of governors of the county attorneys council;

(5) The Commissioner of Corrections;

(6) The Chairman of the State Parole Board;

(7) Four public members appointed by the Governor, at least one of whom shall have been previously incarcerated as a result of a felony conviction.

(b) One of the members shall be designated by the Governor as Chairman of the Commission.

(c) Each appointed member shall be appointed for four years and shall continue to serve during that time so long as he occupies the position which made him eligible for the appointment. Each member shall continue in office until his successor is duly appointed. Members shall be eligible for reappointment, and appointment may be made to fill an unexpired term.

(d) Each member of the commission shall be reimbursed for all reasonable expenses actually paid or incurred in the performance of his official duties. The public members of the commission shall be compensated at the rate of $100 per day or part thereof spent on commission activities.

3. Sentencing Commission
Guidelines: Promulgation

Not later than 18 months after the date of enactment of this Act, the commission shall publish in the state register, in every major newspaper, in the state bar journal, and in each legal newspaper proposed rules to carry out the provisions of this Act. Not earlier than 60 days, but not later than 90 days, after the date of such publication, the Commission shall hold public hearings to afford interested persons a reasonable opportunity to present data, views, or arguments concerning such proposed rules, in an oral presentation, or in writing prior to the hearing. The Commission shall consider fully all submissions respecting such proposed rules, revise such proposed rules on the basis of such submissions to the extent appropriate and consistent with the policy of this Act, and issue a concise statement of the principal reasons for adoption, and the reasons for overruling any considerations urged against adoption.

4. Sentencing Commission
Guidelines: Content

(a) The Commission shall promulgate guidelines for sentencing, based upon the principles enumerated in Section 1. These guidelines shall establish a schedule:

(1) setting forth gradations of gravity of criminal offenses;

(2) prescribing an appropriate gradation of gravity for each criminal offense; and

(3) prescribing a presumptive sentence for each gradation of gravity.

(b) The severity of each presumptive sentence prescribed as provided in subsection (a)(3) shall be commensurate with the gravity of the criminal offense to which such presumptive sentence is assigned.

(c) The Commission shall also promulgate guidelines establishing sanctions for offenders for whom imprisonment is not proper, which shall make specific reference to noninstitutional sanctions, including but not limited to the following: payment of fines, day fines, restitution, community work orders, work release programs, curfew, community-based residential and nonresidential programs, and probation and the conditions thereof. The terms and conditions of such penalties prescribed by the Commission may include the duration, scheduling, and place of residential programs; the amount or method of calculating or determining any restitution, fine or forfeiture, and the nature, type and extent of any supervision, curfew, travel restriction or community work order.

(d) The Commission shall prescribe a presumptive sentence of imprisonment only for serious criminal offenses, and prescribe, with respect to serious criminal offenses, no presumptive sentence in excess of five years imprisonment. A criminal offense is serious for purposes of this subsection if, as determined under *subsection (a),* it entails a substantial degree of harm or risk thereof and a high degree of culpability on the part of the offender. In determining whether the harm or risk thereof is substantial, the Commission shall consider whether the conduct:

(1) involves the infliction, risk or threat of substantial bodily injury;

(2) involves the infliction or risk of substantial harm (other than of bodily injury), including but not limited to the substantial abuse of a

public office, of a public or private trust, or of governmental processes, or the deprivation of a substantial portion of the livelihood of a victim of such criminal offense; on

(3) was undertaken purposefully, knowingly, or recklessly.

5. Sentencing Commission Guidelines:
Aggravating and Mitigating Circumstances

(a) The Commission shall establish, in accordance with the provisions of section 4(a), a schedule of rules

(1) Prescribing variations from any presumptive sentence established under section 4(b) on account of mitigating or aggravating circumstances;

(2) Specifying which types of circumstances shall qualify as mitigating or aggravating circumstances that require or permit a variation from such presumptive sentences;

(3) Specifying, with respect to each such type of mitigating or aggravating circumstance, a particular amount or a maximum permitted amount of variation from such presumptive sentence; in no event shall the cumulative increase or decrease from the presumptive sentence be more than 10 percent.

(b) For the purpose of subsection (a), the Commission

(1) shall not consider as an aggravating or mitigating circumstance the anticipated affect on the future behavior of the convicted offender, or of any other person, of imposing a sentence more or less severe than the presumptive sentence;

(2) may specify as a mitigating or aggravating circumstance any particular acts or circumstances surrounding the commission of a criminal offense which renders the degree of harm or risk of harm of the criminal conduct, or the degree of culpability of the offender engaging in such conduct, greater or less than the gradation of gravity prescribed for such criminal offense under section 4(b).

6. Sentencing Commission Guidelines:
Present Practices

After determining a schedule of offenses and punishments using the criteria of Sections 4 and 5, the Commission may increase or decrease the entire schedule to take into account present correctional resources, overcrowding, and present practices involving time actually served for specific offenses.

7. Sentencing Commission Guidelines:
Concurrent and Consecutive Terms

The Commission guidelines shall provide that where an offender is convicted of more than one offense under either the same or separate case number and where all of the offenses occurred prior to the imposition of sentence on any of the other convictions for the offense, the sentences for all of the other convictions shall run consecutively, subject to the following limitations, and each judgment and sentence shall state any limitations under this section applicable to the sentence:

(1) Where the offenses were committed through a single act or omission, or through an act or omission which in itself constituted one of the offenses and also was an element of the other, the aggregate of the sentences for those crimes shall not exceed 150 percent of the presumptive sentence for the offense which carries the highest presumptive sentence; and

(2) In all other cases except as otherwise limited, the aggregate of all consecutive sentences shall not exceed 200 percent of the presumptive sentence for the offense which carries the highest presumptive sentence; and

(3) Where sentence is imposed for two or more offenses, none of which is a violent offense, the aggregate period of total confinement shall not exceed three years.

7A. Habitual Offenders [Optional][1]

(a) The Commission may, but need not, provide for increased sentences for offenders who have previously been convicted of an offense whose presumptive sentence is incarceration. If the Commission so chooses, it shall establish a schedule of such increases which shall, however, in no event exceed the following:

Second Offense—increase the presumptive sentence for the current offense by no more than 10 percent.

Third or Greater Offense—increase the presumptive sentence for the current offense by no more than 40 percent.

(b) For the purpose of this section, two or more convictions arising out of a substantially contemporaneous course of criminal conduct shall be considered as one conviction.

(c) In no event shall an offender convicted of an offense whose presumptive sentence is a non-incarcerative sentence be sentenced to incarceration on the basis of a prior conviction.

8. Sentencing Commission: Plea Bargaining Guidelines

(a) The (state association of prosecuting attorneys) shall formulate guidelines and procedures which are designed to afford persons

---

[1] As indicated in Chapter 5, I believe this provision to be totally inconsistent with just deserts theory. Nevertheless, in the recognition that it is likely that some sort of provision of this type will be enacted, a suggested version is put forward here.

charged with crimes of similar seriousness equal opportunity with respect to plea bargaining discussions and agreements.

(b) The (association) shall also formulate guidelines and procedures for determining whether to charge an accused with a criminal offense or to place him on diversion or to another agency or to use civil remedies or other means as an alternative to criminal prosecution.

(c) All such guidelines shall be presented to the Sentencing Commission no later than ____; the Commission shall promulgate such guidelines, as revised by the Commission, as regulations of the Commission.

9. Sentencing Commission Guidelines: Effective Date

The Commission guidelines shall be submitted to the legislature on _____ and shall be effective 120 days thereafter unless rejected in their entirety by a concurrent resolution of both houses of the legislature.

10. Sentencing Commission: Powers

(a) The Commission, in addition to establishing sentencing guidelines, shall serve as a clearing house and information center for the collection, preparation, analysis, and dissemination of information on sentencing practices, and shall conduct ongoing research regarding sentencing guidelines, use of imprisonment and alternatives to imprisonment, plea bargaining, and other matters relating to the improvement of the criminal justice system. It may conduct, or arrange for, educational programs relating to sentencing.

(b) The Commission shall from time to time make recommendations to the legislature regarding changes in the criminal code, criminal procedures, and aspects of sentencing.

(c) The Commission shall study the impact of the sentencing guidelines after their implementation, review the powers and duties of the state parole board, and make recommendations to the legislature on the appropriate roles, if any, of the board under the guidelines.

(d) The (Commissioner of Corrections) shall provide adequate office space and administrative services for the Commission, and the Commission shall reimburse the commissioner, for the space and services provided. The Commission may also utilize, with their consent, the services, equipment, personnel, information and resources of other state agencies; and may accept voluntary and uncompensated services, contract with individuals and public and private agencies, and request information, reports, and data from any agency of the state, or any of its political subdivisions, to the extent authorized by law.

(e) When any person, corporation, the United States government, or any other entity offers funds to the Sentencing Guidelines Commission to carry out its purposes and duties, the Commission may accept the offer by majority vote, and upon acceptance, the chairman shall receive the funds subject to the terms of the offer, but no money shall be accepted or received as a loan nor shall any indebtedness be incurred except in the manner and under limitations otherwise provided by law.

(f) The Commission may select and employ a research director who shall perform the duties the Commission directs, including the hiring of any clerical help and other employees as the Commission shall approve. The research director and other staff shall be in the unclassified service of the state, and their salary shall be established by the Commission. They shall be reimbursed for the expenses necessarily incurred in the performance of their official duties in the same manner as other state employees.

(g) No bill introduced into either House of the legislature seeking to increase or decrease the sentence duration or to change the type of sentence applicable to a specific offense or class of offenses shall be enacted into law until the Sentencing Commission has provided a report to the legislature on the impact of the proposal on prison population and upon the Commission's schedule of punishments.

11. Sentencing Guidelines: Changes

(a) Whenever the Commission proposes to increase or decrease the sentence applicable to a specific offense, or to offenses generally, it shall comply with the procedures enunciated in Section 3 concerning newly promulgated guidelines.

(b) No change in the guidelines shall take effect unless agreed to by both houses of the legislature. Any such changes shall become effective no earlier than 180 days after such agreement.

(c) Nothing in this section shall prohibit the Commission, in times of emergency created by overcrowding in penal institutions, from effecting temporary changes in the guidelines scale, for specific offenses, in order to reduce such overcrowding. Such changes shall be effective for no more than 120 days and may not be renewed. A finding by the Commission that there is such an emergency may be reviewed, upon the complaint of any prosecutor in this state, by the state Supreme Court, which shall expeditiously hear the complaint.

12. Sentencing Commission: Reports

During each year of its existence, the Commission shall report to the Supreme Court, the General Assembly, the Governor, and the public. The Commission shall give written reasons supporting each proposed rule and statutory change and shall supplement its proposals with statistical information where possible. The Commission shall maintain and make available for public inspection a record of the final vote of each member on any action taken by the Commission. All meetings of the Commission shall be open to attendance by the public.

13. Sentencing Hearing

(a) At least seven days prior to sentencing, the sentencing court shall provide the offender with all the information, including the guidelines, rules, and regulations of the Sentencing Commission, upon which the court will base its sentence. At the hearing, the offender shall have the right to counsel, to call and examine witnesses (including persons who have given statements which appear in the presentence report), and to present other evidence. The rules of evidence shall apply to these proceedings.

(b) The sentencing judge shall impose the presumptive sentence assigned to the criminal offense of which he was convicted. If a variation from the presumptive sentence is permitted or required by the Commission's rules under Section 5, the judge shall vary such presumptive sentence only as provided in that Section.

(c) If the sentencing judge (1) varies any presumptive sentence based upon the existence of any aggravating or mitigating circumstance, or (2) refuses, upon request by the defendant or the state's attorney, to vary any presumptive sentence, the judge shall disclose in open court and make a statement for the record of the precise reasons therefor.

14. Sentencing Review Panel

(a) There is hereby established a sentencing review board to be composed of three judges of the appellate division assigned by the Chief Justice for terms of two years. Judges assigned to this tribunal shall sit only on matters of sentencing review for the duration of their assignments.

(b) If the trial court imposed the presumptive sentence, the sentencing review board shall affirm the sentence unless the party appealing shows beyond a reasonable doubt that the court erred in failing to find either aggravating or mitigating circumstances.

(c) If the trial court imposed a sentence other than the presumptive sentence, the sentencing review board shall affirm the sentence only if there is substantial evidence in the entire record to support the trial court's finding of facts in aggravation or mitigation.

(d) The state may, within ten days of the imposition of the sentence, file notice of appeal to the Sentencing Review Board. The offender may not file notice of appeal until the state has filed such notice or until ten days have elapsed since the imposition of sentence. The offender shall thereafter have thirty days to file notice of appeal to the sentencing review board. The sentencing review board may increase a sentence only on appeal by the state.

(e) For each appeal, the Sentencing Review Board shall publish an opinion setting forth the reasons for its decision.

15. Good Time

(a) A prisoner committed to the Department of Corrections for a felony shall receive time off for good behavior in the amount of one day reduction of his prison term for every ten days he spends in the custody of the Department without a major infraction of prisoner conduct rules. Prisoner conduct rules shall be issued by the (Secretary of Corrections). The rules shall clearly state types of forbidden conduct, and a copy of the rules shall be given to each prisoner upon entry into prison. Infractions of the rules shall be of two types: major infractions that are punishable by forfeiture of specific good behavior time, and minor infractions that are punishable by loss of certain privileges for specific periods but not by loss of good behavior time or by solitary confinement. All sanctions shall be proportionate to the gravity of the offense.

(b) Within two weeks of entry into prison, the Department of Corrections shall inform a prisoner in writing of the date on which he will be released if he receives the maximum amount of time off for good behavior and of the date on which he will be released if he receives no good behavior credit.

(c) If an inmate violates a disciplinary offense rule promulgated by the Secretary of Corrections, good time earned prior to the violation may not be taken away, but the inmate may be required to serve an appropriate portion of his term of imprisonment after the violation without earning good time.

(d) In no case shall an individual disciplinary offense result in the loss of more than thirty days of good time. The loss of good time shall be considered to be a disciplinary sanction imposed upon the inmate, and the procedure for the loss of good time and the rights of the inmate in the procedure shall be those in effect for the imposition of other disciplinary sanctions at each state correctional institution.

16. Supervised Release Term

(a) Every inmate shall serve a supervised release term upon completion of his term of imprisonment as reduced by any good time earned by the inmate. The supervised release term shall be equal to the period of good time for which the inmate was eligible.

(b) The Sentencing Commission shall promulgate rules for the placement and supervision of inmates serving a supervised release term. The rules shall also provide sanctions for abuse of supervised release, and shall specify the sanction for each violation of supervised release. Charges of violations of supervised release shall be heard in _____ court and shall conform with the rules and regulations for the revocation of probation.

(c) If the court finds that the inmate has violated a condition of supervised release, it may increase the restrictions on the inmate's liberty, including requiring the inmate to reside nightly in a designated penal institution.

(d) Only if the inmate has committed a new crime may he be returned to prison, where he shall serve the remainder of his sentence, less one day credit for each day served on supervised release prior to his new offense.

(e) Nothing herein shall limit the right of the state to prosecute for the new offense.

❋

Bibliography

WORKS ON THE PHILOSOPHY OF PUNISHMENT

Books

CEDERBLOM, J., and BLIZEK, W., JUSTICE AND PUNISHMENT. Ballinger, 1977.

EZORSKY, G., PHILOSOPHICAL PERSPECTIVES ON PUNISHMENT. State University of New York, 1972.

FEINBERG, J., DOING AND DESERVING. Princeton University Press, 1970.

FEINBERG, J., and GROSS, H., PUNISHMENT: SELECTED READINGS. Dickenson, 1975.

FLETCHER, G., RETHINKING CRIMINAL LAW. Little, Brown, 1978.

FITZGERALD, P., CRIMINAL LAW AND PUNISHMENT. Clarendon Press, 1962.

GERBER, R., and McANANY, P., CONTEMPORARY PUNISHMENT: VIEWS, EXPLANATIONS AND JUSTIFICATION. University of Notre Dame, 1972.

HART, H., PUNISHMENT: FOR AND AGAINST. Hart Publishers, 1971.

HART, H.L.A., PUNISHMENT AND RESPONSIBILITY. Oxford University, 1968.

KLEINIG, J., PUNISHMENT AND DESERT. Martinus Nijhoff, 1973.

MORRIS, H., ON GUILT AND INNOCENCE. University of California, 1976.

PACKER, H., THE LIMITS OF THE CRIMINAL SANCTION. Stanford University, 1968.

VAN DEN HAAG, E., PUNISHING CRIMINALS. Basic Books, 1975.

VON HIRSCH, A., DOING JUSTICE. Hill and Wang, 1976.

RAWLS, J., A THEORY OF JUSTICE. 1969.

Articles

Armstrong, *The Retributivist Hits Back*, in THE PHILOSOPHY OF PUNISHMENT 138. H. Acton, ed. MACMILLAN, 1969.

Beardsley, *A Plea for Deserts*, 6 AMER. PHIL. QUART. 33 (1969).

Dworkin and Blumenfeld, *Punishment for Intentions*, 75 MIND 396 (1966).

Ewing, *On Retributivism,* in PHILOSOPHICAL PERSPECTIVES ON PUNISHMENT 137. G. Ezorsky, ed. University of New York Press, 1972.

Gardner, *The Renaissance of Retribution—An Examination of Doing Justice*, 1976 WISC. L. REV. 781.

Hadden, *A Plea for Punishment*, 1965 CAMBRIDGE L. J. 117.

Kellogg, *From Retribution to "Desert": The Evolution of Criminal Punishment*, 15 CRIMINOLOGY 179 (1977).

LaFrancois, *An Examination of a Desert-Based Presumptive Sentence Schedule*, 6 J. CRIM. JUST. 35 (1978).

Lewis, *The Humanitarian Theory of Punishment*, in CONTEMPORARY PUNISHMENT: VIEWS, EXPLANATIONS AND JUSTIFICATIONS 194. Gerber and McAnany, eds. University of Notre Dame, 1972.

———, *On Punishment: A Reply*, 6 RES JUDICATAE 519 (1954).

Moberly, W., *Expiation*, in CONTEMPORARY PUNISHMENT: VIEWS, EXPLANATIONS AND JUSTIFICATIONS 73. Gerber and McAnany, eds. University of Notre Dame, 1972.

Murphy, J., *Three Mistakes About Retributivism*, 31 ANALYSIS 166 (1971).

Rawls, *Two Concepts of Rules*, 64 THE PHILOSOPHICAL REV. 3 (1955).

Stern, *Deserved Punishment, Deserved Harm, Deserved Blame*, 45 PHIL. 317 (1970).

von Hirsch, *Prediction of Criminal Conduct and Preventive Confinement of Convicted Persons*, 21 BUFF. L. REV. 717 (1972).

Wasserstrom, *H.L.A. Hart and the Doctrine of Mens Rea and Criminal Responsibility*, 35 U. CHI. L. REV. 92 (1967).

———, *Punishment and Responsibility*, in CONTEMPORARY PUNISHMENT: VIEWS, EXPLANATIONS AND JUSTIFICATIONS 19. Gerber and McAnany, eds. University of Notre Dame, 1972.

———, *Why Punish the Guilty?*, in PHILOSOPHICAL PERSPECTIVES ON PUNISHMENT 328. Ezorsky, ed. State University of New York, 1972.

DESERT AND DETERMINATE SENTENCING

Books and Reports

AMERICAN FRIENDS SERVICE COMMITTEE, STRUGGLE FOR JUSTICE: A REPORT ON CRIME AND JUSTICE IN AMERICA. Hill and Wang 1971.

CORRECTIONS MAGAZINE, DETERMINATE SENTENCING. September 1972.

COUNCIL OF STATE GOVERNMENTS, DEFINITE SENTENCING: AN EXAMINATION OF PROPOSALS IN FOUR STATES. 1976.

DETERMINATE SENTENCING: REFORM OR REGRESSION? LEAA 1978.

DETERMINATE SENTENCING SURVEY, SENATE SELECT SUBCOMMITTEE ON DETERMINATE SENTENCING, STATE OF MINNESOTA. 1976.

EAGLIN, J., and PARTIDGE, A., AN EVALUATION OF THE PROBABLE IMPACT OF SELECTED PROPOSALS FOR IMPOSING MANDATORY MINIMUM SENTENCE IN THE FEDERAL COURTS. Federal Judicial Center, 1977.

TWENTIETH CENTURY FUND, FAIR AND CERTAIN PUNISHMENT. McGraw-Hill, 1976.

Articles

Allen, *Retribution in a Modern Penal Law: The Principle of Aggravated Harm*, 25 BUFF. L. REV. 1 (1975).

Alschuler, *Sentencing Reform and Prosecutorial Discretion: A Critique of Recent Proposals for "Fixed" and "Presumptive" Sentencing*, 126 U. PA. L. REV. 550 (1978).

Cassou and Taugher, *Determinate Sentencing in California: The New Numbers Game*, 9 PACIFIC L. J. 5 (1978).

Clear, Hewitt, and Regoli, *Discretion and the Determinate Sentence: Its Distribution, Control and Effect on Time Served*, 24 CRIME AND DELINQ. 428 (1978).

Cole, *Will Definite Sentences Make A Difference?*, 61 JUDICATURE 38 (1977).

Coffee, *The Repressed Issues of Sentencing: Accountability, Predictability, and Equality in the Era of the Sentencing Commission*, 66 GEO. L. J. 975 (1978).

Comment, *Senate Bill 42—The End of the Indeterminate Sentence*, 17 SANTA CLARA L. REV. 133 (1977).

Dershowitz, *Let the Punishment Fit the Crime,* New York Times Magazine, December 28, 1975.

Harris, *Disquisition on the Need for a New Model for Criminal Sanctioning Systems*, 77 W. VA. L. REV. 263 (1974).

Kress, *Who Should Sentence: The Judge, The Legislature, or. . . . ?*, 17 JUDGE'S JOURNAL 12 (Winter 1978).

Lagoy, Hussey, and Kramer, *A Comparative Assessment of Determinate Sentencing in Four Pioneer States*, 24 CRIME AND DELINQ. 385 (1978).

Manson, *Determinate Sentencing*, 23 CRIME AND DELINQ. 204 (1977).

McAnany, Merritt, and Tromanhauser, *Illinois Reconsiders "Flat Time"; An Analysis of the Impact of the Justice Model*, 52 CHI-KENT L. REV. 621 (1976).

McGee, *California's New Determinate Sentencing Law*, 43 FED. PROB. 3 (March 1978).

Nagel, Neef, and Weiman, How Might Determinate Sentences be Determined? (unpublished, 1977).

O'Leary, Gottfredson, and Gelman, *Contemporary Sentencing Proposals*, 11 CRIM. L. BULL. 555 (1975).

Oppenheim, *Computing A Determinate Sentence—New Math Hits the Courts*, 51 CAL. ST. B. J. 604 (1976).

Raymer, *Criminal Dispositions for New Jersey: Pre-Trial Intervention, the Model Penal Code and Just Deserts*, 8 SETON HALL L. REV. 1 (1976).

Schullhofer, *Harm and Punishment: A Critique of Emphasis on the Results of Conduct in the Criminal Law*, 122 U. PA. L. REV. 1497 (1974).

Scott, *The Use of Discretion in Determining the Severity of Punishment for Incarcerated Offenders*, 65 J. CRIM. L. & CRIM. 214 (1975).

Tonry, Sentencing Guidelines and Sentencing Commissions—An Assessment of the Sentencing Reform Proposition in the Criminal Code Reform Act of 1977 (unpublished).

Uelman, *Proof of Aggravation Under the California Uniform Determinate Sentencing Act: The Constitutional Issues*, 10 LOYOLA (L.A.) L. REV. 725 (1977).

von Hirsch, *The Aims of Imprisonment*, 71 CURRENT HISTORY 1 (July-August 1976).

———, Book Review, HOFSTRA L. REV. (1979) (forthcoming).

———, *Giving Criminals Their Just Deserts*, 3 CIVIL LIBERTIES REVIEW 23 (April-May 1976).

———, The New Indiana Sentencing Code: Is It Determinate Sentencing? (unpublished, 1978).

Wilkins and Gottfredson, *Is The End of Judicial Sentencing in Sight?*, 60 JUDICATURE 216 (1976).

Zalman, *A Commission Model of Sentencing*, 53 NOTRE DAME L. 266 (1977).

Zimring, *Making the Punishment Fit the Crime: A Consumers' Guide to Sentencing Reform*, 6 HASTINGS CENTER REPORT 13 (December 1976).

SENTENCING AND CORRECTIONS GENERALLY

Books and Reports

ABT ASSOCIATES, INC., PRISON POPULATION AND POLICY CHOICES. LEAA, 1977.

CLARK, R., and RUDENSTINE, D., PRISONS WITHOUT WALLS: REPORT OF THE NEW YORK CITIZENS' INQUIRY ON PAROLE. Praeger, 1975.

COUNCIL OF EUROPE, SENTENCING. European Committee on Crime Problems, 1974.

FOGEL, D., WE ARE THE LIVING PROOF. W. H. Anderson, 1976.

FRANKEL, M., CRIMINAL SENTENCES. Hill and Wang, 1973.

GAYLIN, W., PARTIAL JUSTICE: A STUDY OF BIAS IN SENTENCING. Vintage Books, 1974.

GOTTFREDSON, D., WILKINS, L., and HOFFMAN, P., GUIDELINES FOR PAROLE AND SENTENCING. Lexington Books, 1978.

KASSEBAUM, G., WARD, D., and WILNER, D., PRISON TREATMENT AND PAROLE SURVIVAL. Wiley and Sons, 1971.

KNOPP, F., INSTEAD OF PRISONS, A HANDBOOK FOR ABOLITIONISTS. Prison Research Education Action Project, 1976.

LAW REFORM COMMISSION OF CANADA, STUDIES ON SENTENCING. Information Canada, 1974.

LIPTON, D., MARTINSON, R., and WILKS, J., THE EFFECTIVENESS OF CORRECTIONAL TREATMENT: A SURVEY OF TREATMENT EVALUATION STUDIES. Praeger, 1975.

MORRIS, N., THE FUTURE OF IMPRISONMENT. University of Chicago, 1974.

O'DONNELL, P., CHURGIN, M., and CURTIS, D., TOWARD A JUST AND EFFECTIVE SENTENCING SYSTEM. Praeger, 1977.

ORLAND, L., PRISONS: HOUSES OF DARKNESS. Free Press, 1975.

ORLAND, L., and TYLER, H., JUSTICE IN SENTENCING. Foundation Press, 1974.

PARTRIDGE, E., THE SECOND CIRCUIT SENTENCING STUDY: A REPORT TO THE JUDGES. Federal Judicial Center, 1974.

SANSONE, J., SENTENCING, CORRECTIONS AND SPECIAL TREATMENT SERVICES IN SWEDEN, DENMARK AND THE NETHERLANDS. Hartford Institute of Criminal and Social Justice, 1976.

SILBERMAN, C., CRIMINAL VIOLENCE, CRIMINAL JUSTICE. Random House, 1978.

SLATTERY, B., A HANDBOOK ON SENTENCING. East African Literature Bureau, 1972.

UNITED STATES PAROLE COMMISSION RESEARCH UNIT, SELECTED REPRINTS RELATING TO FEDERAL PAROLE DECISIONMAKING. 1977.

VON HIRSCH, A., and HANRAHAN, K., THE QUESTION OF PAROLE: RETENTION, REFORM, OR ABOLITION. Ballinger, 1979.

WALLER, I., MEN RELEASED FROM PRISON. University of Toronto, 1974.

WHINERY, L., NAGY, T., and FISHER, K., PREDICTIVE SENTENCING. Lexington Books, 1976.

WILKINS, L. EVALUATION OF PENAL MEASURES. Random House, 1969.

WILKINS, L., GOTTFREDSON, D., AND KRESS, J., SENTENCING GUIDELINES: STRUCTURING JUDICIAL DISCRETION. LEAA, 1976.

Articles

Coffee, *The Future of Sentencing Reform*, 73 MICH. L. REV. 1361 (1975).

Comment, *Parole Release Decision-Making and the Sentencing Process*, 84 YALE L. J. 810 (1975).

Dershowitz, *Indeterminate Confinement; Letting the Therapy Fit the Harm*, 123 U. PA. L. REV. 297 (1974).

Heinz, Heinz, Senderowitz, and Vance, *Sentencing by Parole Board: An Evaluation*, 67 J. CRIM. L. & CRIM. 1 (1976).

Hoffman and Stone-Meierhoefer, *Application of Guidelines to Sentencing*, 3 LAW AND PSYCH. REV. 53 (1977).

Kastenmeier and Eglit, *Parole Release Decision-Making: Rehabilitation, Expertise and the Demise of Mythology*, 22 AM. U. L. REV. 477 (1973).

Kaufman, *The Sentencing Views of Yet Another Judge*, 66 GEO. L. J. 1247 (1978).

Neithercutt, *Parole Legislation*, 41 FED. PROB. 22 (March 1977).

Newman, *A Better Way to Sentence Criminals*, 63 A.B.A. J. 1562 (1977).

Note, *Appellate Review of Primary Sentencing Decisions: A Connecticut Case Study*, 69 YALE L. J. 1453 (1960).

Palmer, *A Model of Criminal Dispositions: An Alternative to Official Discretion in Sentencing*, 62 GEO. L. J. 1 (1973).

Robin, *Judicial Resistance to Sentencing Accountability*, 21 CRIME AND DELINQ. 201 (1975).

Sacks, *Promises, Performance and Principles: An Empirical Study of Parole Decisionmaking in Connecticut*, 9 CONN. L. REV. 347 (1977).

Samuelson, *Sentence Review and Sentence Disparity: A Case Study of the Connecticut Sentence Review Division*, 10 CONN. L. REV. 5 (1978).

Van Dine, Dimitz, and Conrad, *The Incarceration of the Dangerous Offender: A Statistical Experiment*, 14 J. RES. IN CRIME AND DELINQ. 22 (1977).

Zalman, *The Rise and Fall of the Indeterminate Sentence*, 24 WAYNE L. REV. 45, 857 (1977, 1978).

Zeisel and Diamond, *Search for Sentencing Equity: Sentence Review in Massachusetts and Connecticut*, 4 AM. B. FOUND. RES. J. 881 (1977).

PLEA BARGAINING

Books

DAVIS, K., DISCRETIONARY JUSTICE: A PRELIMINARY ANALYSIS. Indiana State University Press, 1969.

———, DISCRETIONARY JUSTICE IN EUROPE AND AMERICA. University of Illinois Press, 1976.

HEUMANN, M., PLEA BARGAINING. University of Chicago, 1977.

PLEA BARGAINING: A SELECTED BIBLIOGRAPHY. LEAA, 1976.

PROSECUTIONAL DISCRETION: THE DECISION TO CHARGE, AN ANNOTATED BIBLIOGRAPHY. LEAA, 1975.

Articles

Alschuler, *The Defense Attorney's Role in Plea Bargaining*, 84 YALE L. J. 1179 (1975).

———, *The Prosecutor's Role in Plea Bargaining*, 36 U. CHI. L. REV. 50 (1968).

———, *The Supreme Court, The Defense Attorney and the Guilty Plea*, 45 U. COLO. L. REV. 1 (1975).

———, *The Trial Judge's Role in Plea Bargaining, Part I*, 76 COLUM. L. REV. 1059 (1976).

Bubany and Skiller, *Taming the Dragon: An Administrative Law for Prosecutorial Decision Making*, 13 AMER. CRIM. L. REV. 473 (1976).

Finkelstein, *A Statistical Analysis of Guilty Plea Practices in the Federal Courts*, 89 HARV. L. REV. 293 (1975).

Goldstein, *Reflections on Two Models: Inquisitorial Themes in American Criminal Procedure*, 26 STAN. L. REV. 1009 (1974).

Goldstein and Marcus, *Comment on Continental Criminal Procedure*, 87 L. J. 1570 (1978).

―――, *The Myth of Judicial Supervision Thru "Inquisitorial" Systems: France, Italy and Germany*, 87 YALE L. J. 240 (1977).

Hyman, Bargaining and Criminal Justice (manuscript 1977).

Jescheck, *The Discretionary Powers of the Prosecuting Attorney in West Germany*, 18 AMER. J. COMP. L. 508 (1970).

Kuh, *Plea Bargaining: Guidelines for Manhattan District Attorney's Office*, 11 CRIM. L. BULL. 48 (1974).

Langbein, *Controlling Prosecutorial Discretion in Germany*, 41 U. CHI. L. REV. 439 (1974).

Langbein and Weinreb, *Continental Criminal Procedure: "Myth" and Reality*, 87 YALE L. J. 1549 (1978).

Miller, *The Compromise of Criminal Cases*, 1 So. CAL. L. REV. 1 (1927).

Note, *The Plea Bargain in Historical Perspective*, 23 BUFF. L. REV. 499 (1973).

Note, *Restructuring the Plea Bargain*, 82 YALE L. J. 286 (1972).

Pugh, *Ruminations re Reform of American Criminal Justice (Especially Our Guilty Plea System): Reflections Derived from a Study of the French System*, 36 LA. L. REV. 947 (1976).

Thomas and Fitch, *Prosecutorial Decision Making*, 13 AMER. CRIM. L. REV. 597 (1976).

Vouin, *The Role of the Prosecutor in French Criminal Trials*, 18 AMER. J. COMP. L. 483 (1970).

Index

213

✳

About the Author

Richard Singer has been concerned with questions of corrections and the law for the past ten years. He served as reporter for the American Bar Association Standards Relating to the Legal Status of Prisoners, and for the Model Sentencing and Corrections Act. He holds degrees from the University of Chicago and Columbia University. Along with numerous articles on the legal aspects of corrections, he is the co-author of Rights of the Imprisoned.